18 Tons, 92 Hours
and 175 clouds of dust

Fredric Winton Altman

I was born in Tampa, Florida
March 4, 1947
Tampa Municipal Hospital

Copyright © 2024 by **Ric Altman**

All rights reserved. No part of this publication may be reproduced, distributed, or transmitted in any form or by any means, including photocopying, recording, or other electronic or mechanical methods, without the prior written permission of the copyright owner and the publisher, except in the case of brief quotations embodied in critical reviews and certain other noncommercial uses permitted by copyright law. For permission requests, write to the publisher, "Attention: Permissions Coordinator," to the address below.

Studio of Books LLC
5900 Balcones Drive Suite 100
Austin, Texas 78731
www.studioofbooks.org
Hotline: (254) 800-1183

Ordering Information:
Special discounts are available on quantity purchases by corporations, associations, and others. For details, contact the publisher at the address above.

Printed in the United States of America.

ISBN-13:   Softcover: 978-1-968491-51-2
            Hardback: 978-1-968491-62-8
            eBook: 978-1-968491-52-9

Library of Congress Control Number: 2025917419

The US Review of Books
Professional Reviews for the People

"I firmly believe I grew up in the best possible time in American history"

Tampa, Florida native Altman doesn't do anything in a small way, so readers will find this aptly named autobiography to be immensely entertaining. The titular eighteen tons refers to the biggest cannabis bust in Southeastern history (near Savannah, Georgia, in 1975). Engagingly detailed in one of the largest chapters in the book, Altman was duly rewarded with a one-year and one-day jail sentence that didn't seem to slow him down much.

The overall trajectory of Altman's life is akin to an ongoing Hunter Thompson escapade, though without quite as much literary panache. The episodic reminisces that Altman bills as a collection of autobiographical short stories (175 Clouds of Dust) are compelling, nonetheless. US Boomer generation readers will find much to relate to in terms of shared childhood and young adult scraps and scrapes. The difference is that Altman never really stopped living on the edge, even as his career choices and hobbies turned to legal pursuits such as B&B ownership, mountaineering, and running a scuba diving business.

The final approach of his golden years appears not to have stalled him either. Altman's wife of nearly forty years regards him as a one-of-a-kind renaissance man, and the fact is, the guy apparently can do just about anything he turns his mind to, whether cooking for B&B guests or figuring out how to save life and limb during a scuba trip gone sour in a storm on the Atlantic (the titular ninety-two hours). It takes a man with a big heart and a quick mind to deal with the life situations that Altman created and encountered. Gifted with the ability to squeak through perilous situations, Altman also, in turn, gifts readers with his ability to share his many escapades with sincere, down-to-earth humility. Altman tells it like it is and lets the chips fall where they may.

*Reviewed by **Kate Robinson**, The US Review of Books Professional Review for the People*

"In this riveting compilation of autobiographical short stories, Fredric Altman unveils a tapestry of life experiences that mirror the raw intensity and vivid storytelling reminiscent of literary giants Ernest Hemingway, Hunter S. Thompson, and Jack Kerouac. Each tale varies, ranging from the bizarre and extraordinary to thought-provoking and from hilarious to the mundane. Altman's narrative prowess weaves a thread between the profound and the absurd.

Altman narrates the lead-up to an 18-ton marijuana bust, a narrative that unfolds with the gonzo energy of Hunter S. Thompson. Crooked sheriffs, plane crashes, and the cold steel bars of federal prison set the stage for a gripping tale of downfall and redemption. Altman's words, akin to Thompson's unrestrained chaos, take you on a rollercoaster ride through the underbelly of society, punctuated by moments of transcendence.

In a stark departure, embark on an adrenaline-fueled voyage as Altman recounts four harrowing days lost at sea, the relentless dance with mortality casting a shadow over every page. His prose, Hemingwayesque in its brevity, captures the essence of survival against the vast and unforgiving backdrop of the ocean.

As Altman's narratives echo the spontaneity of Jack Kerouac's On the Road, the reader is invited to traverse the highways and byways of an unconventional life. Through the highs and lows, Altman's storytelling remains a constant, a testament to the resilience of the human spirit and the transformative power of the written word.

"18 Tons, 92 Hours & 175 Clouds of Dust" is not just a book; it's a literary odyssey that immerses you in the thrilling escapades of Fredric Altman, a modern-day raconteur whose tales resonate with the timeless echoes of three literary maestros."

Akhtar Baig Mirza

Dear Readers,

As you embark on this crazy trip through the life of Ric Altman, remember: this is my guy. Nothing in this book could ever diminish him in my eyes.

Everyone has things in their past that they are ashamed of and things they are proud of. One must understand that if you love someone as I love Ric, you realize that this person would not be who they are if it weren't for everything that's happened in their past.

I wouldn't change one minute of our pasts or our life together, as doing so would alter the couple we are today. We've loved, laughed, had adventures, faced death, argued, fought, divorced, reunited, and, above all, forgiven.

My very dear friend Liz calls Ric "The Alien." She says, "He's not of this world." This stems from the fact that the man can do anything and everything he puts his mind to.

In his book, Ric bares all: the highs, the lows, and everything in between. I applaud him for having the guts to "share it all" with the world.

Janet Clemons-Altman

Dedicated to the women I could have treated better.

Especially to Janet, who has put up with me for 36 years.

Preface

There are two big stories in this book and 175 smaller ones. When I would orally tell the two big ones, listeners often said, "You should write a book!"

The two big ones didn't have enough volume to fill a book. However, I would also tell many little vignettes, so I began to write those down, just the funny ones. After that, I realized this was trying to turn into an autobiography. I then started writing about the painful, shameful, embarrassing, and even about my outright lunatic fringe antics.

While writing this, I realized I had been minimizing some of the less honorable things I have done. This has led to my autobiography becoming a double-edged sword. On one hand, it's been cathartic, but on the other hand, it has been emotionally devasting at times and has led to a diminished overall view of myself. Writing about and reading all the negatives in one place has been sobering. Being young is mitigating, but I still had free will to be a better person. As I've grown older, I have become a better person. The experience of writing this book has reinforced that, but a bit of anguish remains. I do hope I can find peace and solace.

PREFACE VII	THE OUTLAWS BAND 40
	AFTER AN OUTLAWS CONCERT .. 41
EARLY ON, '50S AND SOME '60S 1	THE SAMURAI SWORD 42
	THE FLYING CROSS 42
OZZIE AND HARRIET 1	DATING SYLVIA 43
LIFE OF SHORT-CUTS 2	BY THE HAIR 44
WHITEY'S DEMISE 2	TWO QUAALUDES-TWO SOPERS 45
PINKY'S DEMISE 5	FISHING ON GANDY BRIDGE 47
BROWN FAMILY MEMBER 5	M1/M2 47
ROGER SILING 6	M-14 AND THE MERCEDES 49
MY LITTLE LEAGUE CAREER 7	EAST COAST BALE OF POT 50
FIRST JOBS 7	$250,000 51
STORM DRAIN 8	THE SHERIFF 52
SHOOTING MY MOTHER 9	THE GREAT SAPELO BUST 54
RAY FOX AS TURKEY 10	HILLSBOROUGH COUNTY JAIL ... 66
CUBA 10	PALATKA 67
	TALLAHASSEE 67
THE SIXTIES 11	ATLANTA 68
	TEXARKANA 68
MOM'S HALLOWEEN STUNT 11	MY STALKER 70
AUTO THEFT 12	KOSHER FOOD 70
SEBRING 13	LETTER TO JUDGE ALAIMO 70
HUBCAPS 14	BY THE HAIR II 71
THE GEAR SHIFT 15	MY 1978 GASPARILLA 72
PAUL'S CAR 15	END OF THE LAKE 74
ROCKET'S CAR 16	
DRAG RACING 16	**THE EIGHTIES** 76
OXFORD COLLEGE 18	
RAZOR BLADES 19	MARRIAGE NUMBER TWO 76
NO BRAKES TO OXFORD 20	BATHROOM CLEANING 77
THE DRAFT 21	KATHLEEN 78
P-38 22	MY VIOLIN 78
MY AIR FORCE CAREER 23	MY COUNTRY VET 79
FLORIDA STEEL 26	STINGRAYS 79
WOLF SPIDER 27	LOST AT SEA 80
THE AIRPORT 29	ROB'S FUNERAL 105
THE FOREST FIRE 29	KATRINA 105
	THE NEWSPAPER 106
THE SEVENTIES 30	RAY FOX NEEDED A BEER 107
	OUR 3 TRICK ACT 108
MARRIAGE NUMBER ONE 30	MISSION IMPOSSIBLE 108
MUSHROOM HUNT 32	SHRIMPING 109
THE GREAT MARIJUANA THEFT . 33	BEN'S SPECIAL KNOT 109
COZUMEL 34	KEY LARGO 109
ANTI-WAR 35	PHYLLIS 115
CHECKING INTO A PARIS HOTEL . 37	MARRIAGE NUMBER THREE ... 117
MY CAREER AS A PIG FARMER .. 37	
MY DUIS OR LACK THEREOF 39	

Sugar's Jealousy	118
Two Boutonnieres	118
The Propeller	119
Honduras	119

THE NINETIES 122

Some Caving	122
Black Cows at Night	126
Four Corners	127
The Bates Motel	127
Mount Hood, May, 2001	129
Our Nemesis: Mt. Rainier	131
A side story:	133
Are We Taking the Dog?	136
Rum Runners	137
Fall of the Berlin Wall	137
My Fingertip	138
A Snorkeling Trip	139
My Favorite Customer	139
The Glass Bottom Boat	140
Gomez and the Wolf Man	141
Ghost Pepper	141
Smitty	141
'Bout What?	142
The 5k Race	142
Janet's Sea Turtle Suitor	143
Wacissa River	144
The Wedding Ring	145
Our Duct-Taped Airliner	146
The White Eagle Prank	147
McGyver	147
Returning From Bimini	148
Bimini by Air	151
Underwater Fiasco	152
The Northern Light	155
Starbucks	158
Sugar and Sliding Doors	159
Timi's Kittens	159
Silent World III Sinking	160
Evan Jackson	160
Sparky, Liz's Sailboat	161
Cremated Ashes	161
Buck	161
Genteel	161

THE 2000S 163

The Condom	163
Selling the Dive Shop	164
The Black Cat and Wife #4	165
The Monastery	169
Twin Lakes	173
One of My 9 Lives	178
We kept in touch	180
Marriage Number Five	182
Rental Car	183
The Ferry	185
Midgets	186
Adriano and Isabella	186
Tate's Hell	188
'Possums	189
Aneurysm	190
Fake Blood	191
Our Friends, the Dillards	192
Our Friends, the Graysons	193
The DMV Caper	195
Ukraine	196
Family In Need	196
My Favorite B&B Guests	197
5-Star Michelin in Paris	198

BRUSHES WITH GREATNESS 200

"Butch" Gallagher	200
Judy Collins/Stephen Stills	201
Muhammad Ali	202
Reverend Jesse Jackson	202
Jeff Foxworthy	202

PHONE COMPANY STORIES 203

African Bull Elephant	203
The Dairy	203
Giant's Camp	204
The Cucumber	204
The Disconnection	205
B-17	205

THE FAMILY 207

The Holocaust	207
Dr. Mac R. Winton	208
Salomonson Side of Family	209
My Father	210

- The Sea Cloud 211
- Uncle "Eddie" Walsh 212
- Some Cousins 213
- Cousin Frits 214
- Thomas Mayhew 1593-1682, 12th Great Grandfather 217
- Salem 217
- Letter to My Ex-Wives 218

MY FAVORITE QUOTES 221

- D.H. Lawrence: 221
- John Huston in "Chinatown" 221
- Mark Twain (Janet's cousin) 221
- Play it Again, Sam 221
- Unknown: 222
- Unknown: 222
- From Stacey 222
- From Anita 222
- From Janet 223

ACKNOWLEDGMENTS 225

Early On, '50s and Some '60s

Ozzie and Harriet

I opened my eyes for the first time to what would be known in the future as an "Ozzie and Harriet" childhood. Middle-class, working dad, stay-at-home mom, single-family home in a quiet neighborhood, bought and paid for on time, with two children: myself and my younger sister. I was generally a happy child who got a solid public-school education and wanted for little, much like Ozzie and Harriet's kids. There were differences though. I never once saw my parents kiss or show any affection toward each other, public or private. I was scarred for life when I found condoms in my dad's dresser, an image I still have. The lack of affection between my parents may or may not have affected me later in life.

I firmly believe I grew up in the best possible time in American history. I also grew up in one of the best neighborhoods, Beach Park in Tampa. Platted in the 1920s, building began. The Great Depression hit the area hard, but after the war, construction boomed. The original homes were Spanish and Mediterranean influence, but the "Ranch" style took over after the war.

The vast majority of families were like mine. Dads were home from the war with wives and kids around my age. When you went outside, you could always see kids on their bikes. When we got home from school or on the weekend, we took off on our bikes with those in our "gang" to do what seemed like an infinite number of things. We played a lot of games in the streets, played "Cowboys and Indians" with cap-guns, dressed up as Davey Crockett, chased behind the mosquito fogger truck inhaling the chemical fog, bought ice cream from the "Ice Cream Man" and his vehicle that broadcast a jingle to attract us, drank water from a garden hose, played baseball, watched "Howdy Doody" on a brand-new device called a television, explored the woods, ran in the creeks, built tree houses, and played in the mud. We created new games from our imaginations. All this with no adult supervision.

However, there were negatives. We had to do air raid drills in school where we would hide under our desks (duck and cover) to protect ourselves from nuclear attack. An air raid siren would be tested every Saturday at noon. There were bomb shelters at several homes.

At Al Lopez Baseball Field on North Dale Mabry, there were separate drinking fountains and bleacher seats for White and Colored.

One day, I rode on a public bus with my grandmother Mollie Winton's black maid to downtown Tampa. Her name was "Stella," very big and busty and very black. As a seven-year-old, I was dumbstruck by the fact that we could not sit at the front of the bus.

I grew up in the U.S. and had a strong middle-class upbringing. Children were allowed to be out until dark because no one worried about safety, we had never heard of a school shooting, drugs were virtually unknown in most middle-class neighborhoods, and the future looked nothing but bright.

There will never be another childhood like that.

Life of Short-cuts

My first memory is helping my dad at age five or six, carrying hedge cuttings down our driveway from our backyard to the curb in front of our house on Empedrado. While walking down the driveway, I saw a small opening at the ground level of our home, an entry to the crawlspace under the house. I immediately thought, why should I go through the time and trouble to go all the way to the curb when I could stuff the cuttings under the house? It sounded like a perfect plan, but after a few loads, my father realized what I was doing and stopped it. He was not amused, but my mother thought it hilarious. That example of a shortcut became much of my life model for the following decades.

Whitey's Demise

My mother loved cats, so I began a life-long relationship with them early on. I've never been without one. They have literally saved my life at least twice. Much later in my life, I had become so depressed a couple of times, that I seriously considered taking my own life. But, in the internal discussion about doing so, I asked myself, "Who will take care of my cats?"

The answer was, "No one is better than me."

That realization caused me to table my suicidal thoughts.

Whitey was an older cat when I came into his life. I suppose he was originally my mother's. Whitey was a very gentle and tolerant kitty, and I loved him dearly. Empedrado was parallel to Bay-to-Bay Boulevard, on the same block where Bay-to-Bay Hardware still exists, and a barber shop named Ralph's, which is no longer there. The businesses were beside each other but separated by a narrow alleyway leading back to Empedrado.

An unescorted walk, even for one block, by a five-year-old today is unthinkable, but back then, I did it. I liked to visit both stores. My parents knew the owners, and both were friendly, trusted folk. One day, I was walking toward Bay-to-Bay down the alley when I saw a small bench and something under it. I looked, and it was Whitey, dead and stiff under the bench. I remember crying.

Whitey and me, check out the headgear.

That alley today

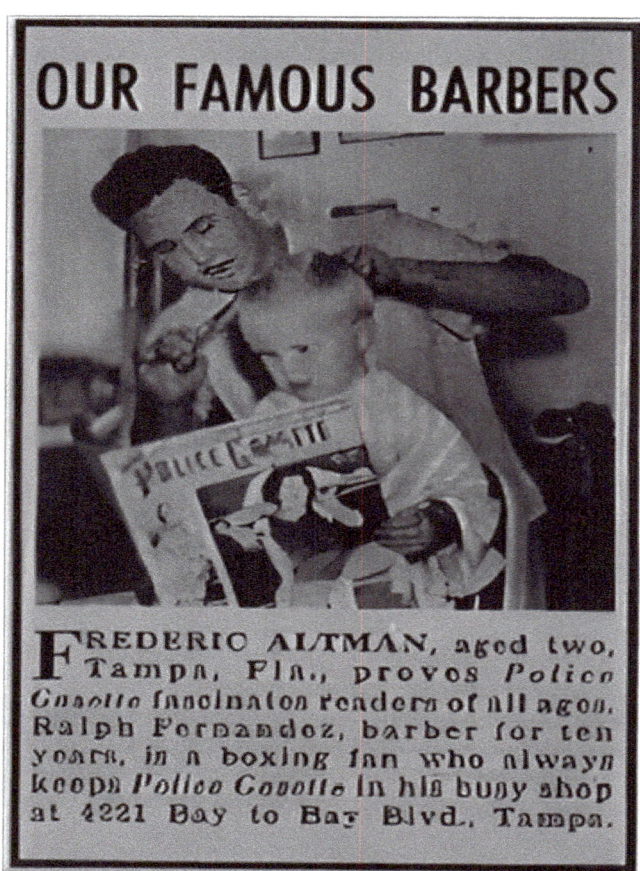

Ralph and me in the "Police Gazette"

Pinky's Demise

At age six, we moved from Empedrado to Swann Circle. Mom had a tortoise-shell Persian female that she had bred, and momma cat had six kittens. I kept an orange male, and we gave the others away. I named him Pinky, but I don't know why. He wasn't pink. He was an indoor-outdoor cat that used to come and go through my bedroom window. We had no air conditioning, so the windows were usually open, and I knew when he wanted in or out. He would jump on the window sill and meow to wake me up.

By the time I was twelve, he and I had had this arrangement for a couple of years when, one day, coming home from school, I found him dead by the side of the road. Heartbroken, I buried him. I went to sleep that night despondent. I heard a meow at the window in the middle of the night. It frightened me at first, but it was him, fit as a fiddle and wanting in. Of course, I let him in, hardly believing what I saw. The next day, we resolved the mystery. I had forgotten Pinky had a twin brother that we had given to friends next door, and he was the deceased, not Pinky.

Brown Family Member

I had a friend, Jeannette Brown, who lived on the next block. We would play at each other's house from time to time, innocent kid stuff. One day, a family member moved in with them temporarily. I don't remember his name, but he was an uncle or cousin. Kids can't judge an adult's age well, but he was probably 25-30.

He owned a car, a VW Beetle. He didn't work, so he had lots of free time to cart the neighborhood's children around to one thing or another in that VW. He was a friendly, entertaining guy. Everyone was so trusting back then.

Whenever he had kids in his car, he would open the glove box, where he always had candy, mostly chocolate, and tell us kids to help ourselves. I remember that glove box to this day. If this is starting to sound like the stereotypical pedophile grooming we have all heard about, it is.

I don't know about today, but 9-year-olds knew nothing about sex in 1956. At least I didn't, and none of my friends did.

One day, after dropping off the other kids, I was the only one in the car with him when he pulled into a vacant parking lot at Dale Mabry Elementary School. It was summer, the school was closed and empty, and no one was around. The grooming now went to the next level in the pedophile playbook. With the candy and gifts comes the touching, the exposing, and the other things. I considered relating the gory details to you, but I can't do it. You'll have to assume.

After a few days of this, I was in the front seat, with him driving and other kids in the car. One of these kids was a friend, Rodney Ricketts, who lived across the street and was two years older than me. Pedophiles do make mistakes. Rodney was in the back seat and took notice when my molester reached over and put his hand down my shirt. Rodney, being older and wiser, recognized inappropriate behavior when he saw it.

When he got home, he told his dad what he had seen, and his dad came over and told my dad. My dad then went to where the guy lived and talked with him. The guy disappeared forever the next day.

None of this was ever spoken of again. My dad didn't call the police; he only threatened the creep and got him out of my life. In the days that this went on, it was bewildering to me, unable to process any sense of right or wrong, but only a vague sense that things weren't right. There was no counseling for kids for those things at the time. The only approach was to bury it, to forget.

That's what I did; I forgot it, buried it, blocked it. I did not remember anything about it until I was nearly 30. One day, without prompting, it came back out of the blue. Until then, I had thought the theory of people being able to block things from their memory was bullshit. I was wrong. I assumed I had no damage from the experience, but I was wrong. It took me another 30 years to grasp the life-long effects. If I knew he was still alive and where he was, I would find him and kill him.

Roger Siling

At age 11, I was a student at Dale Mabry Elementary in the 50s. One of my best friends was Roger Siling. We would regularly get together for a sleepover on Friday nights to watch the local horror TV show "Nightmare," which started at 11:30 pm.

At the time, Roger's dad was an Air Force B-47 pilot stationed at MacDill AFB in Tampa.

One Friday night, we were watching the horror show at Roger's house when suddenly a news blurb came on saying that there had been an Air Force plane crash and all aboard were assumed killed. We knew Roger's father was on a training mission that night and immediately knew it was him. The phone rang, Roger's mom answered, and it was confirmed.

Major Alexander Siling was a B-47 pilot and instructor assigned to the 306th Bombing Wing, MacDill AFB, Florida. Major Siling was acting navigator on this flight in March 1958. He was 37 years old at the time. The aircraft completed a series of low-level bombing runs on the Avon Park, Florida Bombing Range. After completing the runs, the B-47 made a low pass by the control tower and started a climbing roll to the left. The bomber's right wing snapped, and the aircraft burst into flames, killing the four crew members. It is believed that the bomber was overstressed in flight.

My Little League Career

I was a member of a Tampa Little League team called the "Dozier Cats," whose uniforms, to our chagrin, were bright yellow. Dozier was the name of a heavy equipment company in Tampa that sold Caterpillar tractors. I only have two memories from the years I was with the team. My starting position was originally a pitcher until I hit a kid in the head with a pitch. The kid wasn't hurt.

After that, I quit pitching and switched to shortstop. My second memory is of being in a classic situation. It was the bottom of the ninth, bases loaded, two out, and we were behind by one run. I was up to bat and stood at the plate, frozen in place as I watched three strikes blow by me without a twitch, much less a swing at any of them. I struck out with my father watching. The humiliation has been life-long. I feel it today. All I had to do was take one swing, and I probably wouldn't remember the incident, but no.

First Jobs

I worked for two summers as a paperboy for an afternoon newspaper, the Tampa Daily Times. I usually delivered the paper on my bicycle but occasionally would use my go-cart. I would fold the papers and wrap them with a rubber band to make throwing them easier and more accurate. The objective of the toss was to get the newspaper onto the subscriber's doorstep or as close as possible. I remember throwing one toward one doorstep just as the door opened. The paper went sailing into the home past the homeowner, sliding along the floor as pretty as you please and disappearing deep into the house.

I would hand-deliver the paper on Christmas Eve, blatantly attempting to solicit tips. After knocking on one door, I was invited into an ongoing party serving hors d'oeuvres. They suggested trying one particular cheese, which turned out to be Limburger. I had never tasted anything so stinky and delicious at the same time.

Aside from doing neighborhood lawn care, I worked one summer at the Tampa Veterinary Hospital on Grand Central Avenue, now Kennedy Boulevard. Dr. Avery, with the ever-present cigar, was the best. He and his staff trained me as a vet tech and taught me how to hold an angry cat without being permanently maimed.

Part of my work was to clean the place, so while poking around, I came across a ten-gallon trash can. I opened it to find a horrible, putrid, bubbly liquid filled near the brim. I asked another employee what this was. Dr. Avery had a dead monkey submerged in acid to clean the flesh from the skeleton, which the doctor intended to display.

Roger Siling's mom worked as Dr. Avery's receptionist for decades.

This is an actual tag. Me and Stevie Swindall.

Storm Drain

When I was about 12, Drew Smith and I retrieved an 8-foot wooden dingy from a hermit's property on the bay where Culbreath Isles is today. It was in horrible shape, but we cleaned, patched, and painted it so we could use it.

The first use was to explore a storm drainage system that emptied into a canal at the intersection of South Shorecrest and Neptune Way. It was about 8 feet wide and 6 feet tall, but a couple of feet were covered with tidewater. We hand-carried that dingy from the future Culbreath Isles to my house on Swann Circle to be rehabbed. We then carried it to the storm drain, launched it, and climbed aboard with paddles and flashlights. The height from the waterline to the ceiling was about 4 feet, with plenty of room to paddle along, but of course, it was pitch black after going in a distance.

We went from the entrance to our furthest point, the International Inn, about a quarter mile away. That took a few hours, but we hadn't considered the tide. To our eventual horror, this waterway was open to the bay and had tidal movement. We had entered at low tide, but as we went from the International Inn, the ceiling height gradually decreased. As we got closer to the outlet, we became worried. Was the ceiling height at our exit too low for us to get out? We were about 100 yards from the exit when the ceiling became so low, we had to lie down in the dinghy. Eventually, it became too low to continue without pushing up on the ceiling, so the dinghy was lower in the water, and we could push forward a foot or two.

If that wasn't bad enough, the contractor had used a wooden frame to pour the concrete for the roof. When the wooden frame was removed, nails were left embedded in the ceiling, hanging down about 2 inches. The nails were dangerous in themselves, but now, we not only had to push upward to get the dingy to move, but we also had to push the dingy even deeper into the water to get by the nails, then let up, push down again to avoid more nails and inch the dingy along. It was challenging moving forward and we barely got out alive. Well past the point of no return, Drew and I had to continue ahead or drown.

The entrance today.

Shooting My Mother

Roger Siling and I had a .22 caliber rifle that we decided to make into a single-shot pistol. We cut off the handle and much of the barrel, so now we had a pistol. I took it home and showed it to my mother and sister, who wanted to try it. We took it out into our backyard and safely shot it a few times.

When we were finished, I was walking next to my mom, carrying the pistol, which I thought was unloaded. It wasn't. I absent-mindedly pulled the trigger, the gun fired, and the slug hit the pavement inches from my mother and ricocheted into her calf.

Of course, we went to the hospital, and when the doctor realized it was a gunshot wound, the police got involved, came to the house, and confiscated the gun. The wound got infected, and it became a nasty scar on my mother's leg. My mother was a good-looking woman, proud of her shape and legs. My collection of guilt began.

Ray Fox as Turkey

In the late '50s, Ray grew up in North Carolina and liked to hunt. On one turkey hunt, another hunter somehow mistook him for a turkey and shot him, thankfully with birdshot, producing no real, lasting damage. The hospital didn't take any of them out, and you could feel one under his scalp decades later.

Cuba

In 1960, my father had a brother, Harold, who had a family that lived near us in Tampa. He and his wife had three kids, Bev, Chuck and Hal. One evening, our parents went for dinner at Bartke's Restaurant in the Tampa Municipal Airport. My parents took my sister and me to Uncle Harold's house and dropped us off, leaving Bev, at 14 years old, as a babysitter, and the four parents left for dinner.

The phone rang at my cousin's house, and Bev answered it. After a couple of minutes on the phone, Bev announced to us kids that our parents had decided at dinner to take a flight to Cuba that was leaving immediately and Bev would be in charge of us kids for the weekend until they returned. We weren't alarmed at all, we were giddy with the prospect of an un-restrained weekend ahead of us. They did regain control of their senses and from Cuba, called an adult neighbor to come take care of us.

They left for Cuba with nothing but the clothes on their backs. Surprisingly, all went well. They returned and life went on with no police or social services involved.

At the time, this didn't seem out of the ordinary, but if this had happened today, we would all have had brand-new sets of parents.

The Sixties

Mom's Halloween Stunt

In 1960 or so, my mom, for Halloween, filled a pair of blue jeans and a long-sleeve shirt of mine with Spanish Moss from our backyard. She placed it on the road in front of our house next to the curb. My sister, I, and a few neighborhood kids were excited to see the results from passing motorists, so we hid in our carport, huddled out of sight, waiting for dusk.

As it began to get dark, a couple of cars came by, slowed to a crawl to look, but drove off. Then, one driver stopped, got out of his car, realized it was a stunt, and drove off. It was all hilarious until a police cruiser showed up minutes later. We kids scattered, knowing trouble was on the horizon, but my mom got into her car and laid down, hoping all would blow over.

The cop got out of his car, took a look at the "corpse," and walked up our driveway toward our carport with his flashlight. He stopped by her car, shined his flashlight down onto the front seat, and, seeing my mom, asked, "What is going on?"

The red-faced, sheepish reply was just, "Halloween prank?"

He was not amused and asked her to remove the "body."

All of us kids were close by, of course, heard everything and thought it was the most hilarious thing of all time. Mom was a lot of fun.

Mom in her Mountain Man costume for Halloween 1965.

Auto Theft

In 1963, I had a friend who was as car crazy as I was, Dickie Brazzeal. We had just been given driver's licenses and had the idea we wanted a car to tinker with and drive. While driving around in our parent's cars, we frequently passed a used car lot on Gandy Boulevard. This was a barebones car lot.

There was no permanent structure, just an empty, vacant lot with about 12 cars. There was a 1950 Chevy sedan among many newer cars with no price tag on the windshield, so Dickie and I stopped to look. I don't remember the price, but almost everything was out of our price range, so we drove on.

A bit later, we were driving by and noticed a wrecker hooking up one of the newer cars on the lot. We stopped to see what was happening. One of the guys doing the loading said they were moving the lot. We asked about the '50 Chevy, and he said the thing didn't run and we could have it for no charge. We were overjoyed. Before we left, Dickie asked about a car part Dickie's older brother needed for his 1950 Ford. The guy said he had one and gave Dickie his phone number and address.

We took off, looked for a chain to tow the Chevy home, and returned to the lot with my mother's station wagon. The Chevy was the only thing left on the lot at dusk. We backed up to it and began attaching the chain to the car.

Within moments, two Tampa police cars screeched up, cops jumping out with guns drawn, ordering, "Hands up!"

We complied while they searched us and my mom's car. After finding nothing, one of them asked, "Where have you been taking the cars?"

We told him we hadn't been taking cars. We were only taking this one. That was enough for them. They handcuffed us, took us downtown, and booked us for Grand Theft Auto. God knows why, the car was worth about $50.

When our parents arrived, a detective sat us down and wanted to hear what we had to say. We told him we weren't stealing the cars. The car lot owner had given us that one because it wasn't worth towing. He said someone had stolen all the other vehicles on the lot and that the actual owner was in the hospital. He said it looked to him that me and Dickie had been stealing the cars. We told him about the "owner" giving us the vehicle and that the "owner" had provided Dickie his phone and address.

The detective looked at Dickie, and Dickie said yeah, that's what happened, and promptly pulled out the note with the phone and address. That stopped the detective in his tracks. He said he would look into it and released us to our parents.

Later the next day, the detective called to say that the tip we had given him had panned out, that they found all the stolen cars and arrested the perp. He said the charges would be immediately dropped, which they were.

Decades later, when background checks for employees were becoming more routine, at more than one job interview, the prospective employers asked, "What about this Auto Theft arrest?"

I've had to explain that more than once; apparently, expunging records was not done or even mentioned at the time.

Sebring

In 1964, Philip Alonso and I went to the "12 Hours of Sebring" race in his brand-new Corvair, a rear-engine car with a trunk in the front that served us well on that trip as a beer cooler. The 12 Hours of Sebring is an annual motorsport endurance race for sports cars held at Sebring International Raceway on the site of the former Hendricks Army Airfield World War II air base in Sebring, Florida.

We had a hotel room in Sebring the night before, drank too much alcohol that evening, and had a hangover in the morning. The race started at 10:00 am, but it didn't take long for us to get bored. You can't see much of the race, and mostly, you hear engines roar as they go around the course. So, as they say, an idle mind is the devil's workshop.

When you entered the track and paid, it was cash only, and they gave you ticket stubs so that you could leave the race and come back in without having to pay again. We surmised that many patrons would want to leave the race and not return. We exited the track, which was immediately next to the entrance. Lines were going in, and lines were coming out, but you didn't need stubs to leave, so we walked along the exit line and asked for stubs from those leaving. People handed them over easily. When we had enough stubs from those exiting, we walked out the gate, walked up the entrance line of cars, and sold the stubs at half-price to those coming into the race for the first time. Most bought the tickets without question, but some didn't believe the deal, so we would get in the car with them and go through the entrance without a hitch, where we got paid. This scam continued for a few hours while we made several hundred dollars without questions.

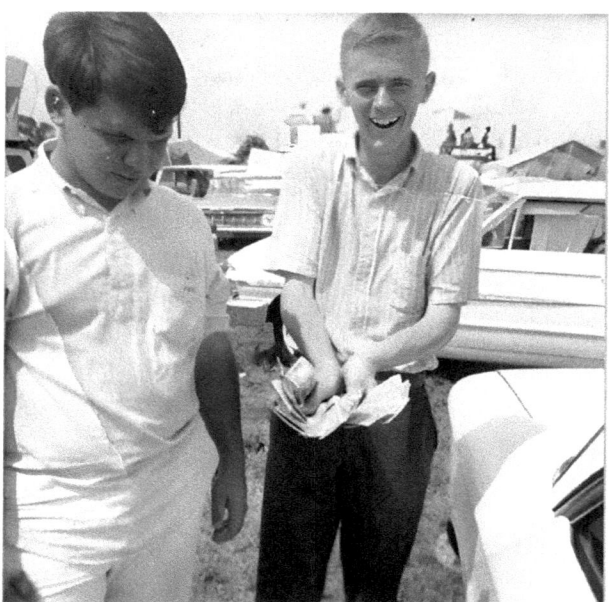

Philip Alonso and me.

Hubcaps

In 1965, wire wheel hubcaps were the rage, especially Chevrolet 14" ones, which fit many cars, not just Chevys. Working for peanuts as a pump jockey at Larry's American at the corner of Dale Mabry and Swann, I always needed a little extra money. My friend, Ben Ellis, could always use a little extra cash, so it dawned on us that those hubcaps, so easy to steal and sell, were tempting. We began looking for opportunities in big parking lots, including the Tampa Airport long-term parking lot. We found them everywhere, and it takes less than a minute to pop them off. I always had one on display in the gas station window and sold tons of them. We made lots of money.

One afternoon, we boosted a set in the parking lot of Britton Plaza. That evening, I got a call from a detective who said I needed to meet him at Larry's American. When I got there, just two minutes from my house, Ben was there too. The detective told us that he tracked us down about the hubcaps stolen that day. We were seen and tracked to Ben as we had used his car in the theft. The detective told us we were going to get a big break. The hubcaps were stolen from a county prosecutor willing not to press charges if we brought them to his house, put them back on, and apologized to him. This we did, embarrassing as it was. That was the end of the hubcap thievery.

The Gear Shift

We stole something unusual before leaving the petty thievery hubcap racket. At the time, the Hurst Competition manual transmission gear shifter was the best and is still popular today. We were cruising the Hillsborough County Junior College in Clearwater for hubcaps when we saw a '63 Chevy Impala. We looked in, and the owner had installed one of those shifters. We had enough tools, so Ben got under the car and removed the shifter. He was proud to say that he had left the transmission in second gear so the guy could get home without having his vehicle towed.

Paul's Car

Late in the decade, I had a friend named Paul who owned a Ford Fairlane he used to race around town with. All of us were chronically short of money, so Paul came up with the idea that we should fake the theft of his car, take it to a remote spot, remove the transmission, report it stolen, and get some insurance money, then sell it.

At the time, we were all very familiar with manual transmissions and how to remove and re-install them, but we had no experience with automatic transmissions. Paul's car had an automatic transmission, but that didn't deter us from attempting the plot.

We drove out to the country one night down a remote dirt road, stopped the car, and with no jack, got under the car with tools and began removing the transmission. We had no idea the transmission didn't come out like a manual; it was much more complicated than we knew. We only got it partly dismantled before giving up, abandoning the car, and fleeing after hours of strenuous work. It always amazes me how stupid I can be. You would think I would become aware of it at some point. This caper didn't result in much monetary success for Paul.

Rocket's Car

In 1968, a friend of ours, Dale Rocket, had a 1966 Chevelle SS 396, a nice car. He decided he needed some money and thought the best way to do that was to defraud his auto insurance company. We were all for it. We took his car to Sarga's garage on Hillsborough Avenue, pulled the engine and transmission, and then stripped the entire interior out. We did all this carefully, ensuring we did not damage the car. We towed it to a parking lot late that night and abandoned it. Dale reported the vehicle stolen, and the insurance company paid dearly when it was found. Dale got the shell of the car back, and we put everything back together just the way it was.

Drag Racing

I was interested in fast cars, so my father said he would buy me a car when I graduated high school. Instead of buying me something sensible for transportation, I convinced him to give me the money to construct one. I bought a '55 Chevy with no engine from Herschel Biggers on MacDill Ave. and a 327 engine and transmission from J&J Auto on Grand Central. Twins Joe and Jack Abene had a machine shop and some local fame as drag racers with a wildly erratic Anglia with far more horsepower than was safe.

I got the vehicle together and running but immediately blew the engine and had to sell the remaining hulk.

My grandmother Salomonson/Winton came to the rescue with a brand-new 1966 Chevelle SS-396. This got me started on street racing, which went on for two years, and then five years of professional drag racing with my street SS-396 and then a 1967 SS-396, strictly a trailered racer. It had a lot of local success but none on the national stage.

In 1972, we bought a 1971 Camaro in partnership with Lee Montgomery and began remaking it into a drag car. I soon decided this was too much money and effort with little return and sold my half to Lee. I was now entirely out of the drag racing scene.

The remnants of this fetish remain today with my love for old Chevy trucks and their required attendant work. I liked the 1960s Austin-Healey Sprites from early on and recently bought one. Their nickname was "Bug-Eye" here in the States and "Frog-Eye" in England.

Me and my 1966 and (Above) 1967 SS-396s (Below).

> **Double Drag Program Slated At Sunshine**
>
> A double program of drag races will be featured tonight at Sunshine Dragstrip with action at 8:30.
>
> Rick Altman of Tampa will be a favorite in the modified division. Wayne Dokken of Clearwater and Jimmy Barr of St. Petersburg will battle it out for super-stock honors while national record-holder Gene Norris of Orlando will be the favorite in the stock division.

Oxford College

I graduated in 1965 from Plant High in the top third of my class, but only by the barest of margins; I was #222 out of 666 students. The Vietnam War was accelerating, and the draft was in full swing. If you were in college, you were exempt. The classification was II-S.

Before Congress reformed the draft in 1971, a man could qualify for a student deferment if he could show he was a full-time student making passing grades in virtually any field of study. He could continue attending school and be deferred from service until he was too old to be drafted. That changed in 1971 with the institution of the lottery system. So, there was a huge incentive to go to college.

My father had for some time urged me to go to the Oxford College of Emory University. He had some connection to the Director of Admissions and Registrar at the school, Dallas Tarkenton, father of Minnesota Vikings quarterback Fran Tarkenton. I did not want to go; I had a girlfriend I didn't want to be without, and I had no desire to go to college; I couldn't see the point. But between the twin pressures of Vietnam and my father, I agreed to apply to Oxford, landed an interview with Tarkenton, and was accepted.

My performance at Emory was nothing short of shameful. I never studied.

All I wanted to do was drink beer and raise Hell with classmates at school. The hell-raising was mostly getting stupid drunk at local bars with homemade fake identification and playing pranks. After the first quarter, when grades were published, I earned the nickname "007" because my grade point average was 0.07. This was courtesy of failing everything but PE, where I got a D. I might have achieved the "D" for setting the school record for pushups at 119. That could still be the record.

The greatest trick ever played on me was in my first class of the day, Spanish. Aside from the professor being one of the most boring people I've ever encountered, I had one of my common hangovers that morning. It wasn't long before I fell asleep when my friend David Cosgrove jabbed me in my side with his elbow and said under his breath, "He called on you to read the first paragraph!"

Well, what was going on was the professor had asked the class to read a passage silently. So, in the middle of the silence, I read the passage out loud. Of course, it was hilarious to everyone but the professor and myself.

I continued through the second quarter without any improvement. Tarkenton called me into his office at the end of that dismal stretch. After scolding me for throwing my father's hard-earned money away, he pointed out that even if I posted straight As in the third quarter, my overall average would not be high enough to be able to attend the next session. So, it would be pointless to start a third quarter. Thus, that stellar educational career came to a halt. I packed and went home.

Razor Blades

One thing I did learn in college at Oxford was how to eat razor blades. In the day, all razor blades were blue steel, hence, Blue Blades. I learned this trick from David Cosgrove, one of the more insane inmates. You break the blade in half lengthwise, fold the two pieces together, place them between one side of your molars, and bite down. A loud crunch is heard by any onlookers, which sends them into wide-eyed disbelief. You must move the pieces to your tongue and open your mouth to show them. Then, you crush the more significant pieces between your molars until they are smaller, then swallow. Your stomach acid takes care of the rest, so there is no subsequent painful horror the next day. I have won hundreds of dollars in bars with this trick. The Blue Blades are no longer made, so I've stockpiled some for future performances. You cannot do this with today's stainless blades. I sent a letter to David Letterman, hoping he would use me and my trick for a "Stupid Human Tricks" segment, but I never heard anything back.

No Brakes to Oxford

While a student (so to speak) at Oxford, I got tired of hitchhiking the 500 miles from near Atlanta to Tampa on Friday and back again on Sunday. So, on one trip, I bought Kirby Hiers' 1957 Ford Fairlane with a Police Interceptor 312 engine.

Drew Smith, a friend and student at Oxford, was with me that weekend when we drove to Oxford on Sunday. The brakes failed On Highway 41 in Brooksville, just north of Tampa, the same highway sung about by the Allman Brothers Band. We stopped and realized we had a significant leak from a wheel cylinder, which was not a quick fix. We mulled it over and decided our best choice was to continue, just being very careful. This was not the Interstate, so we had to go through many small towns. It was nerve-wracking, intense, and dangerous driving, mostly at night.

At about 9:00 pm, we came over a hill crest, looking down the narrow 2-lane road with no shoulder on my side, just a steep drop-off. At the bottom of the slope was a side road intersecting the one we were on, dead-ending there. There was also a gas station on the left at that intersection. Maybe a quarter-mile ahead, approaching the gas station, was an oncoming vehicle. A car going in my direction ahead of me stopped with his blinker on, waiting for the oncoming vehicle to pass so he could turn left.

I was going about 50 miles an hour and headed downhill rapidly. I couldn't stop, and I couldn't pass on the right shoulder. The only option was to veer into the other lane with the oncoming car. Just before the oncoming vehicle got to the gas station, which would result in a head-on crash with me, I veered further left onto the gas station property, between the pumps and the highway, still at fifty miles an hour. This instinctual maneuver let the oncoming car speed by, passing the stopped car. I swerved back onto the road, never having slowed, and continued on to Oxford, just like in the movies.

I kept the car at the local gas station for a week until the temperature had dropped well below freezing for the first time that winter. I walked to the gas station and saw a puddle of frozen water below the engine. It dawned on me that a water-cooled engine with no anti-freeze mixed with the water could freeze, expand, crack the block, and then destroy the engine. That's precisely what happened. Repair was far outside my budget, so I just abandoned the vehicle.

The Draft

According to the rules, Emory reported my educational status to the draft board. My classification soon went from 2-S to 1-A, so I was immediately subject to the draft. It didn't take long before I received my induction notice from the US Army, informing me to report to the induction center in Jacksonville the following week.

I packed and took a bus to Jacksonville, leaving my mother behind, distraught and convinced I would get killed in Vietnam, as was I. I arrived early and walked from the bus station to the induction center. The center was a vast open building with thousands of young guys waiting for induction, which meant infantry.

I was there with those thousands, waiting until an Army Sergeant stood on a platform, introduced himself, reviewed why we were all there, and asked if anyone in the room felt they shouldn't be there. I was the only one to raise my hand. He was surprised but pointed me to a room to the side. I walked over to it and found another sergeant at a desk. He pointed me to a seat, and as I sat down, he asked, "Why do you think you should not be inducted?"

My mother had a friend named Boling, an orthopedic surgeon in Tampa. She wrangled from him a fraudulent letter he signed stating that I had a condition called a calcaneal spur, commonly known as a heel spur, which occurs when a bony outgrowth forms on the heel bone. The letter said I needed surgery and, indeed, had surgery scheduled in three weeks with six months of required recuperation. I pulled the letter out and handed it to him. He looked it over for a minute or two, then said I would get a temporary medical exemption and be recalled to be inducted in six months. Exuberant, I left the building and hitchhiked home to a teary-eyed mother.

The above scam is how our esteemed Donald Trump got out of the Vietnam-era draft. Bone spurs.

Military reservists were rarely called up then, so getting into a reserve unit became an urgent priority. A problem with this is that these units stayed full of those wanting to stay out of Vietnam. Vacancies were rare and filled quickly.

My father had been a P-38 pilot in World War II, operating first in North Africa and then in Italy. The P-38 was designed and built as a fighter aircraft, but there was a version that my dad flew that was used in photo-reconnaissance. He was still in the Air Force Reserve based at MacDill Air Force Base in Tampa and attended meetings there every month. There were three of my friends also looking to avoid the draft.

My father got a phone call early one morning and was told by one of his friends that some openings were coming up that very day and that he should get me to go in as soon as possible. My dad came to my room and said to get my friends together and go to MacDill right away. The openings would be filled on a first-come, first-served basis. I called all three and told them about the opportunity, and we all but flew down there.

We were all accepted into an Air Force Reserve unit in the hospital right there at MacDill. The word "relief" doesn't fully describe the feeling of us all.

My Dad in his P-38, North Africa.

P-38

My father fought in WWII as a P-38 Lightning pilot. Most configurations of the P-38 were fighters, but some were built as photo-reconnaissance he flew over Africa and Italy.

On a trip driving through Middlesboro, Kentucky, we saw a small, temporary sign on the side of the road saying, "P-38 Restoration, turn right." We had time and followed the signs to an airport aircraft hangar.

We found a fantastic sight. A P-38 Lightning fighter was sitting there in the process of restoration. The P-38 had been found under 268 feet of ice in Greenland. On 15 July 1942, due to poor weather and limited visibility, six P-38 fighters and two B-17 bombers were forced to return to Greenland en route to Great Britain during Operation Bolero. They made emergency landings on the ice field. All the crew members were subsequently rescued, but Glacier Girl, the unit's five other fighters, and the two B-17s were eventually buried under 268 feet of snow and ice that built up over the ensuing decades.

Fifty years later, in 1992, the plane was brought to the surface by members of the Greenland Expedition Society after years of searching and excavation. The rescue crew had to dig down 268 feet, hollow out a cavern around the aircraft, disassemble it, hoist the pieces to the surface, and eventually transport them to Middlesboro, where it was restored to flying condition in 2002. The excavation of Glacier Girl was documented in an episode of The History Channel's Mega Movers series titled "Extreme Aircraft Recovery."

My father was still alive, so I took him to see the aircraft. They graciously allowed him to sit in the cockpit, and I will forever regret not taking a picture of him sitting there, overwhelmed.

My Air Force Career

Basic training in the Air Force is done at Lackland Air Force Base in San Antonio, Texas. Ben, Ray, Ron McDavid and I enlisted in the same unit and went to Lackland into the same basic training unit. The physical training was every day, most of the day. I weighed 135 pounds going in, and six weeks later, I came out at 155, all muscle.

The TIs, Training Instructors, hold your life in their hands. In the Air Force, no one will shoot at you outside of aircrews in Vietnam, but if you flunk out of Air Force basic training, being shipped to the Army infantry was the next step, then into the gristmill of Vietnam, an ever-present looming threat. The TIs were Gods. We did our best to avoid their attention. On the other hand, not paying strict attention to them was a life-threatening act.

During Basic, they also tested aptitude to determine your best role for the Air Force. After testing, they decided I was best suited for a stint in a psychiatric hospital while the rest of my crew would continue back to the hospital unit in Tampa. Ironic, I thought. Their instinct was to put me in a psychiatric hospital. After the end of my Basic Training, I would be shipped to Sheppard AFB, Northwest of Dallas, 145 miles for my psych training. That got derailed as soon as I got to Sheppard. I became sick with the flu and missed the start of my psych class. That put me back on the path to the hospital at MacDill in Tampa.

As described earlier, you pay attention and believe everything your TI says to the letter. So, when a fellow recruit told me that the TIs had dictated using only one sheet of toilet paper per episode, I immediately believed, with no thought or hesitation. This is a small example of how military training gets in your head.

A fifth friend, Parky Myers, was to be with us when we got the emergency go-ahead to go to MacDill. He missed our phone call and his opportunity to get into the Air Force unit with us. He did join a local Marine Reserve unit, but the minimum active duty for Marines is two years, not six months. He never spoke to any of us again.

I successfully avoided the draft and probably the Army Infantry in Vietnam. After Basic Training, I began my six years in the Air Force Reserves. My stint started in a hospital unit stationed at MacDill Air Force Base in Tampa. It was a cushy deal. We were orderlies, carrying bedpans, cleaning, and changing linen. They taught us some things, including how to draw blood, administer positive pressure breathing, and give an injection.

Injection training came to me one day. The ward nurse called me to follow her to a bed occupied by an unconscious black male who needed an injection. She handed me the syringe and said, "Treat this syringe like a dart. You "throw" it, but still holding it, of course, into the upper, outer quadrant of one of the subject's buttocks."

I did just that, but it startled me how easily it went in, and instinctively, I jerked it right back out without injecting the drug, then after a brief, wild-eyed look around, stabbed it right back into his butt, finishing the procedure. It's good he was out cold. I received less than high marks from my instructor.

After two years of the hospital gig, they split the unit. The hospital unit remained, and they created a new squadron to be an aeromedical evacuation unit, which meant far more training and being on flight status, meaning you regularly fly to maintain that. We were to miss the hospital, at which the day's work sometimes consisted of grabbing a clipboard and a pen early in the morning and just walking around the place, pretending to take notes. No one ever questioned it.

One Saturday, those on the lowest link in the chain of command were sent to a storage building and asked to wait for further instructions. We waited there with nothing to do with our curious minds, so we rummaged around. We found a stack of gas masks and thought, "They'll never miss these," so several of us split them up and put them in our cars. I put four in my VW van.

Sunday morning came with a change in the general atmosphere of the staff. We were assembled and told there had been a theft of gas masks and everyone's car was to be searched. The other thieves had the presence of mind to take the stolen masks out of their respective vehicles the night before, but not me. I began to sweat as I realized the masks I had taken were still in my car, mere yards away.

They sat me down in a chair in the Master Sergeant's office with him sitting at his desk, a stack of papers in front of him and the four gas masks. They were dead serious about the gas masks. I knew prison was coming. He looked through his papers and asked, "Where did you get the gas masks?"

I responded, "I bought them at an anti-war rally in Washington, D.C., some weeks ago."

He continued to look at his papers and soon seemed perplexed. The mask serial numbers on the ones I had did not match the ones on his manifest, so they had to let me go. The terror subsided.

Every summer, we spent two weeks at Pope Air Force Base inside Ft. Bragg in Fayetteville, North Carolina. These "summer camps" were scheduled at the end of the physical year in the middle of the summer. At some point, someone with the higher-ups realized that if they scheduled our 1970 two weeks at the very end of the physical year and scheduled the 1971 two weeks at the very beginning of that physical year, we could have our reservists for a whole month of training. When that realization crept in, we underlings were fried, and the staff was joyous.

When Ben, Ray, and I arrived with the rest of our unit at Pope AFB that summer, we had all arrived by an antique C-124 military cargo plane from MacDill. The last ones were built in 1955 and long ago dismissed from the regular Air Force, relegated to Air National Guard and Air Force Reserve units. The one we were in lost an engine on the way to North Carolina, but we forged on, unruffled.

We were marooned for a month with these sadists. The first day we had off, we walked into Fayetteville and immediately spotted a used car lot. It took just a minute to find and purchase a 1959 Chevy Bel-Air for $125. It eventually took us to the beach and otherwise relieved us of the monotony and drudgery of the base. We sold it back to the used car dealer for $75 before we departed.

They would call our unit without warning and tell us to be on the base at any time of the month, not just on the scheduled weekends, to get on a plane and fly around for an hour so that we could remain on flight status. Everyone in the unit submitted to this but me. I was the only one who was off flight status. It was a mark of excellence for a commander to have all men in his unit on flight status.

My commander called me into his office to ask why I refused to attend these flights. I told him I would not do it, and if he forced me, I would sabotage the airplane. He digested this for a minute and then told me how I could, and should, get out of his hair without repercussion. He said to apply for a transfer to another unit but never show up. There was a glitch in the system that not many knew about, so that's what I did. This method of getting out of the remainder of your Air Force time was also used by George W. Bush to get out of his.

Florida Steel

At the end of the '60s, I worked at a Florida Steel smelting plant on Orient Road. I was a yard monkey with many assignments in the "yard."

The plant produced almost exclusively rebar and angle iron of all sizes. One of my jobs was using a cutting torch to cut any defective product into smaller chunks to be melted down again for immediate recycling. However, much of my job was helping load bundles of 60' rebar or angle onto rail cars for shipping to various customers. The steel was melted in huge cauldrons about 16' across and 10' deep. These were brick-lined, wore out regularly, and needed to be refurbished. There were only two or three of these at the plant, so getting these giant pots refurbished and back online quickly was a number one priority with management.

You might imagine it takes extraordinary heat to liquify a batch of ten tons of steel. Hence, this mass of brick and steel naturally wanted to stay hot for a long time. When doing this, the only way to remove the old brick was with a jackhammer operated by human hands, hands belonging to me and other low-echelon employees. Management would order 12 of us to come in on Saturday and line up in front of a ladder leading to the upper lip of the cauldron. This equipment was only shut down the night before, so it was steaming hot. They would have the first in the line climb up and into the massive pot, grab the jackhammer, and hammer away. It was so hot that we could only hammer for about a minute before the remaining heat would force us up and out, going to the end of the 12-man line and then waiting our turn to get back in to continue to hammer away. It was horrific, grueling, and exhausting, but they paid me $.95 per hour, so I didn't mind the back-breaking work.

One day, I was helping the crane operator hoist bundles of 60' rebar up and down into an open-top rail car. These rail cars were about 12 feet high. We had almost finished loading a freight car to within about two feet of the top lip of the car when things went wrong. I was up in the car, guiding the bundles into place. The crane operator was a hot-shot who would begin to lift a bundle off the ground, bounce one end of it off a corner of the crane, giving it some extra speed while hoisting it and flopping it into the car. It was a highly unorthodox and dangerous way to do things, but he liked it, and those working with him didn't mind.

I was standing on a bundle with my knees at about the top of the upper rim of the car when I saw a bounce and lift gone wrong as he began to flop it in. I saw it coming but only had time to lift one leg out of the car when the bundle struck me on the other leg. This resulted in me being flipped head over heels off the top of the car and down to the ground. I did a 360-degree flip and landed on my knees, unhurt but freaked out. One of my nine lives had just been punched from my ticket.

Wolf Spider

I worked operating the front counter and repairing magnetos and distributors in an auto racing speed shop in Tampa, Triangle Automotive on Fig Street just off Dale Mabry, in the late '60s. The shop was a 1950 vintage home converted into commercial use. In the rear was a tiny, dingy, dark, bathroom with a toilet and sink. It was small. While sitting on the commode, you could touch the sink and the opposing wall at the same time.

One day, sitting on the toilet with my pants down around my ankles, I reached for the toilet paper next to my knees and pulled down on the paper. Unknown to me but soon to be known, a giant Wolf Spider was clinging to the back side of the roll of toilet paper. As he came around the top as I pulled, he lost his footing and arched gracefully directly down into my pants on the floor. I was so chock full of adrenaline at that instant that I don't remember what happened next. I do remember a lot of commotion.

Unknown gunman sporting a Triangle Automotive t-shirt. Nice toilet.

The Airport

In the late Sixties, the Tampa Airport Security was very lax. At night, we would park outside the fencing on the far side of the airport from the terminal, walk through an unlocked gate, and walk out onto the runways. The first runway we came to was an auxiliary runway with about 50 feet of grass between it and the next runway, the main runway. We would lie down on the grass near the active runway, smoke pot, and wait for the planes to take off right in front of us, just a few yards away. We were so close that the tips of the airliner's wings would go right over us. It was a blast.

One night, however, instead of an airliner approaching us and turning left onto the main runway, it continued to taxi right toward us to get on the auxiliary runway. This was frightening. The plane was right on top of us as we ran when it finally turned right onto the second runway. We left somewhat spooked, but in all the action, I had left a bag of pot in the grass between runways, so I returned the next afternoon, found it, and left.

It wasn't long after that security tightened up the fencing. We would still jump the fence.

The Forest Fire

Larry Enos and I went to shoot pistols one day, northwest of Tampa near Bay Colony. There was a vast wooded forest with a WW2 machine gun training area and a massive concrete wall for a backstop. The place had some dirt roads where a lot of illegal dumping occurred.

We parked the car and began walking along one of the dirt roads, shooting things like old washing machines. We had walked in the same direction for several hundred yards when we happened to look back. We were shocked to see a large forest fire burning and spreading from where we came from. We ran back down the dirt road we had just come from, running through the fire. We got back to the car unhurt, drove to the nearest payphone, and called in a fire alarm, not giving names, of course. Firing our pistols through one of the washing machines ignited the fire.

The Seventies

Marriage Number One

I met Michele in high school. We fell in love immediately and dated for about five years until her father told me to get with it or go away. We married soon after that conversation. We moved into a house in Hyde Park on Delaware Avenue that my mom bought us by putting some money down and financing the rest. The home cost twelve thousand, and after my mom's down payment, the monthly payment was $78.

Michele and I, 1971.

Within two years, I revealed myself as a damn fool and wanted a divorce. I had been seduced by an alcoholic, divorced woman with an 8-year-old child. I could not for the life of me see what was best for me, so I forged ahead with the divorce. I moved into an apartment not far away.

Somehow, months into the divorce proceedings, I knew Michele was dating someone and bringing him home to "our" house. One night, and I don't remember how I knew, but I knew she was on a date with him and would bring him home afterward.

I had a .44 Magnum pistol at the time, so I unloaded it to be sure nothing would get deadly, went over to our house, let myself in, hid in the bedroom closet, and waited.

Sure enough, they got home, entered the bedroom, stripped down to nothing, and got in bed. That's when I jumped out of the closet, brandishing the weapon, and ordered him out of the house. I'm sorry to say it was probably the most frightening moment of their lives.

The guy was gone in a flash. Michelle ran out the front door and down the street to a friend's house, with me behind her, brandishing the pistol the whole way. Michelle rang the doorbell with me right behind, and me then banging on the door with the butt of my gun. Now, mind you, I'm stone sober. Astutely sensing something amiss, the friend opened the door and asked if all was well. Michelle and I both said yes and walked back to our house.

The boyfriend had gone straight to a payphone and called the police. Within minutes, the police showed up and knocked on the door, asking what was going on. I told them I lived there, was on the deed, and had a right to have the pistol. Somehow, I assured them nothing else would happen that evening, and they went on their way.

In another stellar incident, still trying to remember how I came by all this top secret (from me) information, I knew she would meet another guy at his house. I locked myself in the trunk of her car just before she left for her date and waited until she pulled up into his driveway. He came out to the car, and I popped out of the trunk and introduced myself. Michele tells me she never heard from him again.

Yet another time, she was on a date at a restaurant, having arrived in the date's car. I opened the hood of his car and disabled the vehicle. These stories are heart-wrenching to write. I own it, though. Sad and painful to me as it is. I know it was far more painful for Michele and her dates.

However, a reflection of my appreciation of Michele and our good times together can be found in the fact that I have a long-sleeve shirt she hand-made for me nearly 60 years ago.

Male plant behind my home on Delaware

Through no fault of hers, Michele and I divorced two years and two days after marriage. I got the papers on Valentine's Day. I gave her the house, everything in it, and went to live in bliss with the town drunk.

Mushroom Hunt

One of our group's favorite pastimes was to hunt for mushrooms. A specific variety of psilocybin mushrooms, Stropharia Cubensis, was what we looked for. The active ingredient for a psychedelic trip is psilocybin, similar in effect to Timothy Leary's LSD. The trip would last about six hours with visual, spiritual, and mystical hallucinations.

These hunts were in North Hillsborough County farmers' cow pastures, looking for cow patties (bovine waste material), a preferred medium for our magic mushrooms. We pick the 'shrooms off the top of the patty. We usually sauteed them, but if we were in a hurry, we ate them raw.

Me and a mushroom.

The Great Marijuana Theft

1971, I bought a new Volkswagen bus from Lindell Volkswagen on Kennedy Boulevard in Tampa for my hippie lifestyle. After some time, it needed some routine service, so I took it to Lindell. When they called me to tell me the service was done, I arrived, picked it up, and drove home.

While on the way, I remembered that I had left a lid of marijuana in the glove box. I immediately looked, and sure enough, the lid was gone. I quickly turned around and headed back to the dealership. When I arrived, I demanded an immediate meeting with the general and service managers. We sat in a conference room, and I explained the theft in detail. To their credit, they all kept a straight face throughout, listening to me vent my anger. They said they took this seriously and would investigate, then get back to me.

Sometime later, they called and told me they had yet to learn who stole the pot.

Cozumel

Gary Woodworth had some friends in St. Pete who had a small sailboat and the desire to sail it down to Cozumel, an island off the Yucatan coast. Gary wanted me to go with them, so I met the "sailors" to discuss the trip. They were enthusiastic about the journey, had charts and a plastic sextant, but had no sailing experience other than in Tampa Bay, in full view of land.

The plan was for the guys to go on the boat and for wives and girlfriends to fly down to meet them. I thought, "What could go wrong?" and flew down with the girls.

We flew into Merida and got hotel rooms, and then the next day, we went to Uxmal, a famous Mayan ruin. That evening, back in Merida, we went for dinner, then drinks. One of the girls caught the eye of an older, dapper, Castilian gentleman who bought us drinks. He was very enamored, but our girl didn't bite. He was undaunted, however. He knew the hotel where we stayed and showed up after we got to our rooms with a Marichi band, who proceeded to serenade this poor girl outside her room for an hour. She was steadfast and stayed in her room.

One of the sailor's wives liked me, and we spent the night together. The sex was good, but when we woke the following day, she began to cry and begged me to "save" her. She said her doctor/husband had her hooked on drugs and was keeping her in slavery. I had my own problems and didn't need another, so I kept my distance.

We drove the next day to the coast and took a ferry to Cozumel. We got rooms for two dollars a night, spent the night, and met the arriving mariners the next day. They were no worse for wear, unscathed, and on time.

Our rooms were a block off the street along the harbor. After a few days of being familiar with us in the mornings, the locals would have beers already open for us when we came off the side street and headed toward the bar.

I flew back with the girls, unknowingly harboring "Montezuma's Revenge."

From left, Gary, then me on Cozumel dock.

Anti-War

Sentiment against the Vietnam War and the spread of "hippie" thinking and culture both rose in the middle to late sixties, forever linking them. The "Peace" in the "Peace and Love" mantra was about general peace, but specifically the Vietnam War. Our anti-war stance was just one of the things we stood for: sexual equality, women's rights, personal freedom, racial equality, indigenous rights and gay equality, among them. We did change the world, but let's not forget our hippy coalition was only half of our generation. Half of the population our age was pro-war, anti-women, and the rest. Our problem today is that many of those knuckle-dragging white supremacists are the very ones in power.

There were anti-war protests everywhere, many in Washington, D.C. There were yearly ones, with one big one called the May Day Celebration. I went to two of those, 1970 and 1971. Gary Woodworth and I went together to the 1970 protest for two days. The camaraderie with the hundreds of thousands of attendees was just fantastic. There were speeches, marches, and lots of music on the Mall. The scent of marijuana filled the air. We slept a few hours each night on the ground. Police were everywhere, many on horseback, but they were friendly, smiling, and talkative. Every event, and everything in between, was peaceful.

Gary wanted to go again in 1971, but I did not. The event started on Saturday, and I agonized about going up Friday afternoon. While at work, I decided to go. I left work, drove straight to Tampa International, walked up to the ticket counter, and paid cash for the first flight to D.C. Gary had already left, so he had no idea I was coming. With a half-million protesters, it would be tough to find him.

I arrived at Washington National Airport (now Reagan) in the early evening and walked the three miles to the National Mall, where everyone gathered and camped. I had nothing with me except the clothes on my back. I walked the length of the Mall and stood in front of the White House. While I was standing there, a young guy walked up to me and said, "Open your mouth and take this," holding a pill.

Those days were filled with trust, so I opened my mouth and swallowed the pill without a thought. About twenty minutes later, I felt the onset of psychedelia from the LSD tablet I had eaten. It was wonderful. The mood in the air with those thousands of like-minded people was euphoric, hopeful, and full of promise.

It wasn't more than an hour until I happened on Gary sitting at a campfire. Surprised to see me and having coincidentally taken LSD earlier, we both sat for hours watching the campfire, drinking Boones Farm.

Much like in 1970, Saturday and Sunday were filled with music, marches, and speeches, but this event had an additional protest march scheduled for Monday. The idea was to block strategic intersections throughout D.C. and bring Washington to a halt. The police were aware, as was the Federal government. While the mood of the police throughout the weekend was amiable, the mood on Monday morning was quite different. Gary and I decided to join the May Day Tribe.

Our anti-war movement was split on whether or not to block traffic and create a potentially violent scene. Those of us who liked the idea called ourselves the Mayday Tribe. Our slogan was, "If the government won't stop the war, we'll stop the government." Out of the half-million, we were down to about twenty thousand. There was organization and a tactical manual printed and distributed. The Nixon Administration knew about these plans, and even though it was a great rallying cry, it was mostly hyperbole. Stopping traffic in Washington for a day or two would not stop the war.

Still, this was alarming to the Nixon administration (Nixon's White

House chief of staff, H.R. Haldeman, called it "potentially a real threat"). The D.C. police were on high alert and told to be "firm."

Our "tactical manual" highlighted twenty-one intersections and bridges in and around D.C. Gary and I went to the Arlington Memorial Bridge.

The Politzei was ahead of us thanks to the tactical manual. Under Nixon's direct order, Attorney General John Mitchell mobilized the National Guard and thousands of troops from the Army and the Marines to join the Washington, DC police in the mayhem, rounding up everyone even suspected of participating in the protest. There is no "Probable Cause" here. As one protester said, "Anyone and everyone who looked at all freaky was scooped up off the street."

A cosmic number of people, more than 7,000, were locked up before the end of the day in what is still the largest mass arrest in U.S. history.

Gary and I never got onto the bridge; the chaos and intent of the police were apparent from a distance, so we fled on foot, crossed the bridge to his car late that night, and left for home.

Washington was barely affected, but we got the media attention we wanted.

Back in Tampa, Gary and I were at a Japanese restaurant having a meal and a bottle of wine. Our waitress noticed just an ounce left in the wine bottle and playfully asked Gary if she could pour the remaining bit directly into his mouth. We all thought that was a great idea until the waitress put the bottle up to his lips and knocked one of his front teeth out.

Checking into a Paris Hotel

The only class in school I ever really liked was French, starting in the seventh grade and continuing through high school. I got nearly fluent and even subscribed to a French newspaper. I've since lost most of it. French is not a language you use in Florida.

My sister and I went to Amsterdam in 1970 to see my cousin Frits but spent a few days in Paris. When we arrived, I hailed a cab and got us to a hotel, all done in French. I checked with the pretty young girl at the reception desk and did everything in French. As I turned to go to the room, the girl looked at my registration and realized I was American. She was an American also! Both of us thought the other was French!

My Career as a Pig Farmer.

In the late 70s, I lived in Land-O-Lakes in a 25-acre orange grove off Highway 54. The house was so old it had live electrical wires on porcelain insulators in the attic. I wasn't too surprised that it burned to the ground not long after I moved out.

I got the idea to raise pigs and built a couple of pens on the property. I loved them all and named them, but I was able to compartmentalize things and took them one by one to the local slaughterhouse in a special trailer I built. They can be affectionate, and they are intelligent.

At one point, I had three, one nearly 300 pounds and two probably 50 pounds. I had a friend at the time who owned a restaurant and would save the table scraps for me to take to my pigs. I had them all in one pen and would dump the table scraps over the fence into one of those large dog bowls. They loved that stuff, but you would think that the larger pig would get all the food. However, the little ones got everything, and the way they did it was they would be on either side of the big one (Arnold).

One of the little ones would dart in from the side to try to get some, and the big one would nerf him out of the way, but that gave the little one on the other side a clean shot at the food, then the big one would nerf him out of the way and the first one would get a mouthful. This went back and forth a time or two without the big one getting anything.

One day, he realized that if he turned around and sat on the bowl, covering all the food, he would seal up the bowl so the little ones couldn't get any food. He sat and waited until the little ones lost interest and walked away, then Arnold would get up off the bowl and eat everything. I am still trying to figure out which branch of science, but there is some science in that pig's head.

I eventually split the pen in two and had a wooden gate with horizontal slats and a release on top that you pressed down to open the gate. For a week, when I went out in the morning, it was the strangest thing, the pigs had switched sides. I thought a friend was pulling a trick on me, but it turned out the little pigs would climb the fence, press down on the release, and they would swap sides.

They can also be stupid. I was in the house one day when I heard a blood-curdling scream outside. I thought one of my pigs was being killed. Turns out, with again a horizontal wooden slat fence, this one had stuck his head between the slats but had to turn his head sideways to do it, then turn his head upright, but he then realized he couldn't pull his head straight out and didn't have the brain power to turn his head back sideways and then pull himself out. I went out and had to twist his dumb-ass head sideways and push him back through the fence.

Steve and Melissa being scratched.

My DUIs or Lack Thereof

1. I was stopped one night at about 2:00 am for erratic driving on Nebraska Avenue while looking for a quickie blow-job. The Tampa Police officer, after administering a blatantly failed roadside sobriety test, said, "I should arrest you, but it's so close to my shift ending, how about you lock your car, then I'll take you with me to the Tampa Police Department, have you sit in my car while I punch out, then I take you home with no charges? Sound OK?"

   Of course, my answer was, "Most certainly, thank you."

   That's what we did. He took me home, which at the time was my parents' house on Swann Circle. He pulled up in the driveway, and I got out and went to the side door where I usually entered the house. I waited a moment while I faked unlocking the door while he backed out, waited until he was out of sight, then walked the five miles back to my car, started it, and drove home.

2. After closing the bars, I got stopped again on Westshore Blvd. just North of Kennedy Blvd. I was hammered, of course, and should not have been driving and indeed gave them cause for the stop. Again, I failed the sobriety test badly, but while I was tottering along to the cop's amusement, a second police officer pulled up, then a third. Within seconds, something came over their police radios, and all three jumped in their cruisers and took off, leaving me dead drunk standing

by the road, so I got in my car and went home.

3. I turned off Kennedy Boulevard one evening after closing the bars, drunk driving, even to a casual observer. When the flashing lights went on, I took off in a ridiculous attempt to evade. After a block or two, I regained sense after running over a curb and pulled over one block from my house on Swann. The police were courteous while watching me fail yet another roadside sobriety test, while a friend of mine just happened by and also pulled over. The police then said I was being arrested for a DUI and that they were going to impound my car after they searched it. Standing close by and hearing this, my friend said he would happily drive my car to my house just a block away. The police said no; they searched the vehicle and then impounded it.

4. So, in the search process, they found a lid of pot in the glovebox, which got them very excited, so they decided to arrest me for possession of marijuana and not the DUI, which they did. When in front of Judge Harry Lee Coe, he gave me a year's probation for the felony. After many months and many thousands of dollars, the Florida Supreme Court overturned my conviction because it was an illegal search and seizure, primarily because I had a friend there at the scene offering to take charge of my car. The case is a precedent-setting ruling, still used for citation in other similar cases.

The Outlaws Band

In about '73 or '74, I saw the rock band The Outlaws many times at the North Tampa Whipping Post and other bars. Seeing them so many times, I became familiar with the band. One evening, I told one member, I can't remember which, that they needed to get a demo tape and send it around. The response was that they needed recording equipment or access to some.

I had a top-end reel-to-reel and microphones, so I offered to make a tape for them. Soon, I set things up with overhead mics and recorded one of the gigs at the Whipping Post. It turned out very well and had a brief, hilarious moment between songs when you could hear a glass breaking and the laughter of the band and those watching. I gave them the tape, sadly, without making a copy. The band thanked me profusely soon after listening to the video. Not long after, they had a record deal with Arista. I am still waiting to hear from them again.

After an Outlaws Concert

I had moved in with Tricia Plastic in 1973. We both loved the Outlaws. Tricia and I left an Outlaws concert late one evening from the Hitching Post Bar on Nebraska Avenue. I kept a .44 Magnum, long-barrel revolver under the seat of my VW. We had been drinking far too much.

With Tricia driving, I thought it would be a good idea for her to fire the pistol out the window. She had never fired any gun before and had no idea you had to hold something like a .44 very tightly. I neglected to mention that as she fired it out the driver's window on Interstate 275. The recoil slammed the barrel into her forehead perfectly down the middle. She was stunned and hurt, so I drove home.

The next day, she had a vertical lump on her forehead the size of an egg. It took forever to go down, and when it did, there remained a three-inch scar down the middle of her forehead that never went away. She wore bangs the rest of her life to cover it.

On another trip to a bar, Tricia and I went to one on Kennedy Blvd for a drink. During our stay at the bar, Tricia went to the restroom. Shortly, another female patron complained to the bartender that someone was in the ladies' restroom, had been there for a long time and would not respond or unlock the door. I realized they were talking about Tricia and went to see what was going on. The door was locked, and there was no response to repeated knocking. Before breaking the door down, I looked for another way in. I walked outside and saw a small transom window about eight feet off the ground, open and with the window frame slanted inward. I pulled a trash can under the window, stood on top of the trash can, pulled myself through the window, and dropped down into the restroom. Tricia had passed out while sitting on the toilet. She would get so drunk she would go out like a light, and nothing would wake her. She would literally go comatose. I unlocked the door and carried her out to the car.

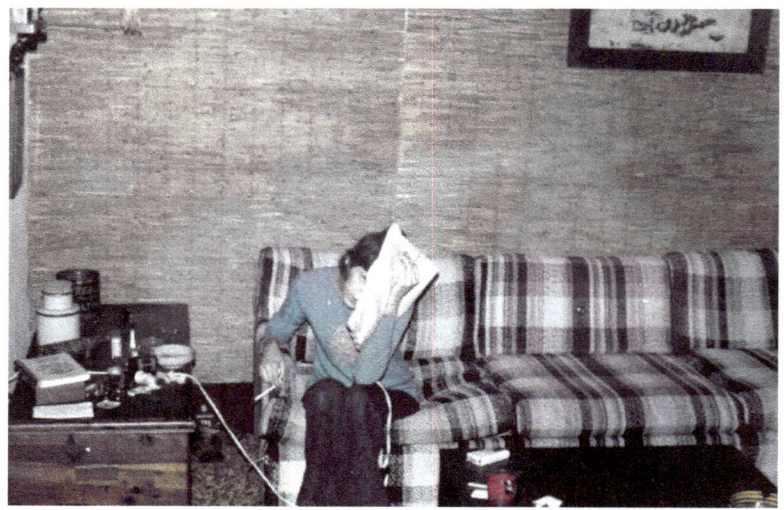

Tricia applying heat to her head wound.

The Samurai Sword

While I lived at Tricia's house on Morrison, I slept completely naked. Our bedroom had large casement windows that opened outward with no screening. I awoke late one night to the sound of what I was sure was burglars going through things in the living room. I had no pistol in the house, just a Japanese WWII military sword that I kept near the bed.

I jumped up, grabbed the sword, opened the window, and thought if I went outside and came through the front door, the burglars could not escape. Completely naked, sword in hand, I leaped through the window and came around to the front door, only to find the burglars had departed through the back door.

The Flying Cross

Back in the day, and maybe still, Harley-Davidson motorcycles had a throttle nicknamed the "Suicide" throttle. This meant it had no return spring. Wherever you set the engine speed, that's where it stayed, even if you took your hand off the throttle.

This feature was useful if you wanted to cruise at fifty miles an hour, let go of the throttle, stand upright on the seat, and spread your arms in a "flying cross." You could maneuver the bike, but only minimally. This trick became a specialty of mine.

My primary venue was on the four-lane Dale Mabry Highway in front of Steak and Shake across from Plant High School. Steak and Shake was a big hangout, and I would alert everyone before a performance. I would start from Bay to Bay, and when I got near Steak/Shake, I would set the throttle, stand on the seat of my Harley, and do the flying cross past Steak/Shake and out of sight. The pavement was badly broken up there, making the trick somewhat sketchy.

Flying Cross practice.

Dating Sylvia

I dated Sylvia for a couple of months until I blew it. Sylvia was a dark-haired beauty from a Cuban family in Tampa. This relationship had real possibility. I met Sylvia's mother at her home and we hit it off, mom really liked me. She liked to make me Cuban coffee whenever I visited.

Sylvia had an apartment, and she had friends over. One evening, some friends and I were over, including her best friend, Jeannie. Jeannie was blond, tall, and beautiful, too. She lived on St. Pete Beach, where she owned and operated an Insty-Print. We called her the "Insty-Princess."

That evening, Sylvia said she wasn't feeling well and was going upstairs to lie down. She said we didn't have to leave right away and that we could stay for a while. Jeannie and I had been eyeing one another for a while and took this opportunity to go outside to have sex in the back seat of her VW, a feat on its own.

While in the middle of this activity, I heard a knock on the window, looked up, and saw Sylvia looking down on us. That was the end of dating Sylvia. She died recently and is missed.

Sylvia

By the Hair

I dated a girl I'll call Alise. She worked as a dental hygienist and I met her through friends. At the time, doctors and dental assistants wore cute little white uniforms that some men found sexually attractive. If you haven't heard that before, it's true. She was the ugliest girl I ever dated, but she had a body to die for and long black hair to her waist. I won't go into detail, but she did a thing with her hair that I will remember with affection until I die.

It was sex, all the time for months – always at her house. I've never before or since had that much concentrated sex in my life. I never lived with her but would stay over at times. She liked Jack Daniels, so we drank a lot of that. She would act weird at times, completely out of character. I just dismissed it so as not to spoil the party, so to speak.

We went to Morrison's Cafeteria one afternoon. I was driving with her on the way home at about forty miles an hour when she suddenly, for no reason, opened her door and began to get out of the car. As she began to slide out onto the pavement, her feet bouncing along the highway, I grabbed a handful of that long hair and dragged her back into the car. Incredulous, I continued to drive until we arrived at her house.

She had no explanation for her conduct. It wasn't the first of the odd behaviors. One thing that had me suspicious of what was happening was, while sitting at her house, she would get loopy sometimes for no reason. The only time I couldn't see what she was doing was while she was in the bathroom. Skeptical about what was going on, I followed her to the bathroom and opened the door after she had been there for a minute. She had her foot up on the toilet lid and was injecting a liquid drug into the space between her toes. The drug was Dilaudid.

I had my own set of problems at the time and couldn't take on another one. I called her brother, told him the situation, and said he should get over here immediately to address the problem. After he arrived, I washed my hands of her and left. I never heard anything about her until much later.

Forty years later, while in Key Largo, I decided to try to find her. I found her brother working in Miami and contacted him. He said she was living in Miami and gave me her phone number. I called her, talked briefly, and agreed to meet at a café in Miami. We met and had a great talk about friends and some old times, but at one point, she asked me, "Did you and I ever date?"

Stunned and humbled to this day, I stammered, "Yes, for a while."

She remembered nothing. I remember myself as a good stick-man, but this has made me wonder. Was I that forgettable while it was unforgettable for me? There is a disconnect somewhere.

Two Quaaludes-Two Sopers

At the house in Land-O-Lakes, I lived in, Mike Sarga had lived there for a while and had installed a waterbed in his bedroom, very close to one wall below a "Miami" window.

Miami windows are generally composed of three horizontal panes, enclosed by aluminum railings, hinged at the top, and rotate outward at an angle to keep rain from falling into the room. It was an old house, so old that it had live, open electrical wires in the attic supported by glass insulators. The walls were skinny also, and with the windows installed, there was no window ledge, the screens on the windows being nearly flush with the walls.

We consumed many Quaaludes at that house. One day, when they ran short to zero, I had the recollection that previously, one had fallen between the bed and the wall below the window. I tried to look down into the space to the floor to see if there was a Quaalude. I couldn't get my head and eye close enough to the window screen to see the floor. Water beds, you might know, cannot be moved without days of work, so I removed the screen and rolled the window out to get my eye close enough to the gap. When

I got my right eye into position to look, my eyeball was only an inch from the railing containing the glass. The horizontal railing had a groove about three-quarters of an inch wide running the length.

As I tried to look down into the gap to the floor, I saw something move in the periphery of my right eye. I pulled back and saw a Pygmy Rattlesnake wiggling its tail at me threateningly. My eye was only an inch from his fangs when I pulled away. He had somehow slithered up the wall inside, and into the window frame to sun himself. I let him go. Thank goodness these snakes aren't very aggressive. By the way, there was no Quaalude.

Kieffer Harris came out to that house quite often, where, at times, cocaine and Quaaludes were on the menu. His father had recently given Kieffer a mint 1970 Buick. Now, a scene in the movie "Wolf of Wall Street" involves Leonardo DiCaprio taking Quaaludes. This scene is absolutely one hundred percent accurate and a perfect example of why you should not take narcotics and drive.

One evening, Kieffer and I had taken at least one Quaalude and decided to go to a convenience store. Kieffer was driving on Ehrlich Road approaching Highway 41, which had no traffic light, just a stop sign. At 50 miles an hour, Kieffer never saw the stop sign or saw it way too late for his addled mind to react and, therefore, ran across a somewhat busy highway at full speed. We responded when it was too late and were across the road without incident.

After a quick visit to the corner convenience store, we headed home again with Kieffer driving. We were on 41, turning left onto Highway 54 in Land-O-Lakes. Kieffer misjudged the turn, turning about sixty feet too late, and slammed into a power pole in the far corner. No one was hurt, and even though the car was severely damaged, it would still drive. So, not wanting to wait for the police, we backed up away from the pole and drove home. That beautiful car was too damaged to repair.

I had been trying to get a date with a beautiful girl I had met while working for the phone company in Clearwater. Finally, she agreed to meet me for dinner at the Mullet Inn one evening. I was taking a shower and getting ready for the date when I stepped out of the shower to find a friend of mine, Michael, standing there. He had come by to share a new drug with me and insisted I take two of them right at that moment, just before the date. They were "Sopers," which, at the time, I didn't know were equivalent to Quaaludes, the same drug, just a different manufacturer.

Life is about choices, and this was a bad one. I took two, got dressed, got in my car, and drove the fifteen minutes to the Mullet Inn. That is precisely the amount of time it took for the drug to take full effect. By the time I met this poor, unsuspecting girl at the restaurant door, my legs were rubber, and I was incoherent. After accurately assessing my condition, she left, and I somehow had enough cognition to drive home. At least, I think I did. When I woke up, I was home, and my car was undamaged in the garage. Refer to the above-described scene in "Wolf of Wall Street" for my condition.

Fishing On Gandy Bridge

Several of us, including Ray and Ben, used to go night fishing with live shrimp on the catwalk off Gandy Bridge from the Tampa side. We would load up everything, drive all the fisherpersons and gear out to the spot on the bridge, and drop everything off. Then I would go to the St. Pete side, back to the Tampa side, park the car, and walk out to meet everyone.

One evening, we had been fishing for a while when a car drove by at probably sixty miles an hour and threw a full beer can at us that narrowly missed my girlfriend, smashed into the railing, and splattered all of us with beer. Hitting someone in the head with a full beer can at sixty miles an hour could easily be fatal.

I carried a .357 Magnum revolver with me for shooting sharks had we ever caught one. Angry, I pulled the pistol from my shoulder harness, stepped out on the highway, pointed my handgun at the fleeing car, and asked everyone, "Should I shoot them?"

As ridiculous as that may sound, that's what I did. I fired at the retreating car but aimed purposefully high so I wouldn't kill anyone. I didn't tell anyone I had deliberately missed, but we felt it best to gather our stuff and leave for home.

M1/M2

I've owned guns all my life, starting with my grandmother buying me a Baretta pistol at an auction when I was about 12 years old. My interests were mostly rifles and pistols from 1870 through WW2.

At one point, roughly in 1970, I bought an M1 Carbine, a lightweight semi-automatic carbine issued in the U.S. military during World War II, the Korean War, and the Vietnam War. The M1 carbine was produced in several variants and was widely used by paramilitary and police forces worldwide after World War II. The M2 carbine is the selective-fire version of the M1 carbine, capable of firing in both semi-automatic and full-automatic. The only difference between the two was a few interior parts that were widely available if someone were disposed to convert from M1 to M2. This was highly illegal unless you had the proper Federal license. Fully automatic weapons are not allowed in the hands of your average American.

The Bureau of Alcohol, Tobacco, Firearms and Explosives (BATFE) is commonly called the ATF. Its responsibilities include the investigation and prevention of federal offenses involving the unlawful use, manufacture, and possession of firearms (fully automatic weapons being one focus) and explosives, as well as acts of arson, bombings, illegal trafficking, and tax evasion of alcohol and tobacco products.

I owned the M1 for a while when I realized that the full auto conversion was possible, cheap, and easy, so I did the conversion and test-fired it a few times in remote places.

I was living alone in a friend's home in Tampa while seeing a divorced girlfriend with a daughter about eight years old. I'll leave the names out. I was at her house often and witnessed how the girl's father would disappoint her by saying or promising something and then not following through. Her father was a good man then as he is now, but sometimes, we let important things slide.

I know the following is a moronic idea to act out, but so it went. I was upset at how he treated his daughter, so one evening, after drinking a little too much, I thought it would be a good idea if, when he fell asleep on the couch, I would unload my .357 pistol, wake him up with the gun to his forehead and tell him if he didn't stop disappointing his daughter, I would use the gun on him. So, I did precisely that. I suspect the message got through. I should have stayed out of it, I'm sorry I did it, it wasn't my place.

What's this nonsense got to do with an M1/M2? Not long after the above incident, I had a break-in at the home I was living in. Two pistols were stolen, an M1911 and a German Walther P-38, both from WW2. I suspected the father was pissed at me over the threat and came to avenge. I blamed him with no evidence whatsoever. In retrospect, he certainly had not done the theft, but at the time, I accused him.

Now, most of the craziness that follows is the result of too much disposable income and, therefore, a lot of discretionary spending on a wide variety of drugs. It's horrible, embarrassing, and shameful, but here we are.

I was mentally impaired most of the time in those days, and being pissed about being robbed, I hired a private investigator to stay at the house for a couple of nights while I was away. I was convinced the thief, the friend I spoke of earlier, would strike again, with no evidence at all that would happen.

When the investigator showed up at the house, I explained I wanted him to sit quietly in the dark and wait for the thief to show. He quickly realized I was expecting him to kill the intruder, and he immediately bolted.

I was so pissed a couple of weeks later that late one night, I took the M2, now fully converted to automatic fire, to the private investigator's office, where the company cars were parked, and shot one of the cars to pieces with the M2.

As I write this, it's hard to believe that it was me doing this ridiculous, dangerous stuff.

M-14 and the Mercedes

Being a gun collector, I've always been fascinated with the Thompson submachine gun. The originals had a selector allowing them to fire in a semi-automatic and fully automatic, making it highly illegal to possess by an unlicensed citizen.

The Thompson submachine gun, also known as the "Tommy gun," "Chicago typewriter," and "Street sweeper," was invented by United States Army General John T. Thompson in 1918. It was initially designed to break the stalemate of World War I trench warfare, but early models did not arrive in time for combat.

The Thompson saw early use by the United States Marine Corps during the Banana Wars, the United States Postal Inspection Service, the Irish Republican Army, the Republic of China, and the FBI following the Kansas City Massacre.

The weapon was also sold to the general public. Because it could be obtained so easily, the Thompson became notorious during the Prohibition era as the signature weapon of various organized crime syndicates in the United States in the 1920s. It was a common sight in the media, used by law enforcement officers and criminals alike.

In 1975, I started looking for one at gun shows, knowing full well that possession by me was a felony. I approached several sellers at different gun shows but had no success other than one who said he would keep an eye open for one, so I gave him my phone number.

A couple of weeks later, I got a call from him saying he couldn't find a Thompson but had an M-14 with a thousand rounds of ammunition. The M-14 was also a selective fire weapon issued to the U.S. Military in 1957. Again, this, too, was highly illegal to possess without a license. We agreed to a price and then met on the roadside on the St. Pete side of the Howard Franklin Bridge.

My mother died two years prior and left me some cash, with which she told me, "Spend it and have some fun," so I did just that.

With $11,000 in cash, I bought a brand new 280C Mercedes, a spiffy silver coupe.

I drove that car to the roadside gun sale and was met with a guy that I didn't recognize. He said he came instead of the seller, saying the seller had some emergency. I fell for that and handed him some cash, and then we put the rifle in the trunk of my Mercedes. That's when the rest of the ATF agents swooped in and put us both in cuffs.

At that point, I didn't realize the seller was also an agent, but off we went to the Hillsborough County Jail in Tampa. I was booked and released the next day, with them telling me that my Mercedes was being seized. The official charge was "Conspiracy to Possess an Un-registered Weapon," carrying a ten-year sentence and a $10,000 fine. The seizure and fine were final.

ATF agents began using my car in their operations. One evening, I happened to pass it on Interstate 4. I recognized it immediately because I had placed an unusual sticker on the bumper, which was still there. I slowed, pulled in behind them, and, at a distance, trailed them to a bar on Fletcher Avenue and waited for the two agents to go inside. After seeing them go inside, I got out of my car and put a very heavy key scratch along the side. It wasn't very satisfying.

A few months after completing my sentence and returning home, I got a call from a parking garage in downtown Tampa, saying my car had been sitting there for a year and asked if I was coming to retrieve it. Still in possession of a set of keys, I brought Ray and jumper cables to the garage, paid the parking fees, and drove it off. I couldn't risk trying to keep it, but there was an expensive car phone installed that I knew I could sell. I drove it home, removed the car phone, returned to the parking garage, and parked it, never seeing it again. I sold the phone.

East Coast Bale of Pot

In the middle of our importation of organic materials from Colombia, I had to drive over to the East coast of Florida, a bit North of Cocoa Beach, to the house of one of our distributors to pick up a bale of pot. The reason is lost in the fog.

I arrived at the house in the middle of a rockin' party. I partied with them for an hour but then had to get the bale of pot and return to Tampa. Incidentally, I met Warren Zevon at the party right before he hit the rock music scene big time with his album "Excitable Boy."

The homeowner and I rode up US1 for a mile or two, stopped, and waited for the light traffic to disappear. Some stretches of the East Coast were undeveloped at the time. With the traffic gone, we went up into the scrub oaks off the highway for a few yards, where the bale was stashed. We put it in my trunk and went back to the party. I stayed a bit longer before getting back on the road. Drinking some alcohol and smoking some pot will make you sleepy, and as tired as I was, I began falling asleep at the wheel.

I knew I couldn't continue, so I stopped and parked on the shoulder for a nap on Interstate 4. I was lucky, again, because the smell of the weed was overpowering. If a cop had walked up to the car, there would certainly have been an arrest. I tried to sleep for about fifteen minutes, but even though I was dog-tired, I was so wired that I couldn't. No sheriff pulled up, my luck held, and I arrived home safe and sound.

$250,000

After a shipment arrived from Colombia, we would distribute bales to our "wholesalers," who would split the bales into pounds, which would get sold and further split. No strangers were involved. We all knew each other from high school, mostly Plant High in Tampa.

After everything had filtered down and sold to the end users, we would drive around to collect. Ben and I were on one of these roundups where we collected $250,000 in cash. We needed to take it somewhere other than where we lived to count and sort it. We took it to a good friend's apartment who lived on Armenia Ave. in Tampa. Becky and her husband smirked as they watched us count all that money on her kitchen table.

On another collection route ending in St. Pete, we finished counting the quarter-million at another friend's home. We left there that afternoon with the cash neatly bundled into $10,000 stacks of twenties and one $10,000 bundle of $100s. The $100s bundle was about a half-inch thick. This filled a brown paper bag that was used in grocery stores at the time. We left that afternoon with Ben driving my big purple Caddy we called "Moby Grape." The bag sat between us on the front seat. I took the $100s bundle from the bag and set it on the seat beside me.

Before crossing Tampa Bay, Ben and I decided we needed a Heineken, so we stopped at a convenience store near the St. Pete airport. We left the bag in the unlocked car, went into the store, bought the beer, got back in the car and drove down the highway.

We were only two miles down the highway when I realized the $10,000 bundle of $100s was no longer in the car. We turned around and sped back to the convenience store and did a perfectly controlled four-wheel drift into the empty parking lot. The bundle was right where I had dropped it, lying on the pavement in the mid-day sun. I grabbed it and we drove on.

We arrived shortly in Tampa in the mood for a celebration. We picked up Po and Sharon and took them to Bern's Steak House in Tampa. Bern's was and still is high-end. It was dark as I parked the car on the street about a block and a half from Bern's, with the bag of cash now safely in the trunk.

As we left Bern's and walked toward my car, I felt for my keys in my pocket. To my horror, I realized I had left the keys in the ignition. The keys, the car and the money were still where I left them.

The Sheriff

PCP was a briefly popular drug in my circles back in the early seventies. It is also known as "Angel Dust," a street name for phencyclidine. Angel dust was developed in the 1950s as a surgical sedative but was later discontinued due to its severe side effects. Phencyclidine (PCP) is a mind-altering drug that may lead to hallucinations (a profound distortion in a person's perception of reality). It is considered a dissociative drug, the consumption of which leads to a distortion of sights, colors, sounds, self, and one's environment.

Herschel Biggers, a local biker, was my supplier, from whom I would buy small, high-quality quantities. A friend in Savannah tried it and said he would buy all I could muster. Having no cash, I had a new Harley Davidson Sportster that I figured I could leverage, so I worked out a trade with Herschel for an ounce of PCP. I did just that. I traded an excellent bike for a baggie of dope.

With a baggie of PCP in hand, two friends and I drove my car to Savannah for the sale. Only a couple of hours out of Tampa and deep into a bag of cocaine, we decided it would be more fun to fly to Savannah. I got on my car phone and somehow booked a small, private plane out of Ocala with a pilot and co-pilot. Within minutes, the aircraft was ready, and we got on board.

Fifteen minutes into the flight, I realized I had left a tote bag on the floor next to the tiny airline counter containing the dope and a .357 Magnum pistol. This immediately became, of course, an emergency. I determined we should continue to Savannah, drop my two friends, fly back with the pilots, grab the bag, get in my car, and drive back to Savannah. So, that's what we did.

Thankful for not having police meet us at the terminal, I picked up the bag from where it had not moved, got in my car, and headed north.

After driving through Jacksonville in the middle of the night, I found myself on a two-lane highway in MacIntosh County, Georgia, with flashing red and blue lights behind me. I knew nothing before this about the notorious speed trap I found myself in. I knew I was not speeding and was profoundly unhappy I would get a speeding ticket. But things got way worse immediately. I had put the dope in the glove box and the .357 pistol under the driver's seat, not realizing it had slid back to the floor between the front and back seat, in full view of anyone glancing down there. Of course, as the officer began to write the ticket, that's where he looked, and the whole tenor of the activity we were involved in changed dramatically.

The officer dropped his ticket book, stepped back, pulled his pistol, and, pointing it at me, ordered me out of my car. I put my hands up and got out of the vehicle. The officer proceeded to spin me around, cuffing my hands behind my back, and placed me in the back of the police car. The officer called for backup, and my vehicle was searched when they arrived.

One of the officers found the baggie of powder in the glove box, and things got even more serious. I might have been able to explain away the pistol, but not the dope. I watched as the officer looked at the drug and then opened the bag to smell it. I hoped I would see him stick his fingertip in the powder and taste it like you see in the movies. Thankfully for him, he didn't do it, or soon after, he would have been on another, very unfamiliar planet.

After the commotion at the highway stop, I was taken to the Sheriff's Office. They sat me in the sheriff's office, which was tiny – barely room for his desk and two chairs. I was left alone for a few minutes when the sheriff, Tom Popell, walked in, apparently pulled out of bed by his excited deputies. Sheriff Tom walked into his office with my pistol, sat down with my weapon in front of him on his desk, and began the interrogation.

First off, he asked me if I was a hitman, a drug dealer, or both. He arrived at the hitman idea from a shoulder holster that matched the pistol. While we talked, he casually unloaded my gun and set it and the bullets down on the desk. After another minute or two, he stood up, said he would be right back, and walked out of the office, leaving me alone with the pistol and bullets within arm's reach, directly in front of me.

Hyper-aware at that point, it took just a millisecond to realize what was going on, and the hair on the back of my neck stood up. Tom and his deputies were setting me up, thinking I might grab my pistol, load it up, and shoot my way out of the sheriff's office. I was severely spooked and knew they were immediately outside the office door with pistols drawn, waiting for my move. I froze in my chair. Another minute or two went by, and Tom came back, sat down, and told me I was about to be booked for possession of a controlled substance, not having any idea what the substance was.

It was about three in the morning when they put me in a cell. At seven-thirty, a deputy came to my cell saying I had a visitor. I thought, "What the fuck?"

Not a soul I knew had any idea where I was. Turns out the visitor was John, a local attorney. Now, I was aware this entire thing was a scam. John spoke for a minute and said he could get me out of this for five thousand dollars. The previous night, when I realized I was being pulled over, I had eight thousand dollars in cash in the car with me that I quickly stuffed into my underwear as I pulled over. The deputy's subsequent search didn't include my groin. I said OK, let's talk to the sheriff. I was let out, walked with John to the sheriff's office, and sat in front of his desk. Sheriff Tom asked if I was agreeable to paying a five thousand dollar "fine."

I said yes, stood up, reached into my underwear, pulled out the eight thousand, counted out five, set it on the stunned sheriff's desk, and waited. He and John were momentarily speechless. Then the sheriff picked up the money, called for a deputy, and told him to give me my belongings and let me go. The belongings they gave me included the pistol and ammunition but not the drugs. I walked out into the broad daylight, got in my car, and continued to Savannah. With the loss of the PCP, my Sportster, in effect, was given away.

Now, I knew a crooked sheriff in a sparsely populated coastal county.

The Great Sapelo Bust

I first tried marijuana in about 1968 with my first wife, Michele. One evening at the Red Dog Saloon in Tampa, a friend, Jerry, offered for us to try some pot he had at his apartment a couple of miles away. We sat in his apartment while he rolled and lit up a number. After a bit, when we began to feel high, Jerry stood up, took his shirt off, and began flexing his muscles while walking around the apartment.

Being high and watching Jerry, we were stunned and slightly afraid of him. It wasn't very long until we left, but I was afraid of Jerry for a long time. To give you an idea of how wacky he was, his nickname in our group was "Albert DeSalvo," an American serial killer.

Being young with no money and limited income, it began to dawn on me and a few friends as well that if we bought a larger quantity of pot, we could split it up, sell most at a small profit, and smoke for free. Several of us did that for a while. We then decided to step up our game, buying an even larger quantity and making a sizable profit. At the time, to go even bigger and import from South America seemed like the easy and logical thing to do.

Of course, there are a couple of huge problems with this. First, who do you buy from, and how do you do it safely without getting killed or ripped off? Second, after assuming a successful purchase in South America, how do you get the product back to Florida? These are insurmountable problems for most aspiring drug kingpins.

However, it wasn't long before a friend of mine, Pedro Alvarez, told me he had a friend who had a friend in Columbia who had a friend who could arrange hundreds of pounds or even tons of Columbian marijuana, which had a worldwide reputation of being the best. Jamaican pot was almost as good, and Mexican dope was considered to be trash.

Pedro, Mike Sarga, myself, and an unnamed other discussed how and if we could pull this off. We could meet with the suppliers and come to an arrangement, but how do we get merchandise back to Florida? That would take more thought and some recruitment of talented and trusted friends.

My dear friend, Ben Ellis, and another mutual friend, Doug Dery, both had multi-engine pilot's licenses but owned no airplanes. Both were interested in the budding enterprise. The natural extension from there was to look for a relatively inexpensive aircraft that could carry some cargo, not just a couple of passengers.

Of course, setting up a supplier in Colombia comes first. We had the meeting set up, flew commercially to Medellin, and were met at the airport by Pedro's friend's friend, but I can't remember his name. He drove us to a Medellin hotel, where we met two Colombians at the bar.

After brief pleasantries in broken Spanish and broken English, we arrived at a deal. When we had an airplane, we would ask for some poundage, and they would ask for a deposit. They then took us out to a nice spread somewhere in the country where there was too much to drink, showed us some horses, and had several pretty Colombian women who joined the party. I don't remember much, but I assume we had loads of fun. We left Colombia the next day, full of hope and very hungover.

One of the principles in the deal turned out to be Pablo Escobar before he turned into a vicious but wealthy murderer a few years later. He seemed like an ordinary guy about our age and was lots of fun. I'm not sure the pot was his. He could have been brokering the deal, I can't say. At this point in his career, he was involved with pot but was soon transitioning into cocaine, where he built the Medellin Cartel in '75 or so. As you will see, we were out of it by then. We never saw Pablo again.

Pablo's mugshot, 1976.

We found an airplane broker with a top-notch DC-3 for sale in New Jersey that the 1950s TV personality Arthur Godfrey owned. It was named "Matilda" then, but we soon removed the name. As I remember, we paid $42,000 for it, which was not an easy sum for us. We test-flew it and brought it to Tampa to a secluded dirt field near Brooksville, where we stripped the interior and installed extra fuel tanks. There was no fueling station at that strip, so we had to ferry aviation gas to fuel the airplane, which was a significant problem.

Over three years, we flew ten trips to Columbia, with Mike and Pedro doing the logistics. I never again went down to South America; I was involved with distribution in Florida. We did use the plane for other things. We flew it to Mexico a couple of times to buy Quaaludes in bulk and traveled to Colorado three times for Coors beer.

Coors beer was trendy at the time in Florida and elsewhere, but it could only be bought in Colorado. We flew to Denver twice to load Matilda up with dozens of cases of beer with no problem, but the third time, on the way back, we stopped to refuel in Midland, Texas. The scene when we taxied up to the fueling station was out of a movie, a dozen vehicles of all sorts screeched up with lights flashing and then guns drawn. The DEA and other drug enforcement authorities were somewhat inept at the time. They assumed we were carrying drugs of some kind. You would think they would stop us on our way from Colombia, but they stopped us flying from Denver. They weren't happy about finding nothing but beer aboard, so after about an hour of conference, they announced they were seizing the airplane for "Non-Payment of Alcohol Tax."

The seizure held up, and we lost the plane and the beer. We replaced the beloved "Matilda."

There was a second DC-3 that Doug Dery and Ben Ellis piloted on two trips south. Doug and Ben were fueling a DC-3 that they were test-flying at an airport when they got "ramp checked" by the FAA. An agent went into the aircraft and yelled out he had found drugs. He had found sandbags above the tailwheel used for ballast when the plane is empty. They contained sand.

Doug and Ben used Hubert Rutland's Inverness, Florida ranch, to prep their DC-3 for a trip south. Bladder tanks had to be installed because you had to have enough fuel to make a round trip. The aircraft was loaded with pampers and trash requested by the farmer. Hubert Rutland had no knowledge. Several young ranch hands were paid well. When they landed the aircraft in Colombia, it was damaged and was not flyable. The farmers used a backhoe to dig a hole and bury the plane. The farmers used their personal Cessna Skymaster to fly Doug and Ben to Aruba and drop them off.

We then bought another WWII-era cargo plane. Her maiden voyage ended in disaster when she crashed, fully loaded. One engine quit within an hour of take-off, and the crew had to crash-land on a remote Colombian beach. Everyone was buckled in, and luckily, there were no injuries. They torched the plane and disappeared into the jungle. Ben and the other pilot contacted our Colombian partners, who sent a crew to help them survive in a jungle camp until fake passports could arrive. The Colombians provided food and water while they waited.

One of the Colombians had a dog with a litter of puppies. As the days progressed, the litter became fewer and fewer. No one asked questions. The crew managed a quiet return to the States in a circuitous route, running through Aruba and Haiti. That had to be done quietly, without drawing attention.

On another trip, they flew out of a ranch in the Green Swamp near Lakeland, Florida. When they returned at night, they missed the approach and had to do a "go around."

The plane was low and heavy, and when they applied full power, the two radial engines were extremely loud. People living close by called the authorities and reported a possible downed aircraft. They landed on the 2nd attempt but clipped the fence near the runway. The airplane was not flyable. Doug and Ben were paid pilots, $75,000 for the pair. They say they should have gotten in their car and left but stayed to help unload the plane. They had many trucks to unload that quantity. When the sheriff, who was on the lookout for a possible downed aircraft, saw all the trucks pulling out on the highway, he said to himself, "This ain't right," and he busted them.

The pasture they used to land had cars lining the landing area with headlights on high beam. The fence they had to go over to touch down had high-intensity flashlights on top of the fence posts pointing up.

Even with the seizure and three total-loss crashes, we had completed enough trips to have more money than anyone I ever knew. As a perk, the Colombians would save the best of the crop for our personal use, separating it specifically for us. My friend, Phil Alonso, had a coffee mill where we would go at night to vacuum a lot of our personal pot into sealed coffee cans with "El Aguila" printed on them.

All this income needed to be laundered through legitimate businesses like the "Sound Room" on Kennedy Boulevard, owned by Pedro and Mike but with a phony front-man owner.

We decided to ditch the airplane smuggling and bought a shrimpboat, the Hazel B., from a shrimper in South Carolina. Although slower than a plane, it could carry far more and be safe from airplane crashes. They are not safe from sinkings, but sinkings are more survivable.

Docking and unloading a shrimpboat with eighteen tons of marijuana was more complicated than landing a small plane with one ton, so we had to find a private, secure dock somewhere in the Southeast. Pedro had found one we used twice in 1974. We were also constantly looking for other places to use.

After encountering Sheriff Tom Popell, I met with Mike and Pedro and told them of the potential. They asked me to run up there and see if he was interested in an alliance. I had a 1967 Chevy Bel-Air with inflatable airbags under the rear suspension, able to carry two hundred pounds of pot in the trunk without the vehicle looking as though it had weight in the trunk. The car was fitted with highway gearing, and though it had a 427 engine, it was capable of twenty miles to the gallon on the road.

Today, there is surveillance in every gas station and convenience store in America. Back then, there was not as much, but there was some. We thought not creating a paper trail to Georgia was in our best interest, so I drove unannounced to the Sheriff's Office, carrying twenty gallons of extra fuel in my trunk. No phone calls and no gas station stops.

I arrived at Tom's office at 7 am, hoping he was there. He was and ushered me into his office. I was blunt about what we were looking for. The meeting lasted ten minutes, and I was out the door on my way back to Tampa with no response from Tom, who simply said, "Thanks for stopping by."

I got a call from John ******, my impromptu attorney for my prior encounter with Tom Popell, asking that I return to Georgia and meet with Tom's nephew, Bobo Thagard. Days after that, Ray and I drove to meet him. He had a girl in the car who turned out to be candy for me. He showed us a remote, wooded area that backed up to a sheer bluff where he said we could pull the boat up to unload directly onto land without ferrying the goods from ship to shore.

He said the area was a popular camping and drinking spot on the weekend but that Tom would cordon off the site for us to do the deed for a $50,000 fee. Bobo and Ray were in the front seat, driving to town, while I had sex with the girl in the back seat, them smirking in front. It didn't seem like it was an unusual thing to do at the time.

We returned to Tampa without incident, and I relayed the outcome to Mike and Pedro. They liked the idea, but I was cautious. I suggested testing it before committing to a real deal is best. I said we should pay him the 50k, unload hay bales, and see what happens. They thought that was a good idea, so we tabled it. We had a boat headed to the old spot south of Savannah and would test Tom later.

I got a panicky call late one night from Pedro, who told me they couldn't use the intended offload dock south of Savannah because there was another boat already there unloading. He thought it would be too much commotion for two offloads and would likely attract law enforcement. He said we needed to use the Sheriff's offer. I said, "Jesus, Pedro, we were going to verify the deal before committing."

Pedro said, "This is an emergency, take $50,000 to him right now."

He told me to pick up the money at his house from his wife and get up to Georgia immediately. I called John and asked him to meet me. "You know where" and "You know with whom," and hung up.

I went to Pedro's house at 3 am, picked up the cash, and drove to meet John and Tom. The meeting was brief, with only John there, telling us when Tom could arrange the offload. I went home, called Pedro, and the deal was on.

Days later, late at night, things were going quite well until Sheriff Tom realized there were Customs and DEA officials there in the woods behind him. After an intense, brief exchange of pistol fire where no one was hurt, in effect, the DEA had tapped Sheriff Popell on the shoulder and asked, "What are you doing here?"

Tom said, "I'm here to arrest these drug pirates, of course."

This wasn't true, but what could he say? Customs and DEA were involved because Tom's nephew had been caught by the Feds doing an unrelated dirty deed. To save himself, he gave up his uncle and all of us. They arrested nineteen of us on site, and Pedro and I three days later.

A hot-shot Tampa attorney, Arnold Levine, who had been with us since the beginning, advised us to come clean with everything. Sheriff Tom was well known by federal authorities as a crooked sheriff but was beloved by his constituents in the county. Arnold found that the Feds wanted Tom badly and were willing to make a deal if I were to testify truthfully in a trial of John ******. Since I was the only link to John, who was the only link to the Sheriff, the theory was that my testimonial pressure on John would make him flip on Tom.

The deal was that we would get only a year and a day in prison. I was reluctant but had no choice. I didn't want to look over my shoulder for the rest of my life, but I didn't want to spend more than a year in jail. Customs questioned us all, but mostly me. During this, the agent mentioned they found an FBI file relating to my anti-war activity, which was not much, a lot of talk and two trips to Washington, but there it was. Our organization was very tight, we all knew each other well and for many years. The agent commented, "What was this, Plant High School Goes Drug Smuggling?"

Most of the twenty-two indicted attended Plant High.

The trial went forward in Brunswick with a jury of John's peers. There was no paper trail linking me to him or Tom, just the drug arrest the year before, so it was a "my word or his" circumstantial evidence case, and he got off.

I was relieved and thankful. Tom died peacefully years later, still a hero, a legend, and adored by his constituents who remember him to this day. Bobo disappeared forever, days after the bust.

Largest S. E. Haul, 18 tons of Marijuana Confiscated (Aiken Standard, Aug 25, 1975)

Savannah, Georgia (AP) The customs agents watched and waited as the 65-foot shrimp boat turned across the dark sound to a waiting launch. The launch, a 22-foot inboard/outboard, led the larger boat into a nearby inlet, and in the dead of night, a score of men began unloading 50-pound sacks of marijuana from the shrimp boat, the "Hazel B" agents said. Forty-two customs agents slipped into action, surrounding the unsuspecting men early Sunday. The result was 22 arrested on smuggling charges in the confiscation of nine camper trucks, a sedan, a van, the launch, the shrimp, a boat, the houseboat, $11,000 in cash, and some 18 tons of marijuana – the largest seizure of the illegal weed ever in the southeast, customs officials said.

They placed the street value of the marijuana at $10 million. The Hazel B and the launch took off toward nearby Sapelo Sound when the agents jumped, but officers and boats stopped about an eighth of a mile from the bluff, agents said others ran for the woods, "they just took off like a covey of Quail," said Charles Perkins, Director of the regional patrol office of the US Customs Service.

Some of those arrested were taken on the scene. Others were apprehended later. The ones we got during the day were mostly ready to come out. Morris, the Customs Patrol Supervisor for this area, said, "They had them a night of thrashing around the woods with all that and all the mosquitoes. They were pretty well scratched up."

Perkins said the campers had been spotted in the uninhabited area for several days. We knew something was going on; we had been staking it out. He said authorities differ as to how the shrimp boat took on the marijuana, which he said came from Columbia, judging by the markings. Perkins said he believes it was loaded from another vessel beyond the United States territorial sea limit. Morris said the shrimper could've made the journey from Columbia, a South American nation at the Western end of the Caribbean Sea. Customs agents said late Sunday that the shrimp boat was registered as belonging to William Destler of Savannah. An agent said one of the men charged was identified as William L. Destler, Jr., but they said they did not know if he was on the boat. The raid was the fourth and largest in a series of drug raids in Georgia, and recent ones have cost the illegal drug visits some 50,000 pounds or more marijuana worth $15 million.

PICTURESQUE BUT NOT PEACEFUL
The Hazel B, a shrimpboat loaded with 18 tons of marijuana piled on the stern, sits in a marina near Savannah. (AP Wirephoto).

Shellman's Bluff Amused by Smugglers
(Atlanta Journal Constitution Aug 26, 1975)

"I don't know how that boy made it through a mile of mosquitoes, cats, rattlesnakes, bears, and 1 million seed ticks."

To fight the evening heat and the bugs here in this tiny, coastal fishing village, Mr. and Mrs. Hinton Deloach usually take a walk down the sandy lane, then shut the windows, turn on the air conditioner, and go to bed. This past Saturday night, though, they sat out on the screen porch of their little cottage for a couple of extra hours, watching as the full moon lit up the greatest cops and smugglers saga ever to unfold in these parts.

But long before the $10 million in marijuana had been seized and several of the 23 suspected smugglers in custody were still running through the tick-infested bogs or stealing getaway boats from local marinas, Mr. and Mrs. Deloach got bored by it all, "shut the windows and turned on the air conditioner and went to bed."

Fact is, the largest marijuana seizure in the history of the southeast United States has left the residents of this picturesque little town about 50 miles south of Savannah Little more than amused. Collie Wilkes, for example, operator of Kip's Fish Camp, which, like everything else at the Bluff, looks out on acres of green marsh grass and Sapelo Island, sums up his feelings about the whole session with these three thoughts:

- They stole two of my boats.

- I don't use marijuana anyway

- I'm sure they didn't catch anybody but the peons.

62-year-old Woodrow Wilson, one of the local landmarks, also known as Good Time Shirley, was amazed at the stupidity of the would-be smugglers.

Excerpt from the 1979 book "Grass Roots: Marijuana in America Today" by Albert Goldman from his in-person interview with Robert Perkins, U.S. Customs:

Off-loading a shipment of smuggled goods is the moment of truth, the D-Day that even veteran smugglers anticipate with a lump in their throats. Those who have organized the operation and brought it this far have much to lose—maybe even their lives. The odds against getting nabbed don't quell the quick churning in the guts that begins when the whole unloading scene starts to reel off like a movie.

The best picture I obtained of an off-loading was provided by Robert Perkins, director of the Charleston Patrol, an armed and specially trained unit of U.S. Customs charged with interdicting dope smuggling into Georgia and the Carolinas. In August of 1975, Perkins received word from an informer that a big load of dope was coming into Sutherland's Bluff, down near Sapelo Island, one of the most remote and thinly inhabited sections of the Georgia coast. (Customs will pay any informant a "moiety:" half the value of the seized merchandise up to a maximum of $25,000.) Marshaling all his people into a convoy of trucks and cars, he took off on a suffocating Saturday afternoon for Savannah. There, he briefed them on the operation. Then, the CPOs piled into their vehicles again and rolled down 1-95 until they were near Shellman's Bluff, a popular Saturday night drinking spot about a mile from the smuggling site.

Perkins needed to get his men into the area before the smugglers began unloading, but he was afraid to infest the area with a big posse lest some spy spots them. He could not contact the local police because lots of redneck sheriffs are into the smuggling game, just as their daddies were into bootlegging. So, he ordered his people to pull off the highway into a rest area where no one would ever think to look for them. Then, he dispatched four specially trained scouts to slip up to the smuggling site and spy out the operation. These men had gone to Navy Seal school. They were trained to cross rough country, swim for miles underwater, and get close to a criminal operation without being seen. Their orders were to wait until they saw the dope coming off the ship. Then, they were to signal the rest of the officers with the code word "Eyeball."

The area the smugglers had picked to land their load was a classic bit of Southern coastal scenery. Sutherland's Bluff is a stretch of twenty-foot-high bank along the Sapelo River, which winds down to the ocean through a landscape of gnarled live oaks streaming with Spanish moss. On this hot, humid night, a smuggler's moon rose like a giant orange ball from the swamp. When it got higher, it turned into a silver disc beaming down like a floodlight on the narrow, sandy riverbank.

Around ten o'clock, the patrol scouts were scoping out the position. They reported that there were many police in the area: both the local sheriff and his deputies and some Georgia highway patrolmen. As some of the Customs men were undercover agents wearing civilian clothes, the presence of the police posed the distinct possibility that in the confusion of the raid, some of the "good guys" might be shot as "bad guys." Perkins ordered all his people to take out white rags and tie them around their right arms.

Then, the scouts approached the riverbank and began reporting the scene there. About twenty smugglers were scrambling all over the bluff. They had nine campers and vans. They had moored a houseboat at right angles to the beach to act as a floating dock.

A big shrimp trawler, led by a little pilot boat, was seen coming up the river. The shrimper was the Hazel B, her port of registration Savannah. She was coming to anchor adjacent to the houseboat. The smugglers were swarming out to meet her. The cargo was coming off. The word was "Eyeball!"

Perkins ground out his last cigarette and gave the order to attack. The convoy dashed across the highway and down the local road until it hit the narrow, sandy track leading to Sutherland's Bluff. Suddenly, Perkins stared through the windshield in disbelief. There, blocking the road squarely, was a Georgia highway patrol car. Its occupants were standing on the side of the road looking straight at the oncoming Customs men. Shrieking to a halt, the lead vehicle of the Customs caravan disgorged a furious Customs man.

"Robert Perkins, director, Charleston Patrol, U.S. Customs," snapped Perkins, flipping open his leather ID wallet with its gold-and-blue badge. The sergeant who had been driving the car looked perplexed. He explained that he could not get his vehicle out of the road. "Well," growled Perkins, who was now beginning to have his suspicions about this inopportune roadblock, "if she's not gonna go that way," jerking his thumb backward, "she's damn well gonna go that way," jerking it forward, "or you're under arrest for obstructing a federal officer in the performance of his duty!" The astonished highway patrolman stared for a moment; then, without saying a word, he jumped behind the wheel and drove the car furiously down the rough country lane, tearing off bumpers, fenders, scraping and smashing the undercarriage, until by the time the vehicle reached the creek bank, it had been totaled.

Meanwhile, many of the CPOs had jumped out of their vehicles and ran on foot toward the river. Firing broke out at once. One smuggler rolled out of a van with his pistol blazing. A CPO got off three fast rounds from the hip with a shotgun. The local sheriff, who claimed to be leading a raid on the smugglers, was caught in the river in a small boat. Spouts of water erupted around him. When he stumbled ashore, he found out Perkins and accosted him. "Your goddamned bastards been shootin' at me!" he snarled. Perkins laughed. "Sheriff," he replied, "if my 'bastards' been shootin' at you, you wouldn't be standin' here talkin' to me." The sheriff promptly disappeared.

Half the smugglers surrendered after minutes of violent scuffling; the others tried to make getaways. They raced into the bushes, stole boats, and got onto Sapelo Island. They spent a dreadful night contending with mosquitoes, bobcats, rattlesnakes, bears, and a million seed ticks there. One or two escaped; the rest gave themselves up the following day.

When the final tally was made, Perkins had bagged twenty-one men, a sixty-five-foot shrimp boat (whose real name was Gemini II), nine motor vehicles, a houseboat, a 25-foot launch, $11,000 in cash and eighteen tons of marijuana worth about $10 million. It was the biggest dope bust up to that time in the history of the Southeast.

The Great Sapelo Bust by Vic Waters

There was a full moon shining on the river
when the boat came in with the goods.
The high sheriff was a hidin' in the marsh grass,
while the customs agents waited in the woods.

Well, the sheriff didn't know about no customs men,
and they did not know about the sheriff,
and the shrimp boat didn't know nothing 'bout nobody.
When the lights came on, it scared them half to death.

Well they were running through the woods trying to figure out
a way to get out this mess they'd all done got in to.
Looking for some cover, shooting at each other,
bumping in to one another, calling for their mother you hoo.
I know that's what they's doing cause they's all runnin
Round the woods goin "Mutha ...!"

Well the boys commenced to unload the trawler
When the law moved in and grabbed em fast.
Its pretty damn hard to conceal the evidence.
Lawd you just can't eat eighteen tons of grass.
Not even if there's two of you.

Compliments of songwriter and singer Vic Waters on Youtube

Hillsborough County Jail

On October 31, 1975, Halloween, I surrendered myself at the Hillsborough County Jail in Tampa for the year-and-a-day Federal sentence for Conspiracy to Import Marijuana and Conspiracy to Possess an unregistered Weapon, an M-14. I was at the zenith of my drug and alcohol abuse days and thought it was a good idea to smuggle in a Quaalude in my socks to ease my first day in incarceration.

I made it inside with the Quaalude without a problem. They weren't particularly thorough in the inspection, although they did have me bend over and spread my ass-cheeks, looking for contraband. They didn't find anything, and I was placed in a private cell for a couple of weeks. During the day, an inmate would come by with a "library" cart with books for inmates. I picked out "The Rise and Fall of the Third Reich" by William Shirer, the most complete account of that war in existence. One thousand pages. I found it so fascinating that when I finished it, I returned to page one and reread the entire thing.

In a couple of weeks, I was transferred to the general population, which consisted of dangerous thugs and assorted low-lifes, not your average federal white-collar criminal. Things didn't go badly, thank goodness for the figs they fed you every morning. I have a taste for them even today. The only thing that happened out of the ordinary of watching inmates take a dump in plain view was that one day, while I was lying on my bunk, face down, right at the bars where guards would walk by, a guard stopped and looked at me. He said, "It's not a good idea to lie prone like that on your stomach, especially for a young, good-looking guy like you."

That point was well taken.

I was in the County Jail for six months, a very long time indeed for federal inmates not to be transferred to a federal lockup. The reason was that I had to continually go up to Savannah, Georgia, for the lawyer's trial. It was just logistically easier for them to hold me there, in the town where my attorneys were, so we could fly up to Savannah when needed. It was easier for my keepers to keep me there rather than ship me to a federal prison, then back to the county, then to Savannah. It's easier for everyone but me, of course. County jails, in general, are far more dangerous than federal prisons due to different types of crimes. County and state crimes are far more violent and vicious.

It took six months in the county jail for the trial appearances to finalize, and then they began my transfer to federal custody.

Palatka

When the federal inmate bus picked me up in Tampa to get me out to FCI (Federal Correctional Institution) Texarkana, Texas, we stopped at a county jail in Palatka for the evening. It was March, so it was chilly. We were put in a cell for the evening with no bedding, sheet, pillow, or mattress, just a flat, solid steel bunk bed. The only clothes I had were jeans and a thin silk shirt that I wore when I surrendered six months ago. I still have a picture of me with that shirt. The jail had no heat, at least for the inmates, so we were cold. I shivered all night and barely slept on that cold steel plate. The federal bus showed up in the morning, and we lumbered on.

Tallahassee

On the way, the bus began to have engine trouble outside Tallahassee, so they stopped at FCI Tallahassee, a juvenile facility. Adult inmates cannot mingle with juveniles, so I was put in a private cell. After a few days, I wondered when the bus trip would resume. I would ask the guards about it, but they knew nothing. After about ten days, with no answer about my travel plans, I went on a hunger strike, using only the pipe tobacco and rolling papers they issued you daily.

After three days, someone higher up the food chain stopped by my cell and asked what the fuck my problem was. I explained everything to him. Two days later, the feds found a bus somewhere, loaded me up in all my refinement, and we departed for Texarkana, but not directly.

Atlanta

A stop on the way to Texarkana was USP Atlanta. The United States Penitentiary, Atlanta, is now a low-security United States federal prison for male inmates in Atlanta, Georgia. However, in 1975, this was a maximum-security facility housing the most dangerous lifers the system has produced.

When the bus dropped about ten of us in USP Atlanta, we were only to be there for a day. Another unknown problem would eventually keep us there for ten days. When prison officials decided we shouldn't be kept in isolation for an extended period, they agreed to let us go out into the general population but needed a bit of an orientation to the facility first. This was a maximum-security facility at the time, with primarily lifers with nothing left to lose, so they said never to walk alone and maintain heightened situational awareness. After the orientation, the officer looked me in the eye and said, "Especially you."

His point was well taken. Nothing out of the ordinary happened, and one day, we got on the bus to Texarkana.

Texarkana

The rest of my co-defendants were sentenced to the minimum-security facility at Eglin Air Force Base which was notoriously called a "country club" due to having no barbed wire or even a gate. It was for non-violent inmates with minimal sentences. I was the only one out of nineteen defendants who went to a medium-security prison due to probably the additional machine gun charge that I pled to at sentencing. They thought meek, mild-mannered old me, was some gangster.

My five months at Texarkana were mostly uneventful except for one unsettling event. Just days after I arrived, a new inmate was admitted to our dormitory. This would not be unusual except for late that evening, after lights out, he invited everyone into the bathroom for some sex. There was a long line waiting but I stayed in my bunk. Otherwise, it was clean and quiet, with no fights and little arguing, just dull, day-to-day getting by.

There are many inmates who, after being acclimatized to treatment in Federal prisons, decide that it is their preferred lifestyle. Especially the gay ones. Free room and board and an unlimited supply of horny males to choose from.

A local gay inmate who differentiated himself from the straight population with a bandana over his mostly bald head had taken notice of me and began to make sultry glances at me, hoping I'd take him up on whatever proposition he had in mind. I was one of the horny guys there, so after minimal resistance, I took him up on his offer, which turned out to be a blow job.

Now, I'm with Bill Clinton on this one, BJs are not sex, so don't get your gay-dar going. I never met a man I wanted to have sex with. One could argue males who look like females could be a gray area, but once it boiled down to two penises in the same bed, the second penis would be difficult to ignore.

We went to his cell, and he gave me an expert blow job. Now, a blow job is a blow job, and it doesn't matter where it comes from in the final analysis as long as there is no expected reciprocity, which, in this case, there was none. With a lookout to keep the guards away, all went well, except that I am confident this was the moment I contracted Herpes. I swear I could feel it getting into me.

This class of inmate, often when released, immediately commits another Federal crime to get back into the system, and this is what my blow job benefactor did. A couple of months after he was released, he was right back home in prison, having threatened a bank robbery. He was happy as a clam, having an array of penises eagerly awaiting him in Texarkana. All was well again.

Genital herpes (HVS-2) was new to most Americans, having begun to spread dramatically in the late '60s and into the '70s. Clinical studies started then when not much was known and there were no treatments. There was the occasional story on television news. Early symptoms can be bad, and during one of those, I caught a news story about it saying the NIH (National Institute of Health) had a hotline you could call for information.

I called, and a doctor named Anthony Fauci answered the phone. I described my symptoms, and he confirmed my suspicion that I had genital herpes. He said he would like to check on my symptoms after a few months. He called three months later for an update, and an unusual aspect of my symptoms caught his interest. Even though his attention soon turned to the surging HIV epidemic, he continued to call over the next six years.

My Stalker

When you arrive at a federal prison, the management will look at you to determine if you would be a good fit for a job in the administration. There are good reasons, keeping you busy and out of trouble and avoiding having to pay a civilian to work among them.

They put me to work in the inmate intake area of the office. I worked administering psychological and literacy tests to incoming inmates. My boss was a young civilian female from rural Texas. It's in your best interests to schmooze everyone in power, so I did so with her. I might have overdone it because after I was released, for 25 years, she regularly drunk-called me, proclaiming her love.

Kosher Food

An interesting development came about one day when a prison official stopped by my bunk to talk. He told me a recent Federal lawsuit had been ruled in the plaintiff's favor. The plaintiff was a Jewish inmate who had sued the prison system to have them provide Kosher food for Jewish inmates. Incorrectly assuming from my last name, Altman, that I was Jewish, he said I was to no longer report for meals with the rest of the inmates, that I was to report to another area with a smaller dining area and a kitchen, separate from the ordinary kitchen and dining area.

There were only six of us, five real Jews and one phony Jew. The kitchen was staffed by a real kosher chef who provided excellent meals for us in a quiet, private dining room for the rest of my stay at Texarkana—a unique and welcome turn of events.

Letter to Judge Alaimo

Six months into my sentence for the smuggling charge, the light bulb went on, and I realized I never wanted to go to prison again. In the five years leading up to the bust, "we had enough money to buy Miami, but pissed it away so fast," as Jimmy Buffett sang. Cocaine, Quaaludes, women. We rented penthouses at high-end resorts for parties. We had phones in our Mercedes, which was rare in the early seventies.

I realized after six months of being dry and away from like-minded friends that the trajectory of my life wasn't going in a good direction. It could have easily, and soon, ended my life. I wrote the letter from my dormitory at FCI Texarkana to my sentencing judge, thanking him for putting me in prison. I never heard from him. When I was released from custody, I ditched many of my friends and began a straight, law-abiding life.

Me at Texarkana

By the Hair II

At the end of my year-and-a-day federal sentence for my misbehavior, I stayed for a month at the Goodwill Industries facility on the St. Pete side of Gandy Bridge. It was a huge facility with a big thrift store, sorting, storage, and a side hustle in the rear, housing federal inmates on work release. I met a beautiful girl there with whom I immediately hit it off. She had just been released from prison too and was as horny as I was. It was forbidden, but we would meet on the roof for sex under the stars.

When we both got out, we agreed for a date to go to a restaurant in Clearwater. I picked her up and drove to the restaurant. After being seated, I asked her what kind of wine she liked. She said she didn't drink and that alcohol makes her crazy. Yes, I thought, it makes most people somewhat crazy.

Sometimes, you should listen to what people say and register it word for word. Sometimes, what they say is the literal truth.

I said, "What can one glass of wine hurt?" and talked her into it. About ten minutes into the glass of wine, she began to act strange, with wild eyes and louder, incoherent talk. I recognized the situation as needing action. I threw cash on the table and hustled her outside. I put her in the car, got in, and began to drive.

Only two blocks from the restaurant, she opened her car door and proceeded to exit the vehicle at about twenty miles an hour. She had long, dark hair, so I grabbed a handful of it and pulled her back into the car.

Immediately, red and blue lights began to blink in my rearview mirror. I thought, "Oh, shit, what fresh hell will issue from this?"

I pulled over, hair in hand. The officer politely asked me what was going on. I explained it, he took a look at her and let me go. We had no further dates.

My 1978 Gasparilla

Pirate José Gaspar's legend has been celebrated in Tampa since 1904. The annual Gasparilla Pirate Festival consists of an "invasion" by Gaspar and his ship, the Jose Gasparilla, and a massive parade along Bayshore Boulevard.

In the '70s, I took friends on my boat, the Rhino, a couple of times to ride alongside the Jose Gasparilla pirate ship as it invaded Tampa with hundreds of other boats. In 1978, several friends were on my boat, the Rhino, on the Hillsborough River an hour or so before the invasion. My pretty girlfriend, Po Morgan, was on the boat's bow when I slowed the boat down too quickly, and she slid right off into the river. When she surfaced, I was doubled over, laughing my ass off. I said, "I knew I waxed the boat for a reason!"

Po

Just days before, I compounded and waxed the hull and gunwale. We went back upriver to Tampa General Hospital which was right on the river. Po was soaking wet, so we went looking for a blanket or something to dry her off. It was a chilly day, not a Gasparilla T-shirt day. We all had tons of clothes on, and Po was soaked. After watching the pirate ship dock, we idled down along Bayshore, where the parade was starting. Ray was sitting on the gunwale and slipped off into Hillsborough Bay, right next to the seawall, forgetting the fresh wax.

Ray Fox after sliding off the gunwale.

Another minor thing that day, I took a picture of a girl sitting on the seawall while watching the parade, oblivious to apparently being in desperate need of a toilet.

Girl

End of the Lake

I had just put a new 200-horsepower Mercury on the rear of my 24' Pro-Line and launched it in Lake Hiawatha behind Ray's house. It was a party, and about eight of us, including Ben and Ray, went out on the boat after dark to test the engine and the electric trim to see how fast it would go. We were not sober and looking at the engine as we trimmed it, when we ran out of the lake at forty miles an hour, up into the slick grass at the lake edge, and onto a neighbor's lawn at full speed. We barely missed some trees at speed and finally did hit one, but we were not going very fast.

No one was hurt, but we thought it best to get the boat off someone's property and back onto the lake as soon as possible. The boat was wedged up against a tree, and we first tried to push it straight back, but the stern dug into the ground. Over two hours, we gradually turned this twenty-four-foot boat, one hundred and eighty degrees around so the more streamlined bow would slide toward the water. It's heavy, so it was back-breaking work. No one ever came out of the house on the property we had invaded. They were there but thought it wise not to inquire.

Ray, myself, and Ben after retrieving the boat.

Ray was in his phone truck, stopped on Dale Mabry, waiting to turn left when he was rear-ended by a tractor-trailer going fifty. Ray's spine was cracked, and while he was in the hospital after surgery, I visited him with four friends, and my girlfriend, Tricia, who had too much to drink.

As Tricia and I stood next to the dresser by his bed, I looked down into the open upper drawer. I saw folding money and pocket change lying at the bottom of the drawer. A full urinal sat on top of the dresser.

Tricia was waving her arms around, ranting. Alarmed, I asked her to be careful not to knock the urinal over. In about ten seconds, she did just that, with the urinal spilling into the drawer.

I looked back down into the drawer and saw Ray's money, awash now in a sea of urine. I looked around at the stunned room and said, "That's why your mother told you never to put money in your mouth!"

The Eighties

Marriage Number Two

I met Stacey (future wifely victim #2), who worked as a Physician's Assistant at the Lutz Clinic, Chiropractic, Podiatry, and General Medicine. She was drop-dead gorgeous and I had it bad for her.

One day, I had gone in for an X-ray and found myself alone in one of the exam rooms. I had a friend at the time named Herschel Biggers. He was a hot-rodder whom I met while looking for a 55 Chevy to buy. He was about ten years older, a classic biker with several bad habits, some involving needles. I never used them, but I knew he had a use for them, and they were very controlled then. In my idle time in the exam room, I naturally rummaged through the drawers under the counter. I found a batch of needles and immediately thought of Herschel. Feeling the urge to ingratiate myself with him, I stuffed a handful of needles and syringes into one of my socks.

Stacey came in and told me I needed to take my clothes off and put on a gown, and that she would return in a moment. I wouldn't be able to walk around, nearly naked, with a bunch of needles in my socks. They would have been pronounced and prone to falling out of my socks while walking, so I quickly put them in one of my pockets. Stacey came in a minute later, picked up my clothes, and immediately, dozens of needles and syringes that were in my pockets spilled out, clattering and scattering all over the floor.

After her eyes bugged out, she walked out and, in a few moments, came back in with the doctor. Knowing the doctor was aware I was trying to steal needles and syringes, he asked, "Why?"

A little quick thinking resulted in me telling him and Stacey that I was in the middle of laying linoleum flooring at a tenant's apartment. It made things far easier to rid the bubbles from poorly installed linoleum with a syringe and needle filled with glue. Somehow, they believed me, and after sheepishly returning the loot, we all went on with our day.

Weeks later, Ray and I were at the Whataburger in Lutz when we bumped into Stacey. He knew I had it bad for her, so he dared me to ask her out, which I did. She accepted. Our first date was to the Café de Paris on Kennedy. On the way there, I almost wrecked my car when she told me what year she graduated from high school. I thought she was a bit older than she was. She was nineteen.

It astonished me, but she agreed to that first date, where we hit it off and were married not long after. We did a lot during four years, many fishing trips into the Gulf and several down to Key Largo. We did have a lot of fun.

Stacey

Bathroom Cleaning

While living out in Odessa with Stacey, I cleaned our bathroom toilet regularly for well over a year with a small cleaning pad I found under the sink. It was oval white and did an excellent job scrubbing. I would use it, wring it out, and put it back under the sink. Normally, I would do the cleaning while Stacey wasn't home. One day, while cleaning the toilet, she walked in and was horrified to see me using her "Buf Puf" facial cleaning sponge she used on her face daily to scrub the toilet. I don't think she is over that to this day.

After four years, my inability to be affectionate or close to her in any way took its toll on Stacey, and we divorced.

Kathleen

Stacey, Kathleen, Ben, and I had dinner at a restaurant in St. Petersburg. Kathleen is a tall, striking woman with long, flaming red hair. She was the epitome of politeness, poise, and manners. When we left the restaurant, I was driving, Stacey was in the front seat, Ben and Kathleen were riding in the back seat. Without warning, Kathleen blurted out, "Stop, stop, I'm going to be sick!"

She exited the car, squatted inches away next to the curb, and became sick. Stacey asked, "Do you need a tissue?"

Even though she was violently ill by the roadside, she stopped, looked up mid-vomit, and answered Stacey's question with a question. Holding her perfectly coiffed, long red hair back to her ear, looked up, sweetly saying, "Pardon me?"

My Violin

While with Stacey, I decided to learn to play the violin. I had been inspired years before by a Jefferson Airplane cut from one of their albums. I don't remember which cut it was, but the artist was Papa John Creach. His play prompted me to take lessons. The violin is not something you should try to learn at age 40, age 4 is a far better starting point, but that was impossible. Now that I think about it, the daily practice is probably a big reason Stacey and I parted. I attended lessons twice a week and practiced daily for four years. I'm sure it was too much for her.

I was never very good, though I did play briefly as a second violin in the University of South Florida Orchestra. To give you an indication of my level of play, before a concert, after we were all seated on the stage, the conductor would come over to me and move any microphone that happened to be near me.

As hard as I tried, I was never any good. I would have to start practicing Christmas carols three months before Christmas to make my play recognizable. However, I could play "Cavalleria Rusticana" by Pietro Mascagni reasonably well. You have heard the entire piece if you watched the opening credits of "Raging Bull" or the closing scene in "Godfather II." It's a beautiful piece.

I gave up forever after I cut off the end of my left index finger while working on my 28' Bertram, but more about that later.

My Country Vet

I've never been without cats, so while living in Odessa, my local veterinarian was an older country vet who did mostly large animals but also cats and dogs. It was a one-person practice in a tiny old building only a mile from where I lived. Odessa has had many horse and cattle farms for a long time.

One of my male cats had a urinary blockage that could ultimately be fatal, so I took him to the doctor. He examined my cat and handed him back to me, then, after rummaging through a drawer, pulled out a hypodermic needle. He told me to bring my cat and follow him outside. We walked out the front door onto the concrete steps. The doctor kneeled and rubbed the point from the needle on the concrete. He stood up, and with me holding the cat, he inserted the blunt needle into my cat's penis, immediately releasing the blockage, resulting in a strong stream of urine coming from a greatly relieved cat. The cost for the visit and procedure was five dollars.

Stingrays

Ray, Ben, and I did a lot of shark fishing off my boat. When we first got interested, we bought a book about shark fishing. The first sentence in the book was, "First, catch a whale."

We took that off the list for several reasons. One of the secondary baits for sharks was listed as stingray, so we always had our eye out for stingray.

We were fishing in Tampa Bay when we saw a school of small stingrays swim slowly by in the shallow water. There were at least a hundred. I had a cast net on board, so we trailed them, idling along until I had a good shot throwing the net. I caught about twenty of them. We put them in a large cooler for our shark fishing.

We finished the day, put the cooler in the trunk of my '66 Chevelle, hooked the boat and trailer up, and went home. I had two vehicles at the time and was primarily using my Chevrolet station wagon, so the '66 sat in the front yard for about two weeks with the windows closed until I got in it. It didn't take me long to realize I had forgotten the stingrays and left them in my trunk to putrefy into a bubbly, rotten witch's brew of stinking flesh. The stench was unbelievable and took about two years to disappear.

Lost at Sea

The Beginning

I have been trying to write this all down since 1986 but have been unable to do so until now. The ordeal was so traumatic, so emotional, that I have been unable to tell the story either orally or in writing, no matter how briefly, without getting very upset. But finally, here it is.

A relatively new-found friend, Rob Harris, and I had been going scuba-diving together for about a year. He lived and went to school in Gainesville, Florida. I lived just north of Tampa and drove up to Gainesville for three hours to dive the freshwater springs and caves with him. We would rent canoes with friends and girlfriends, load beer, food, and scuba gear in the canoes, and paddle down the Santa Fe River. We would stop at various spots along the river and picnic, swim, and dive.

The usual dive spots are Ginnie Springs, the Devil's Eye, and the Devil's Ear. The Devil's Eye and Ear are two entrances to the same cave system that connect twenty yards or so inside. Rob was twenty-seven, doing post-graduate studies at the University of Florida in Gainesville. He was near completion of his Doctorate in Agronomy. He was very bright, and I was sure he had an outstanding future ahead of him. He was very fit, nearly 6 feet, blond, very trim, no fat on him. Rob was energetic and loved to laugh.

I met Rob through his brother Kieffer, who had been a close friend for over ten years. Kieffer was a year younger than Rob. Kieffer and I had a great relationship. He had a twisted sense of humor that we both shared. The brothers lived across the street from me while Kieffer was still in Junior High School. Kieffer and a buddy of his would come over and smoke pot with my wife, which is more commonly known as "contributing to the delinquency of a minor."

Kieffer was a good kid, bright and honest, and turned out fine. I had been in my first marriage at about 24 years of age. I moved out of that house and the marriage after two years, but Kieffer and I kept up our friendship.

A few years later, I bought a saltwater fishing boat, and he and I did a lot of fishing offshore from the Tampa/St. Petersburg area, and we made several trips to the Keys. I also had a ski boat that we did a lot of skiing with. Kieffer was a great skier. He could make cuts so hard that they would stop the boat. We used to have a lot of ski parties out north of Tampa, where I lived. We did a lot of hard partying back then. We had many friends who could always be counted on for a grand weekend bash. Several of us lived on lakes, so the party would migrate from lake to lake, weekend to weekend. We did a lot together. Kieffer was tall and thin, over six feet, and handsome with light brown hair.

Rob and I had dived the springs so often that we began looking around for something different. I had the idea first to dive the Empire Mica. The Empire Mica was a 465-foot British tanker torpedoed by the Germans in 1942. The wreck is one of the finest wreck dives in Florida. It sits in 110 feet of water, twenty-five miles south of St. George Island in the Florida panhandle.

Because the dive was so far offshore and deep, it became a dive where skills, training, planning, and preparation would all play significant roles. It would require navigational electronics to find it. The wreck is not marked on the surface with any buoy or marker. My boat was a 23-foot Pro-Line called the HooLoo. The name comes from a contraction of the words ballyhoo, a baitfish, and hallucination since we had hallucinated so many fish on so many trips. When you do a lot of intense fishing, you see more fish than are actually there. It was my second Pro-Line and had the electronics we needed: a Loran for determining position and a depth finder for looking at the bottom. A Loran unit calculates your position by triangulating signals from several satellites. I also had a VHF radio on board. St. George Island is the closest land to the Empire Mica. I had another old friend who owned a rental house on St. George Island that we could use for a base. It seemed perfect. We planned the trip for months ahead.

The fourth member of our crew was Ben Ellis, one of my oldest friends. We had known each other and had been fast friends since 1965. We were the same age, 37. We were both working for the telephone company as sub-contractors doing installation and repair. Ben is a big guy, six-two or so, two hundred pounds, strong, with black hair – another good-looking guy. Ben was also one of the fishermen usually on my boat along with Kieffer. He was also a great water skier. Ben, Kieffer, and I had spent many days offshore fishing in good and bad weather. Ben had a lengthy background with boats and salt water. He had been around boats, salt water, and fishing since his early teens. We all loved to fish.

My second saltwater boat was a 23-foot walk-around cuddy cabin. It had a small enclosed cabin forward with a narrow walkway on both sides of the cabin that allowed access to the bow. It had a lot of deck space aft for fishing and the occasional dive trip. A single 200-horse Mercury Outboard provided the power. The boat was quick and very functional. It got a lot of use. Many boats will sit in driveways and side yards for months, but not this one. There was always a lot of fishing gear on board, even on the dive trips. It was stored there more or less permanently. There were many artificial rigs, big ones for marlin and such, with huge hooks, all coiled and ready for use.

We all lived in or near Tampa. Eleven days before Christmas, on December 14, 1984, we towed the boat on a trailer to St. George, about a nine-hour trip. I had done many of these sorts of trips, all to the Keys, so getting everything ready wasn't too tough. I had a checklist of about 125 items to go through before we left. The list had things like ensuring everything worked on the boat, testing all the dive gear, and checking the trailer carefully. It's hard keeping a saltwater boat in shape, the corrosion from the salt air is a nightmare. Electrical connections are the most vulnerable. Rob and I had been heavily into brewing our own beer. So, of course, we took a couple of cases with us. I brought some of my Northern Brown Ale. The boat always had a couple of snacks on board with a long shelf life, like a can of sardines.

The trip up was uneventful. The coast road along the panhandle hasn't changed much in forty years. We arrived after dark, found the house, and brought in our bags and beer. The boat was completely ready to go. At 8:00 am the following day, Saturday the 15th, without much effort, we launched the boat from a local ramp in front of a bait store. We bought some things at the Fisherman's Headquarters bait store, and I casually mentioned to the owner, Ann Chestnut, that we would be back well before dark and that a front was coming. We were trying to get the dive in before the Gulf waters got too rough and dangerous for diving. An approaching cold front generates high winds and waves. All boats get smaller as the waves get bigger. A 23-foot boat can be a tiny boat 25 miles offshore.

The boat ramp was on the Inter-coastal Waterway side of the island, so we had to run a few miles down the backside of the island to an inlet to get out to the open Gulf of Mexico. It was a beautiful, bright day with little wind and not much in the way of waves. It was just a perfect day. The run out to the Empire Mica was easy, taking about an hour. The Loran put us on the spot very quickly, and we could see the wreck on the depthfinder almost immediately.

When we arrived, we saw no other boats on the way out and none on the horizon. We were out of sight of land, completely alone on a featureless sea.

The idea was to position the boat right over the wreck as best as one could, so we took some time placing the anchor just so, without actually snagging the wreck with the anchor. It's possible to lose your anchor and line if you cannot get it loose from a wreck. You want to set an anchor in the sand, not in the wreck. We had plenty of anchor rope. Kieffer was on the bow handling the anchor. One unusual thing he did while setting the anchor was, as he was pulling the excess line in, he payed the line over the gunwale and into the water.

Usually, you would coil the excess on the deck of the boat. When I saw him doing this, I said something to him about it, but he wanted to do it like that, so I said "okay," and didn't think anything more about it. We did a great job of getting directly over the wreck. After we secured the anchor, we could see it directly below the boat on the depthfinder. We were all very excited about the dive.

The water temperature was about 65 degrees. That might not sound too cold to a non-diver, but it is plenty cold. If you were submerged in it for two days, it would kill you. Thermal protection is absolutely mandatory. There are two types of thermal protection for divers. Wetsuits, which, as the name implies, are wet, and drysuits, which are, likewise, dry. Wetsuits need to be skin-tight to minimize the exchange of water from outside to inside. You warm up the water that gets in, and you stay warm even though you have water in the suit. Drysuits have sealed feet and a tight seal around the neck and wrists to keep all water out. The drysuit is made of relatively thin rubber. The rubber layer would do little to keep you warm without an inner thermal layer, much like long-john underwear. Ben, Kieffer, and I, all had wetsuits, but Rob had a new drysuit complete with thermal undergarment.

In case of an emergency like the anchor line parting, an oncoming vessel, or your boat starting to take on water, we needed to leave someone on the boat at all times. You cannot leave a boat unattended out on the ocean, too much can happen. If we all went down at once, it is all too possible that the boat might not be there when we surfaced. We split into two dive teams, Ben and Kieffer, Rob and I. Rob and I suited up and got in first. We carried some light spearfishing equipment, pole spears called Hawaiian slings. These are simple four-foot poles with barbs on one end and a rubber loop on the other. The rubber loop is to tension the spear in your hand so it can be shot toward a fish.

When we dropped down, we found the wreck right away. A 100-foot dive is short, 20 minutes maximum, without decompressing or using special gas mixtures. I speared a couple of Amberjack and put them into a mesh catch bag. We looked around at some broken wreckage and then returned to the surface. When you dive off a boat, you typically have a line hooked to the stern that floats with the current out behind the boat on the surface. It is called a current line or tagline. Divers will come to the surface, grab that line, and pull themselves up to the boat. Holding on to the tagline so as not to drift away from the boat, they will remove their gear and hand it up to those on the boat. We did all that and climbed aboard.

When we got on, several inches of water were on deck. This we did not find disturbing. We had been fishing off this boat for years. The style of boat is called a self-bailer. Anytime several of us stood at the stern, the boat would take on water through the scuppers, getting 4 or 5 inches deep in the stern. All we had to do to remedy this was get some of the weight out of the stern, the boat would level, and the water would run back out the scuppers. That is the design of a self-bailing boat. No problem.

When we returned to the boat, Kieffer was the only one on deck. Ben had been seasick and had gone into the cuddy cabin to lie down. When I stuck my head in the cabin, I saw about six inches of water in the well of the cabin. The well is about six inches off the hull, meaning about a foot of water was in the bilge. The boat had taken on water through a hole in the hull. The hole was caused months earlier by the boat not being on the trailer straight while being towed.

The boat is supposed to sit on V-shaped rubber rollers. The boat was off one of the rollers, was bouncing while being towed, and finally settled on a metal U-bolt, gradually wearing a hole in the hull. The hole was only about an inch in diameter. An inch-wide diameter hole is a big hole in a boat. This happened on an earlier dive and fishing trip to the Keys. Rob, two friends, and I were on that trip. We noticed the hole when we launched the boat. We pulled the boat back up onto the trailer and pulled the trailer up into the parking lot of the Caribbean Club bar. The Caribbean Club is a notorious locals and biker bar in Key Largo where the Humphrey Bogart film Key Largo was filmed.

Rob and I looked at the hole, trying to find a quick fix. He said, "Don't worry, we're engineers, we'll fix it."

So, Rob went to the hardware store and bought a hand crank drill, drill bits, screws, and a piece of aluminum plate. Right there in the Caribbean Club Bar parking lot, he drilled holes in the hull, applied some caulk, and screwed the aluminum patch to the hull. The patch worked great, at least on that trip.

On the trailer on the way home, with the jouncing on the road, the hull flexed so many times that the patch split. I noticed the patch had failed only the day before our trip to St. George. The split wasn't too bad, so I just caulked it. Looking back, of course, I know it should have been fixed. The patch, by the way, was on the exposed part of the overturned hull. The split was ragged and sharp and cut my hand several times, causing nasty saltwater infections.

The bilge pump was not working for some reason. The bilge is not very big, so it had maybe 20 gallons of water. Only a little water, but coupled with the water on deck, it made me a little nervous. I encouraged Ben and Kieffer to get into their gear and get going on the dive. We all felt that since the boat was loaded very heavily, if Ben and Kieffer got in the water for the dive, it would lighten the boat considerably and make it easier to get the water out of the boat. Even after they got in the water, though, we still had too much water on deck.

Ben and Kieffer had begun to go down, but at about 15 feet of depth, Ben felt a stutter in the regulator he was using. He was worried there was a real problem with the regulator. He reached for Kieffer's fin, as Kieffer was just below him heading down, and grabbed his fin to get his attention. When Kieffer stopped and looked up, Ben motioned to him for both of them to go back to the surface.

When they got to the surface, they saw me starting the engine. I asked Rob to go to the bow and handle the anchor line. I did not feel we had enough time to bring the anchor line in normally, so I asked him to untie it and pitch it over the side. I got the boat going and, with the forward momentum of the boat, began forcing the water to the stern and out the scuppers. With the water rapidly running out of the boat, I began to feel a little relief. My relief lasted only a second or two. The anchor line, which had no time to sink, became caught in the prop and stopped the engine. The boat then settled quickly and heavily and began to take on an alarming amount of water over one side of the short transom.

Ben and Kieffer swam to the back of the boat and cleared the line from the prop. The stern was about 18 inches underwater at that point, with the engine half submerged. I had doubts whether it would even start for a second try at clearing the deck of water. I was afraid that one or two of the carburetors were underwater. Remarkably, it started somehow, and after I put it in gear again, the boat began to rise on plane and the water began to rush heavily and quickly toward the stern, washing rearward over the deck, up over the transom, and back into the sea.

I was again greatly relieved but the relief did not last long. When I put Ben and Kieffer in the water, I pulled the tagline back into the boat and coiled it on deck. When the water began to rush over the transom, the tagline went with it, snagged the prop again, and killed the engine. Ben and Kieffer watched in shock at what was happening from fifty feet behind the boat. The boat settled very heavily and water began to come in at a terrific rate, pouring over the transom like a waterfall. Almost immediately, it was two feet deep, all over the deck. I began to bail at the back of the boat with my hands, a ridiculous sight with water coming in about a hundred times faster than I could make it go out. It took only a moment to realize we could not recover.

Ben and Kieffer swam back to the boat, reached up, and with their hands and the weight of their bodies, were attempting to hold the gunwale on the side that was rising in an effort to keep the boat from capsizing. It seemed, if only for a moment, that they might be able to stabilize the boat. At that point, I was out of options, standing on the deck, knee-deep in seawater, paralyzed, not knowing what to do, the boat sinking beneath me. Ben had the presence of mind to yell at me to make a distress call.

The VHF radio was next to the helm, just under the ceiling of the cabin. It was only two steps to the helm. When I got there, I had time only to grab the microphone and put it to my mouth before the boat abruptly turned turtle – flipped over, upside down. Not enough time to make the call.

One of my regrets and mistakes of the trip was not to make a distress call at the first sign of trouble. The range of a VHF radio is only fifteen or twenty miles at the most, and we were twenty-five miles offshore in a desolate area of the Gulf of Mexico. We might not have been able to raise anyone, but the effort should have been made. It might be a little embarrassing to make a distress call and then call it off later, but it would certainly be prudent.

The scene was developing so rapidly that I had no time to both make a distress call and deal with the problem at hand. I thought if I acted quickly, I could correct the problem. I felt if I stopped to make a call, the boat would swamp and either capsize or sink. I had seen the self-bailing aspect of the boat work properly so many times before that I only realized our problem's magnitude once it was too late.

I was still in my wetsuit when we went into the water. After getting back aboard, Rob took his drysuit and thermal layer off. When we went over, he could only grab the rubber outer layer. Ben and Kieffer swam to the boat, and we all got together. It didn't take very long for the gravity of the situation to dawn on us. I made the astute remark, "We're in some deep shit now."

The boat was manufactured with some internal foam flotation, so we were pretty sure it would not completely sink out of sight, at least we hoped so. We needed to stay with the boat at all costs. The sea conditions were very nice when we started out in the morning, but gradually worsened throughout the day. When we went over, the wave height was 3 to 4 feet. We knew instinctively that we had to hold onto whatever material we could. One of our coolers containing ice floated nearby, so we grabbed it and tried to hold onto it. I knew immediately we would need water the ice would provide.

The seawater temp was 66 degrees, so we knew hypothermia would be a problem. As I mentioned, being submerged in that temperature of water for 24 hours could kill you. We had to try to stay up on the boat's hull and get as much of our bodies out of water as possible. Ben, Kieffer, and I had our wetsuits, but Rob had only his drysuit shell. The hull was clean and slick, with nothing to hold on to. Only a tiny portion of the hull was above water, a section of keel a few inches high, about six inches wide, and about four feet long.

We crawled up onto the hull, huddled together, and held one another as best we could to keep out of the water. We could get our upper bodies out of the water, but not our waists or legs. The keel was too small, and the waves too rough to stand. As the waves gradually grew, staying on the boat became harder and harder. On the ocean, waves come in sets, with the seventh wave larger than the others. We could stay up on the boat for six waves, but the seventh would wash over the boat and knock us off like bowling pins.

That first day, we had only one line attached to the bow, which we used to try to stay up on the hull. We took turns at what we called the Breakwater Position. Whoever had that spot faced those huge waves first and he did that until he got so tired someone else had to take over. He had to hold on as tight as possible to the bowline when the waves hit, but the waves were almost always stronger than we were, and knocked us off the boat into the cold water. You could hear the big waves coming. This would go on every few minutes for two days.

The waves were four to six feet for the first afternoon, then up to ten-foot waves for about 24 hours. Of course, there was no rest. It was an awful, grinding, endurance test that went on endlessly, but we had to stay with the boat and out of the water as much as possible.

On that first afternoon, we could only hold onto ourselves and the cooler. The cooler had some ice left in it, but it was taking some abuse from all the wave action and the ice was beginning to melt. We knew it was going to become contaminated soon with seawater, so we each sucked some ice and drank some water before it was gone. Not only did it taste like salt water, but it also tasted like bait. It was usually our bait cooler and retained a nasty taste.

Kieffer and Ben began to dive under the boat to see what we could salvage. At that point, we had no scuba gear; it had all drifted away the first afternoon. I can remember seeing my double tank setup with my buoyancy jacket and dual regulators attached drifting away. That rig cost over a thousand dollars and I couldn't do anything but watch. It was impossible to hold onto everything with the sea conditions as they were. So, without scuba gear, Kieffer and Ben held their breath when they dived under the boat. They had no masks either, making it difficult to see anything.

In the semi-darkness, up under the fully flooded boat, there was a tangled mass of fishing lures, cushions, fishing rods, and hundreds of other pieces of equipment. The Bimini top was also up, which at this point meant down, and had to be negotiated to get inside the boat. I was terrified of diving up under the boat. I could think of nothing but being hooked by one of the many lures, held there, and drowned, being unable to get out from under. It was too much for me. Kieffer and Ben were fearless for doing that. I just could not. They first looked for the flare kit, which they found.

Saturday Night

The nights were utterly dark, far from land, and with no moon. The night sky was nothing but brilliant stars from horizon to horizon with no light pollution from cities. Sometime during that first night, we saw the lights of what we were sure were a shrimper about two miles away. He seemed to be heading generally toward us. I fired a flare when it looked like he might be turning away. We saw no reaction from the shrimper. We decided not to waste another flare on him, we had only four left. He continued to motor away.

A little later, we saw another shrimper. This one was a little closer, a mile away. I fired the second flare. We knew within seconds that he had seen our flare. He abruptly stopped his trawling and switched on his searchlight. The light from the searchlight panned across us and lit us up. We couldn't believe it. We were overjoyed, we thought we were found. However, the light continued to pan around. He had not seen us. After ten minutes of looking for us with his searchlight, he fired his own flare. It was a white flare, an apparent attempt to get us to fire another flare. We had two remaining. We fired our next-to-last flare in response. It went up, high in the air like it was supposed to, but did not ignite. Unbelievably, it was a dud. We were stunned. We re-loaded and tried to fire the last flare. I aimed the flare gun straight up and pulled the trigger. It did not fire.

I pounded the hammer of the flare gun on the hull in a desperate attempt to get it to fire. It would not fire, no matter how hard I hammered it. The last flares had become so damp they were useless. I had kept them zipped inside my wetsuit on my chest where I thought they would be protected.

The shrimper continued to pan his searchlight around for about ten more minutes. It was easy to see he was losing his general sense of where he had seen the flare. During that time, we thought the white ice cooler would reflect light much better than our dark wetsuits, so we held the cooler over our heads and faced it toward him. His searchlight panned across us several more times, repeatedly lighting us and the cooler up. Still, there was no sign from him that he had seen us. He gave up and turned away. We were despondent. We were so close to salvation. Even though we were lit up by the searchlight several times, light beams will go farther than the human eye can see. He could not see us, even if his searchlight could.

During that first night, the temperature dipped into the forties. Without his thermal layer, Rob began to get cold. He got so cold I could see his face was blue, even in the dark of night. Kieffer, Ben, and I took turns holding him between us to warm him. We massaged him and held him tightly, but he still shivered uncontrollably. We even pushed a snorkel down into the back of his drysuit and Ben would then blow warm breaths from his lungs into the drysuit in an effort to warm him. Rob spent a harrowing night; the cold took a lot out of him. The lack of a wetsuit and body fat took its toll. The waves still pounded us, but we always scrambled back up on the hull.

We began to wonder how and when we would be reported missing. We hashed over the endless possibilities for hours and hours over the following days. We had filed no official float plan, as it's called. In other words, no one was explicitly told to call for help if we were not back at a particular time. One hope was that the bait shop owner would remember the conversation about being back on Saturday afternoon and call the Coast Guard. We could not see how she could miss, with our car and trailer right in front of her store. We wondered when a search might start. We went over repeatedly who would miss us first and get someone searching. We hoped it would not be as late as Monday when Ben would be due at work.

We learned later that Ben's work missed him early Monday morning and called his mother when he didn't show up for work. Ben's mother called my stepmother, Mickey. She called Drew's mother and got Drew's phone number. Drew Smith owns the house we stayed in on St. George Island before leaving for the dive. He is my oldest friend. Our parents used to babysit for one another. Mickey then called Drew, who was still in bed. He called the bait shop. The bait shop owner looked out their window and saw my car and boat trailer. Drew immediately knew something was very wrong and called the Coast Guard in Panama City, Florida.

Brad Bowen, a friend of Ben's and mine, had been involved somehow. He had been in contact with the Coast Guard. He told us later that the Coast Guard was mainly looking away from our original location (they knew where the Empire Mica was and that we were planning to do that dive). They figured we were drifting south like we also thought. Brad had contacted Jim Menard, a weatherman at a local TV station in Tampa, about our situation. Menard said he felt we were probably still in our original location, drifting in a loop current and still very near the Empire Mica. That turned out to be precisely the case.

Sunday Morning

The next morning, Kieffer and Ben began to dive under the boat again to see what they could salvage. Kieffer found a scuba tank full of air and brought it up. One of the skills discussed but not actually practiced during scuba training was breathing only off a scuba tank valve underwater. I could never imagine a scenario where you would use that skill, but here it was. This means you open the valve and catch the air bubbles with your mouth as they come out. This is a terrifying method of life support. He used this method to thoroughly search under the boat for anything we might find of use.

Kieffer did about 25 dives under the boat over the first two days. He says it was nothing, someone had to do it. I called it heroic. Kieffer found six bottles of homemade beer, one can of sardines, and, most significantly for Rob, a bag of wetsuits that had been brought on board by mistake. The spare wetsuits had been intended to be left at the house. We put the wetsuits on Rob and helped him put his drysuit on over all the wetsuits. He warmed up right away and was his old self. He had begun to lose a little mental alertness during the cold night. After he perked up, we all felt much better about him.

We had a long discussion about whether to drink the beer or not. Some felt the alcohol would accelerate the dehydration that had already begun. Others thought the beer was so thick and full of calories that we had to drink them. We decided to drink one a day. I had hoped the amberjack I had shot would be found, but no. There had been sandwiches, but they were lost when the boat capsized.

The large swells continued all that day, wearing us down. We were constantly knocked off the boat and had to climb back on every time. Ben and Kieffer rigged a couple of lines they found under the boat so we could hold onto them much like a bull rider would ride a bull. The waves that crashed over the boat were so big and powerful that even holding the lines was not enough to keep us from being knocked off. The stern of the boat rode much lower in the water.

We had a toolbox that one of the guys found under the boat and thought that if we could disconnect the engine and let it sink, the boat would ride higher in the water and make things a little more comfortable, drier, and warmer. We struggled with that project for hours before we gave up. It was just too difficult. The day dragged on while we continued to assess our situation and hold on for dear life. We knew we had to conserve energy, and we knew we had to stay out of the water. Not having food or drinking water was terrible, but the seawater was our worst enemy.

We knew the Coast Guard would eventually look for us, so we figured we would be found if we could hold on long enough. I told everyone I thought we might have to survive a week. I calculated it would probably take a couple of days for someone to initiate a search and then several days to find us. I didn't tell them I wasn't sure we could survive a week without drinking water. We could get by without food, but water, no. The water temperature was a wild card against our survival too. At least we were not submerged in it all the time; most of the time, it was just our legs.

The cold front that was coming never entirely made it to us. It stalled just north of where we were. As it was, it was in the sixties during the day and forties at night. If it had been any colder, we would have died within two days from hypothermia. Rob took a hard shot from the elements the first night. Our only genuine warmth came when we urinated into our wetsuits, but that didn't last long. It was just too tricky and nearly impossible to peel the wetsuits down to urinate under those conditions. Later it was calmer, but at that point, we were too weak to remove the wetsuits to pee, nor did we give a shit. The urination into the wetsuits gave a few moments of warmth, but later, a terrific rash would develop. Kieffer would describe it as being on fire. At least it was not so cold in the afternoons. The sun and wetsuits helped give us some warmth late in the day.

We saw no boats or planes that second day. We ate our precious can of sardines that afternoon. The split was one sardine for each of us. They were delicious. We opened one of our beers and very carefully poured each ration into a paper cup that had been saved somehow. That one sardine and one-fourth of a beer would be our only meal for four days.

Ben and Kieffer both smoke cigarettes. One of them found a pack of cigarettes under the boat during one of the dives. They had planned to dry them out and then smoke them. Immediately, they realized lighting them would be a problem. After much pondering, they remembered the dome light in the cabin and thought they could use it to focus sunlight like a magnifying glass and light a cigarette. They soon realized lighting cigarettes was the least of our problems and abandoned the project.

Sunday Night

The second night, we had another opportunity. We saw in the distance what turned out to be a tug towing a barge heading directly toward us. It was traveling relatively slowly, maybe ten knots. We could see no one in the wheelhouse. It was on autopilot and the crew was below decks. Running like this is common for an ocean-going tug and barge in an area with little traffic. As it approached, we thought for a while it might run over us. We crouched and watched as it came, ready to jump and swim away from our submerged boat. We thought it might be good if the tug collided with our boat. We thought it might cause such an impact and vibration that the crew would take notice and stop to see what happened. One problem with that scenario was that it would take at least a mile before the tug could stop, taking them well away and out of sight and sound of us.

One possible way of saving ourselves would be to swim the few feet over to the path of the tug, grab the bumpers on the side, and climb aboard as the tug thundered by. It would be a daring and foolhardy attempt. We had enough time to discuss it and decided that if one were to miss the tug, the barge, which was much bigger and wider than the tug towing it, would run over whomever the volunteer might be, killing him. We decided not to try. I do not know whether it was cowardice or reason that stopped us. Odd as it may be to hear it, we must have not felt that desperate quite yet.

The tug and barge passed within fifty feet of us, lit like a Christmas tree. The wheelhouse was incredibly bright. It was eerie, seeing that boat go by, nobody at the helm, nobody at all in sight. We screamed as loud as we could, but tugs are noisy creatures, and no one on board heard us. We saw no other boats that night.

Monday Morning

The dawn of the third day brought a little hope. We felt that a search might begin that day. We were right. In the middle of the afternoon, after splitting another of our beers, we saw a low-flying plane far off on the horizon. Search and Recovery aircraft generally fly at low altitudes, and aviation aircraft fly at much higher altitudes. We knew it was looking for us.

About twenty minutes later, we saw it again, only closer. We realized it was running a search pattern. We saw it again heading toward shore, closer yet. We did not see it again for about an hour. When we saw it again, we figured it had refueled and returned to continue the search. It was continuing a pattern, getting closer to us at every pass. We began to think we might finally get lucky. As it was getting dark, it made one more pass just a quarter of a mile from us going out to sea. Judging from the pattern he was running, we knew he would be very close to us on his last pass of the day.

We were right. We could see the Coast Guard Falcon jet coming straight for us just after the sun set. There was just a little light left but it was dark enough for the pilot to have his searchlight on. As the jet approached, we could see he was panning his searchlight back and forth on the water. It was dark enough at that point that I knew they would not be able to see us unless the searchlight shined directly on us as he flew over. He was very low. It seemed as though he were only about one hundred feet off the water when he passed directly overhead. The searchlight beam was off to the side about twenty feet. The jet seemed close enough to throw something and hit it. Our hopes were trashed again. We would need to endure at least another night in hell.

Monday Night

Monday night was uneventful. We sat and stood on the hull, crushed by the growing realization that we would not be found. We knew we were watching each other slowly die. We would, one by one, grow delirious, then comatose, and then die. We wondered silently who would be the last to die. We sat silent in the gloom and while doing so, did discuss one wild plan. There were some lights in the distance that we thought were boats we might be able to swim to, but we were afraid that if whoever went could not get there, he would be unable to find his way back. From our search of the hull, we knew there was a very large fishing reel with several hundred yards of fishing line on it, still on the boat. We thought one of us could swim with the line attached to him, and if he could not get to whatever the lights were, we could reel him back in and not lose him. Harebrained, I know, but we discussed it for hours. Finally, we decided it was too risky.

Tuesday Morning

The next day at dawn, we were hopeful again. We knew they were searching for us and may start the search where they left off. We saw a search plane twice in the distance but never anywhere close. The good news of the day was that the wind and waves had slacked and it was almost flat calm. We were worn badly by the constant exertion of staying on the boat.

Sitting on that narrow strip of fiberglass was torture, but sitting or standing on it were the only options. Keeping as much of our bodies out of the water was paramount. We were very cramped and exhausted. Sitting on that narrow strip was very hard for us all. Rob had gotten the idea to give his butt some relief, that he could inflate his drysuit and float in the water next to the boat to relieve the pain of sitting. The problem is that the water would still gradually sap the heat out of him. I told him not to do that under any circumstance, but he did anyway. He would lay on the water for about a half hour until he got too cold, then returned to the boat to warm himself. I talked to him, we all talked to him about the danger in letting the water drain the heat from him. He said it was just too painful to sit on the boat endlessly. He insisted, so we let him repeatedly lie in the water. My greatest regret is not forcing him to stay on the boat somehow. However, I was conserving as much energy and heat as possible, and, did not want to physically restrain him. The others felt the same. I am ashamed to say that I knew what he was doing to himself and did little to stop him.

That afternoon, something dawned on me that made us all laugh out loud. Just a few months before, the divorce between Stacey and myself was finalized. It had been a terrible divorce. I had not wanted it, but she did. There was a terrific battle over property, alimony, and, lump sum payments. Stacey initially claimed half of everything I owned, but in the end, I kept the real estate and the other assets I brought into the marriage, agreeing to pay an amount for her to resettle. The hilarious irony was, as it was looking very likely that I might die, she would get absolutely everything anyway. I had not changed my will since the divorce. Stacey was still my sole beneficiary. We laughed and laughed over that. It was curious how we could laugh so hard at our imminent fate.

We were continually trying to devise ways to help effect our rescue. We had Styrofoam cups that we tore into small pieces and threw into the water every five minutes. The thinking was that the pieces might work as a Goldilocks breadcrumb trail, leading rescuers to us. In retrospect, it sounds ridiculous, but we were desperate. We also jettisoned life vests every couple of hours on the same day.

Another idea was to loosen the fuel tank cap, let the fuel seep out, and leave a gasoline slick that could be seen for miles. Gasoline floats on water. The gasoline on the boat was mixed with oil, so all the better to be seen, especially from the air. Kieffer dived under the boat yet again and loosened the fuel cap. The fuel gradually began to bubble up all around us. We thought this was a pretty good idea, but the problem became immediately apparent. We were drifting with the current with no wind, so the slick we generated stayed with and around us, getting all over us, and we breathed the fumes into our lungs. It made an awful scene even more unbearable.

Tuesday was the most challenging day. The seas were flat calm, but we had lots of other trouble. We had not eaten anything but one sardine each for four days. We drank our one beer for the day. Rob was dying, and we all knew the rest of us were about a day behind him. We felt at that point, the rescue had probably been called off. We had no self-rescue ideas left. We were so weak we could do nothing but sit. We were also getting weak mentally.

I began to hallucinate. I would look up into the sky and see gigantic cypress trees like the ones at home. Then I could see huge power lines and towers, many miles high. I mentioned it to Ben later that night; oddly, he said he had seen the same thing.

Kieffer had been having his own hallucinations. For a while, he was negotiating purchasing several 55-gallon drums of water from a guy who seemed to be right in front of him. Another time, he was driving down a road very slowly. Every house had the water spigots open, and water ran into the street.

My lower legs had begun to swell to the point where the wetsuit was cutting off circulation. I was losing feeling in my feet, and I began to worry about losing my feet if we ever got out of this mess. I used our knife to cut the lower seam to loosen them. We were all getting saltwater ulcers, painful sores that festered and would not heal, only getting bigger. Any weak spot in the skin, whether it was from the smallest of cuts or any chaffed area, would develop them. Even areas with no mark would begin to ulcerate. Ben's fingernails were all black from gripping the line so tightly. He would later lose all the nails.

We still had the cooler tied to us, drifting along about ten feet away. At noon, a seagull flew in and sat on the cooler. We immediately saw the gull as a potential meal. How to catch it? We had no net, nothing. The only thing I had was my hands. I was the closest, so I watched the bird with an intensity that I have never been able to muster before or since. We needed to catch that bird. I slowly pulled the line in, dragging the cooler closer, inch by inch, hoping the seagull wouldn't notice he was getting closer and closer to being eaten alive. As I pulled, I waited, coiled to jump and catch him. Turns out seagulls are quick. At any rate, he was much faster than me. He was never in any real danger.

At times we had sargassum weed floating around us. I picked some up and took a closer look, finding tiny snails clinging to the weed, not much bigger than the head of a pin. I began to pluck them off one by one and eat them. I figured they had to have some nutritional value. There was no cleaning them, no preparation of any kind. I just put them in my mouth, crunched them up and swallowed. They were awful. The crushed shells tasted more like sand than anything else. I tried eating the seaweed too, but I was afraid it had too much salt in it and might only do more damage to me if I continued. You cannot drink salt water even if you are dying of thirst.

We saw no boats or planes that day, but it was an active day around the boat. We saw a pod of dolphins and a shark briefly. They circled the boat for a few minutes and left. The thought of sharks did not even upset us. Sharks did not seem like a threat compared to what we were facing. They might even be a relief if they killed us. Any end, even an awful one, as long as it was quick, seemed preferable to what we were facing.

That afternoon we held hands and prayed, even though none of us was religious. Just covering the bases, I suppose. There are no atheists in a foxhole, as they say.

At the end of the day, another major problem was emerging. We knew that the Coast Guard would only look for someone for a few days, and we knew they had already been looking for at least two. We were fearful the search had been called off.

Tuesday Night

Nights were especially bad. At that time of year, at that latitude, there are fourteen hours of dark with ten hours of light. These were the very longest nights of the year. There was no chance for a rescue at night and the time dragged unbelievably. I had a watch, but having lost my glasses when the boat capsized, I could not read the dial. I would have to ask someone to read my watch for me. I would wait for what I was sure was at least an hour before asking someone to tell me the time. It would only have been five minutes. That's how long the nights were for us—five minutes seemed like an hour. One night was like a week. Ben had the same time stretch that I did. It was excruciating. The night seemed never to end. Waiting for dawn and possible salvation was one of the hardest things to endure. Predictably, our moods always brightened at dawn.

Rob and Kieffer had a running conversation about which one was a bigger girl-chaser. They used the term receptacle for meaningless sexual conquests. Guys can be less than politically correct about women when there are no women around. I'm sure that term was meant never to go beyond us four.

We spent much time calculating where we were in our featureless drift. After hearing a lot of aircraft and estimating a three-knot drift, we thought we were off MacDill Air Force Base in Tampa. We had yet to learn we were not far from where we started.

We did have one magical, beautiful experience that night. It was very dark, and we occasionally heard dolphins surfacing to breathe around us. We noticed a momentary phosphorescent glow directly below us. As we peered into the completely black sea, we saw what looked like a green torpedo accelerating toward the boat below the surface. Then, there would be an explosion of light, a green fireball exploding below, which would fade after a few seconds. It took us a few minutes to comprehend what we were seeing. The dolphins were charging a school of bait fish minnows that were gathered below the boat. Smaller fish will use a floating object as protection against their predators. The charge and the scattering would activate the phosphorus. It was a fantastic light show.

Another odd and wonderful incident happened that night. Rob, Kieffer, and I were facing one direction, and Ben was facing another when a dolphin came to the surface just five feet from the boat. He poked his head out of the water and stood motionless, vertical in the water, looking at Ben and the rest of us. Ben was the only one to see him. He felt as if the dolphin were trying to communicate telepathically with him. Ben felt as though he could tell what the dolphin was thinking, which was, 'I know you guys are in trouble. I'm sorry I can't help.'

The dolphin and Ben looked at one another for a few more seconds, and then the dolphin slipped back beneath the sea.

Dolphins came by every day, whether through curiosity or whether they were merely looking for food. We will never know. They would circle us once, then disappear in the distance.

Tuesday night, Rob took a turn for the worse. Dehydration and hypothermia were getting to him. He began to talk nonsense, talking about his wife back home. He was not married then, nor had he ever been. It was breaking our hearts. At times, he was only about half-conscious. We knew he was dying. It became harder for him to sit on the boat, but not from the sheer discomfort of it. He was losing consciousness and he could not hold himself upright. We tried and tried to hold him up, but we were all very weak and could not continue. At one point, we tied him upright to the boat. He became so combative and began struggling so hard that we untied him. He calmed down and nodded off. We secured a line to him and let him drift along beside us, precious heat being slowly sucked out of him all the while. We knew he was going to be the first to die. We never talked about it, but we all knew it.

Rob had been in and out of consciousness all day and now into the night. We all knew that none of us would survive another day. Rob was in bad shape, but the rest of us were not far behind. The weather continued to be very calm, the water glassy. As the sun went down, we were sure we would all be dead by this time the following day. I had resigned myself to the fact that I was going to die. I was sure of it. We did not talk much that night.

I realized that we were going to arrive at a point when Rob died, and we would have to decide whether or not to eat his body. We did have a knife. I knew it was coming, and I dreaded it far more than I dreaded losing my own life. I spoke to Ben after the ordeal and he said he had planned to drink Rob's blood. I wondered and feared how the decision would go. Rob's brother was on board. What would he think? What would he do? What would I do? Would I be able to eat the flesh of one of my best friends? Would I die first or would the survival instinct prevail? These were the worst thoughts I've ever had, the hardest to bear.

I had weekly nightmares about this for a year afterward. They were all the same. We had just finished cutting and eating Rob's flesh when rescuers found us. We looked up at our rescuers with gore all over us. It was a very ghoulish and guilt-ridden dream. Decades later, I shudder when I think about it.

Early Wednesday Morning

At about four o'clock in the morning, a very thick fog had settled over us; you could not see twenty yards. Unbelievably, we heard what sounded like a large ship's horn. We came out of our daze and began to listen very carefully. We thought we could hear the heavy thumping of a ship, and it sounded close. Ben began blowing SOS on a whistle we had. He blew it over and over again. He could not remember whether SOS was three dashes, three dots, and three dashes, or the other way around, so he alternated it while he blew. He thought it would be ignored if someone heard an OSO being blown. Kieffer quietly believed that Ben was wasting his time, that the ship would never hear him. Thankfully, he was wrong. When their searchlight abruptly switched on, we could hardly believe it.

We did not have high hopes, remembering the shrimper searchlight from three nights before. However, this vessel was much closer, although we could not see it. The searchlight panned across us, then past us. My heart sank. Instantly, it snapped back at us and locked on, unwavering. My first words were, "My God, we're not going to die!"

Ben vividly remembers the depth of emotion in that statement. We had been so sure that we were going to die, that being found was almost anti-climactic. It was almost as if we were cheated. There are several stages of coming to terms with your own death. Something like surprise, then denial, then anger, then acceptance. We were in the final stage that last night. We had accepted it and were looking forward to being out of our misery and having the answer to the Great Question.

At first, we could not make out any shape, only seeing the searchlight that never strayed from us. Then, gradually, a shape emerged from the solid wall of gray fog. At first, it was faint, but then it slowly became bigger and clearer. Even then, it didn't seem real. Our minds had been playing so many tricks over the last twenty-four hours that we had difficulty comprehending what we were seeing and what was happening. We were being rescued, and we knew we were being rescued, but somehow, it didn't seem real.

Kieffer was looking at the ship with his head cocked to the side like the little RCA Victor dog. Is it real? As the vessel maneuvered closer to us, I could make out a large diagonal orange stripe on the side of the vessel's black hull. It was a U. S. Coast Guard Cutter, the White Pine, a 133-foot buoy tender based in Mobile, Alabama.

We were euphoric. The cutter eased up right next to us and dropped a net over the side. The net is designed to be climbed. I grabbed the net and tried to climb up, but I had been sitting on that relatively sharp edge of the hull for four days and my legs had no strength. Ben was having the same problem. Kieffer was holding onto his brother. The captain looked down on us and realized we could not climb. He immediately yelled, "Dammit, someone get in the water and help them."

Some of his men had been putting orange exposure suits on and splashed into the water next to us within seconds after his command. They hauled us over the side and onto the deck. We needed help to walk. They lowered a basket for Rob and hauled him up. Somehow, Kieffer had the strength to climb up on his own.

The USCGC White Pine's crew was bummed out about having to go on a mission so close to Christmas. They would miss the pre-Christmas parties and possibly Christmas itself to repair a stupid buoy on St. Marks River in the panhandle. When they learned they would be looking for missing divers on the way to repair the buoy, they perked up, feeling they had something important to do.

The radar operator on the White Pine saw a weak signal, or target, ahead. Anything other than a buoy tender would not have been able to see us on the radar. They have two types of radar: a conventional radar, which most ships have, and a more localized radar for locating submerged or partially submerged buoys. The longer-range 5-mile radar would not see us, but the 2-mile would. They only saw a faint target. When they got closer, the radar would not pick us up at all, so they lost the image when they got close. Not being sure where the target was at that point, due to drift, etc., they sent Troy Noble out on the bow to listen. Captain Rucker slowed the cutter down to reduce the noise generated by a ship that size. They were not sure what they had seen at that point. Noble apparently heard our whistle.

With a guardsman on each side, they walked the three of us to the Ward Room, where the crew ate their meals. There were booths much like in a diner. Stainless steel and chromium never looked better. Water, food, dry clothes, and helping hands. These were things we knew we would never see again. What a glorious, wonderful vessel this was. There were several crew members assigned to us. They said we could have Gatorade or tomato soup. We chose the soup. The soup was gone in seconds. When we asked for more, they said the commander was in contact with a doctor on shore and was under orders not to feed us anything more for thirty minutes. They were afraid we might go into shock. They gave us more when we kept that first soup down for thirty minutes and said we could have more in fifteen minutes.

After the soup, they helped us to the shower, where they took our wetsuits off us and literally bathed us. What a luxury warm water can be! While other men bathed us, we felt no shame, only gratitude. Kieffer was a little stronger and did not need quite that much attention. We all trembled when we stood, not from cold but from physical exhaustion. They helped dry us and then gave each of us a dark blue jumpsuit to wear. They were much too large for me, but they were clean and dry and felt wonderful. I still have that jumpsuit.

Recognizing Rob was in very serious condition, they took him to the infirmary. The cook, a black man named Duncan, was assigned to help Rob. He cared for Rob as though Rob was his brother. As a buoy tender, the White Pine was a very slow vessel capable of only about eight knots. Rob needed immediate attention, so rather than wait the six hours it would take for the White Pine to get him to port, the captain tried to arrange for a helicopter to pick up Rob.

The fog was still very thick, making landing a helicopter on the White Pine far too dangerous. They then arranged for a high-speed 41-foot launch to rendezvous with us and pick up Rob for a quicker trip back to the hospital. They came and picked him up, and our hopes went with him. We drank and ate more soup, then lay in bunks for the return trip. The guardsmen watched over us every minute, even as we dozed.

Before we got underway, we heard some commotion out on deck. Everyone seemed to be very concerned about something. Being a buoy tender, they could lift something heavy out of the water. They had lifted the HooLoo out of the water and set her on deck. That would have been fine, but the fuel cap was still off and when they set her down on the deck, raw gasoline began to run out on deck. This was a hazardous situation. Any spark could have set it off, turning a happy rescue into a bigger hell. They washed the fuel off the deck and diffused the problem. A while later, we got underway.

The White Pine Engineering Officer was Chief Machinery Technician Ray Evers. When we realized they had retrieved our boat, Ben asked him to see if he could find his wallet, which he did. It was still there with the 500 dollars in it. Ben asked about his gold necklace, which Evers found still hanging on a porthole inside the cabin where Ben had left it.

On the way, we were informed the media wanted an interview. When we docked, there they were. Before we got into the ambulance, we told a reporter a few words on camera. I could walk a little better at that point, but I still needed some help stepping up into the ambulance. I just had no strength in my legs.

After a brief stay in the emergency room, they admitted us and wheeled us toward our room. We went by Rob's room and they let us go in to see him. Rob was more coherent than he had been in two days, but his speech was slow even though he recognized us and made a couple of jokes. He was in bed with some blankets over him. Smiling widely, I wheeled up to him, reached out, and took his hand. My smile disappeared immediately. His hand was very cold to my touch. I was alarmed and thought he needed some help. I told the nurse immediately that he needed to be warmed. I thought he was dangerously cold. Re-warming someone with a very low core temperature can be tricky business. The heart can stop if it is warmed too fast. Hypothermia techniques have improved since then. They warm the blood first by pumping It through a heating device and back into the patient.

Ben and I went up to our room and we began to relax. We ate and drank everything we could talk the staff into bringing. I had lost twenty pounds in four days. Most of the weight was dehydration, but we also lost a lot of muscle and fat. I ate like a wild dog for a month afterward. We were in the room only an hour before I got a phone call from Brad Bowen, who was a close friend of mine and Ben's. He had been following the search for us and saw on TV we had been found. We talked for a minute or two and then he said something strange. He said something about Rob dying. I told him that was bullshit because I had seen him barely an hour before. I told him the media never gets things right and they had this one wrong. Well, sadly, they had this one right. I could hear the TV news over the telephone giving the details. Rob had died of heart failure right after we saw him. I couldn't believe the whole world knew about Rob dying but us. The hospital staff decided to keep it from us, thinking it might trigger heart failure in one or more of us. We went from ecstasy to the depths of sadness. We had been so happy we all had made it.

Most people never have to face their real selves, to find out whether they have the right stuff or can be depended on to do the right thing in a life-or-death situation. Most of us think we could be the hero. It's an awful thing to find out you are not, that you didn't measure up, and that your best friend died.

The way I look at this, in one's life story, there can sometimes be one defining moment, and when it is over, you never get a chance to redeem yourself. Once it is over, it is over. I failed myself and especially Rob in that moment. I've had many failures, wives, education, and potential among them, but this was the big one. There is a saying by a 19th-century German philosopher, Friedrich Nietzsche, "What doesn't kill you only makes you stronger." I think that is true, but I have been permanently diminished in my own eyes, and that makes it hard to live with. I don't think about it all the time, but it is there in the background like a shadow.

Epilogue

Neither the vessel White Pine nor its crewmembers received any commendation or recognition from the Coast Guard. The crew is still bitter.

The White Pine was decommissioned in 1999, sold to the Dominican Republic government, and continues in service to the mariner, as it is said.

It took about two months to regain strength and a year before I could get on a boat again. I saw the world as though it were now in Technicolor, compared to the black and white before the accident. I had a much-heightened sense of awareness. That had faded somewhat but still comes back strong as ever. I feel compelled to watch every survival story I see on TV and read every book about survival. I have a unique insight for those people in survival situations that most people can never have.

Kieffer seems outwardly unaffected by the incident but does not like talking about it. Ben seems to have a little of the life taken out of him. I don't think any of us fully recovered.

A friend, Brad Bowen, retrieved the boat from (I can't remember which port they took it to now) and brought it back to Tampa. It sat in the woods for a year while my lawsuit with the manufacturer was resolved. I sued, contending that the boat was poorly designed, that the deck of the self-bailer was too close to the waterline. Proline changed its design the following year, raising the deck inside the hull in relation to the waterline. I settled for $20k partly because there was no permanent damage to any of us (arguable) and because of the hole in the hull. It produced enough money to get the boat fixed, which I promptly traded for a 28' Bertram, moved it to the Keys, and started chartering dive and fishing trips. I moved to Key Largo two years after the incident, got my Coast Guard Captain's license, became a professional boat captain, and eventually owned a dive shop in Key Largo.

CWO (Chief Warrant Officer in layperson's terms, Captain) Robert O. Rucker retired to Oregon. I tracked Captain Rucker down a number of years ago and dropped in on him at his work unannounced. I had made a Coast Guard hat embroidered with the original White Pine logo and was wearing it when I walked into his workplace. He was working in a plant nursery. He was surprised and pleased.

The Engineering Officer was Chief Machinery Technician Ray Evers, since retired, lives in Mobile and works for the USCG Aviation Training Center in Mobile. I've spoken to Ray Evers. He is talkative and remembers a lot of detail. Evers said the crew was ecstatic over finding us alive, but after they had left port, they heard one had died. He said everyone was badly broken up over it.

Chief Boatswain mate Troy Noble is retired, living in Mobile, Alabama. He is now a captain on a gambling boat on the Ohio River.

The whereabouts of the cook, Duncan, who took such personal care and interest in Rob, are unknown.

From an email from Don Vinson, skipper of the White Pine after Rucker:

I was not the CO of CGC White Pine when you were rescued. I was CO from 1985-1988 and again from 1992-1996. However, when you were rescued, I was the 1st Lt. on the CGC Salvia. We had searched for you for three days before we were dispatched to go elsewhere. We passed CGC White Pine while she was en route to Saint Mark's River. We were near Pensacola when we were made aware of your rescue. The newspaper articles were placed in the White Pines Scrap Books, which have since been sent to the CG Archives.

I tried to get copies of the White Pine records and scrapbook, but they have been destroyed.

I got a phone call from Don Hackney 30 years after the incident. This is his first-person account:

The crew of the White Pine had heard the Coast Guard broadcast of "Securitay, Securitay" of four men missing in the area throughout the day. Chief Noble was in charge of the bridge with two seamen, me, and another on the midnight to 4:00 am watch. The radar was clear when I went to make coffee but when I came back up, that soon changed. Within minutes, at 3:45 am, Chief Noble saw a radar blip and commented, "That may be the missing men."

Chief Noble told me to wake the captain and began blowing the foghorn every two minutes. Noble had slowed down, keeping focused on the blip still repeating on the radar. Chief Noble told me to go out on the bridge. I soon heard "help" and then saw the four men with my searchlight. I ran back to the bridge yelling, "That's them! That's them!"

Noble told me to wake everyone. Soon, the crew was on the buoy deck looking over the side. The searchlight was still on us as the White Pine slowly came alongside. Rob was still tied to our boat. I reached down to pull one of them up, and as I pulled from the elbow, the skin began to pull off, so I stopped and climbed down the rope ladder and hosted him from the waist.

None of us has been tested like this before or since.

The White Pine

Rob's Funeral

Later in Tampa, Ben, Stacey, and I, attended Rob's funeral. Our feet were so swollen; we couldn't wear shoes, just house slippers borrowed from Stacey. Walking was painful. Our legs were still weak, and the steps up to the church were difficult. Stacey held an arm each and helped us up the steps. Once we were seated, the service and the eulogies began. Ben and I were overwhelmed with emotion, and tears streamed down. Neither Ben nor I were Catholic, but at the end of the service, when communion was offered, my emotions were so overpowering, and my need to feel close to Rob so strong; without thinking or hesitation, I stood and motioned to Ben to come forward with me. We walked forward together and kneeled. I'm sure we surprised Stacey and the other mourners.

Katrina

I lived with Tricia Plastic for a year. One of the things we liked to do was go to a gay bar in Tampa on W. Platt Street. The place was always a lot of fun. One night, they had a trivia contest, which I won, but the fix was in. The MC liked me and, with no one looking, gave me the answer, and then the prize; a bottle of champagne.

After having me on stage for a minute to get the award, the music and dancing began again. Tricia had wandered off in the crowd, dancing and talking, when a tall, pretty girl approached me and asked me to dance. I never dance, but with enough alcohol in me, I do. So, we danced, Katrina and I.

After dancing and provocative talk, we went outside for some quiet and sat in my car. We had been passionately kissing and getting aroused when I heard a tap on my window. I turned and saw a uniformed Tampa Police officer. He motioned for me to roll the window down. When I did, he asked for our IDs. He looked at them and asked me if I knew my friend in the car was a man. I said no, but I did know the truth. She gave me her phone number, and we went back inside.

Katrina and I remained friends for many years. She was in love with me and did everything in her repertoire to reel me in. I liked her, but it was just a bridge too far. Stacey and I asked her to a party we had out in Odessa not long after she had her breasts enhanced. While the partygoers were talking to her about it, she whipped off her blouse and showed us. It was an excellent job.

After the full conversion to female, she talked me into having missionary sex with her to "try it out."

I was too drunk to remember much about it. I lost track a few years later and don't know what happened to her. I remember her fondly.

Katrina and Tom

The Newspaper

About 1985, I lived in a ground-floor, single-level condo in North Tampa with a privacy wall and gate, inclosing a small, private courtyard leading to the front door. I subscribed to the Tampa Tribune at the time, with the delivery coming over the fence and landing a few feet from the front door.

It doesn't freeze many days in central Florida, but this morning, it was below freezing when I went out the front door to pick up the paper. The courtyard was very private, and the newspaper was less than ten feet from the front door, so I went out with only my underwear on. When I bent down to pick up the paper, I heard the door close behind me, knowing the lock had been set and I was locked out of my house in tighty-whiteys.

After the initial panic wore off, I remembered being in the habit of leaving my car keys in the car. This was not for exactly such a situation; it was for laziness. I soon realized that I could get in, start it up, heat it, and use my car phone to call for help. The locksmith was greatly amused.

Ray Fox needed a beer

Ray and I became close friends while at Plant High. We did everything together. One of our favorite things was saltwater fishing. In the 80s, I had a 24-foot Pro-Line open fisherman. We used it many weekends locally, but once or twice a year, we would tow it down to Key Largo for a week.

I used my '55 Chevrolet station wagon to tow it, carrying our provisions and a cooler full of beer back on the boat, not in the car. On one trip to Key Largo, our beer in the station wagon ran out. Ray wanted more beer, but I refused to stop. He got so irritated with me, that at 60 miles an hour, he climbed into the rear of the wagon, out the rear tailgate, onto where the trailer was hitched to the wagon. He then climbed up on the bow of the boat, got into the boat, retrieved some beer, and climbed back on board the wagon the way he came. We continued, none the worse for wear.

Ray was a fun guy, physically powerful, strong, and capable beyond average human ability. In the early 90s, he married and had a young son, who was maybe six years old, and a stepson, probably about twelve when this incident I'm about to narrate took place. At the time, he and his family lived in Inverness, Florida, and had a ski boat. Ray and his two sons were on a local lake just goofing around, with Ray driving slowly and the sons jumping off the boat as it went along at a relatively slow speed.

After a while, Ray got bored and said to the older son, "Here, let me show you how this is done."

He had the older son drive the boat much faster so Ray could jump off himself. He did that but landed on the water in an unplanned way, broke his neck, and sank to the bottom, all to the horror of his onlooking sons. It took the Sheriff's dive recovery team several days to find his body.

Our 3 Trick Act

Whenever Ray, Ben, and I would get together, it would come up in conversation that the three of us did different tricks, and quite often, we proceeded to perform them. I would eat a razor blade, Ben would breathe fire with lighter fluid, and Ray would hammer a straight pin into his thigh. It was all very amusing.

Mission Impossible

In the '80s, I had a '66 Chevrolet Super Sport that needed body repair and paint to cover it. The paint job was beginning to fail, and I thought I'd get a quote from the guys I wanted to do the work. I left the car at the body shop for the estimates. The owner soon gave me both quotes. I mulled it over for a week and called him to tell him I wanted the repair, not the whole car painted.

He told me he had painted the entire vehicle and that I owed him $1,000. I was stunned and told him I had not approved that and wouldn't pay him. He said if I didn't, he would confiscate the car. The rear of his body shop was completely fenced in. I called my attorney at the time, Rick Levenson, and explained the situation to him. He told me to get the car and not to pay the body shop owner. Well, that was problematic due to the fencing at the paint shop.

At the time, the Super Bowl was being played the following Sunday. I figured early the following Monday would have the owner and his workers possibly a little hungover and less alert than usual. I had Brad Bowen, another good friend, take me to the body shop early Monday morning, drop me a block away, then go into the office and engage the owner in some body work talk, distracting him from what might be happening at his business.

Brad dropped me, then went to the office as I went through the unlocked and open fence, got in the car, started it, and drove off. The caper came off just like we planned. Of course, the owner was livid and called the police. The police found, arrested, and booked me for "Removal of Property Under Lien."

Of course, I called my attorney, who got involved. He explained to the prosecutor what had happened and why things happened the way they did. My word against his is what it boiled down to. My attorney suggested I take a lie detector test, which I passed, so the charges were dropped. I kept my vehicle without paying the owner.

Shrimping

There is a lot of shrimping on the West coast of Florida, so Ben, Ray, and I bought a shrimp net from T. A. Mahoney Marine Supply by the Tampa commercial seaport. Commercially, shrimp are caught at night on Florida's West Coast in shallow water with a trawling net pulled slowly behind the boat. Late one afternoon, we launched my boat in Tarpon Springs, went out the Anclote River, and turned North after getting into the Gulf.

We set up the shrimp net with outrigger planes that stretched the net on either side of the boat. The idea is to pull the net along the tops of the seagrasses. After trawling all night, we pulled up the net, and when we got the net in the boat, there was only one shrimp! I was so pissed I ate the shrimp on the spot, live and wriggling in my mouth.

We think the catch was limited because our net had caught something sticking out of the seabed floor, resulting in us not moving an inch all night.

Ben's Special Knot

In the 80s, several friends and I were out at Ray Fox's lake house on Lake Hiawatha, sitting in his living room listening to music and smoking a bit. Ben Ellis was always good with nautical knots and others like the traditional hangman's noose. He was sitting in a hanging chair making knots and had some larger rope like what you might make a hangman's noose from, and that was what he was doing.

When he finished, he got up and removed the chair from the hook in the ceiling. He then put the noose around his neck, got on his tip-toes, and hooked the free end of the noose on the ceiling hook. We were all watching, expecting him to return to his tip-toes and free the end of the knot. He had extended himself so far that when he went to free himself, he couldn't raise himself enough to get free. It didn't take long for him to realize what he had done to himself. His eyes bugged out and you could see the panic. We stared at him, frozen until the seriousness of the predicament he found himself in also dawned on us.

We then jumped up, lifted him high enough to get the rope off the hook, and let him down to the floor. If he had been alone, he would have hung himself completely by accident.

Key Largo

After getting my Florida real estate license and a year of miserable failure as a salesman, I decided to pick everything up and move to Key Largo. I had vacationed there many times, diving and fishing, and was familiar with everything onshore and offshore. I had yet to learn how I would make a living. I moved myself and my 19' Bayliner open-fisherman into a canal-front mobile home I rented from a gentleman named Bill Mullins.

I must divert to a "small world" story about Bill. Janet (wife #3) and I were in New Mexico twenty years later doing a big mountain hike, Wheeler Peak. We completed the hike and then headed toward Arizona's highest point. The route there took us through Taos.

After these hikes, we would be ravenous and begin thinking about a big steak dinner afterward. Driving toward Taos, we began looking for a steakhouse.

On the two-lane road toward Taos, we saw a road sign saying, "D.H. Lawrence Ranch." Being a fan of his, I couldn't pass it up. We had plenty of time, so we took the detour and arrived at the ranch, which was open to visitors.

D. H. Lawrence, the author of literary classics such as Women in Love and Lady Chatterley's Lover, and his wife Frieda first came to New Mexico in September 1922 at the invitation of Mabel Dodge Luhan, a New York socialite and arts patron who lived in Taos. While the English-born writer only spent eleven months during his three visits to New Mexico, the state made a notable impression on him. He wrote:

I think New Mexico was the greatest experience I ever had from the outside world. It certainly changed me forever.

In March 1924, Lawrence and his wife, accompanied by Dorothy Brett, an English painter and admirer of the author, returned to Taos a second time. On this visit, Mabel Dodge Luhan gave Frieda a ranch she owned located 20 miles northwest of Taos on Lobo Mountain. The 160 acres were known as the Kiowa Ranch because the Kiowa Indians had used a trail through the property when they traveled south to raid Indian pueblos along the Rio Grande. Nice gift.

Lawrence, Frieda, and Lady Brett moved to the ranch in May 1924 and spent five months there. During the summer, Lawrence completed his short novel "St.Mawr," in which he celebrates the special quality and landscape of the Kiowa Ranch. Lawrence also wrote his biblical drama, "David," and parts of "The Plumed Serpent" during his last visit to the ranch in 1925. New Mexico also appears prominently in other essays and stories, such as "The Woman Who Rode Away."

After Lawrence died near Vence, France, in 1930, Frieda returned to New Mexico to live. In 1934, she had Lawrence's body exhumed, cremated, and his ashes brought to the ranch to be housed in a small memorial chapel.

The journey of Lawrence's ashes from Europe has two differing accounts. One is that the ashes were brought by a friend to the ranch and were incorporated into the concrete used to form the pedestal in the memorial created by Frieda. The other story has the same Lawrence friend, only this time harboring a petty grievance towards Lawrence, for which he dumped the ashes over the side of the ocean liner. Obviously, in this version, the ashes never made it to America. The official story is that the ashes made it to the ranch.

In 1955, eight months before her death, Frieda gave the Kiowa Ranch to the University of New Mexico. She stipulated that the ranch be used for educational, cultural, and recreational purposes, and, that the Lawrence memorial be open to the public. Since then, the ranch has been known as the "D. H. Lawrence Ranch."

Under a mammoth pine tree right outside the door to their home, D.H. Lawrence would spend his mornings writing at a small table. In 1929, five years after Lawrence's final visit to New Mexico, artist Georgia O'Keeffe came to Taos. During her visit, O'Keeffe spent weeks at the Kiowa Ranch and painted the stately pine. O'Keeffe writes that she would lie on the long, weathered carpenter's bench under the tall tree, staring up past the trunk through the branches and into the night sky. The scene is captured in her famous oil painting, "The Lawrence Tree."

You can lie on that same bench, look up into the same tree, and see the same image that O'Keeffe saw many years before—a very cool experience.

We went through Taos without seeing a steakhouse, so we stopped at a convenience store at the far edge of town and asked the clerk where to find one. She told us to drive further out of town and that we'd see it on the left. We drove several miles out of town and saw nothing. Undeterred, we turned around, went back into town, stopped at another convenience store, and asked the clerk. He gave us more specific directions. The restaurant was further out and had a landmark where to turn.

We arrived at the restaurant at 4:50 pm. The sign on the door indicated that the restaurant opened at 5:00 pm. We were fresh off an all-day strenuous hike, so we were caked in sweat and most certainly stinky. The wait staff seemed to know this instinctively and seated us in a remote spot in the dining area. In other words: they seated us in a far corner. We were the only patrons at the time, so with nothing to do, the wait staff assembled at the welcome station and talked. We were close enough to hear bits and pieces of their conversation. I heard "Key Largo" and I perked up. I asked our waiter if the waitress who said "Key Largo" could come to our table.

After a moment, she came over, and we began talking about Key Largo. She mentioned an uncle who lived there and owned some rental property. I asked, "What is his name?"

"Bill Mullins" was her answer.

Yes, small world. How many hoops did we have to jump through to get to her and her uncle?

My resume' in Key Largo starts with being an on-call taxi driver. There were only landlines then, so I had to be home to get a fare. I realized soon that this employment wouldn't sustain me for long. I had fished offshore Key Largo for many years with great success, so I thought real employment could come by becoming a sea captain and charter fishing. I signed up for a captain's course in Miami and soon passed the Coast Guard test, becoming a licensed mariner capable of legally taking guests out for hire on the ocean.

I began that career by answering an ad for a fishing mate on a private 25' boat owned by Bill Cohen, owner of a candy company in New Jersey that made Gummie Bears. The job was for the winter, paying me full time to be available as a mate to them for sail-fishing. He was not there full-time but paid me to be available. This is where I got my live bait, light tackle sail-fishing experience. His fishing was geared to finding and cast-netting a baitfish called ballyhoo, keeping them alive in a baitwell, and using them offshore to attract sailfish. We were very successful. We always released sailfish alive.

I had recently purchased a 28' Bertram with flybridge and was anxious to sailfish on it, which I did many times with Janet and friends. Bill owned a condo at the Ocean Reef Club, so, being there all the time, I began to make my sailfish captaining available to other guests at the club through the tackle shop. It was lucrative, but only four months a year while the sailfish ran. I also ran a fishing charter all year on my Bertram: sailfish in the winter and dolphin (Mahi Mahi) in the summer.

Even though winter was good, summer was spotty. Needing more income, I began to take note of the scuba trips going out every day, regardless of the weather. Stay-at-home days are rare for divers. I gave up most of the fishing and the Cohen's gig to hire on with Captain Slate's Atlantis Dive Center located on the same canal where Janet and I lived.

I worked relentlessly for him, sometimes fourteen days in a row, until I left a snorkeler out at the reef. There had been a miscount at the dock that led to that disaster. The snorkeler was fine, having been picked up by one of the many boats on the scene, but that was the end of my job with Slate. I was reprimanded by a Miami Coast Guard review board, and my license was suspended for a year. Dejected, I drove home.

The year before, I had found a small, well-worn 14' Boston Whaler with an outboard motor drifting just outside of the canal that we lived on. I confiscated it. The boat had been anchored somewhere in the Caribbean and drifted across the Gulfstream into my hands after breaking anchor. It ran perfectly. When I was suspended by the Coast Guard, a friend and I began to make a living by free-diving for lobster. I was only middling good at it, but Andy was a wizard. It became my job to stay on the boat, drop him off in the mangrove waterways, and keep watch while he hunted. We did surprisingly well. He was fearless and would dive under bridges and other places with heavy boat traffic where others dared not go. We made a decent living with this.

After my suspension was up, I answered an ad for a captain's job at a smaller dive shop that I took. It had three smaller boats with only six and twelve diver capacities, compared to the forty-diver capacity of Slate's boats. The pay was the same, so it was a no-brainer. Silent World was the name of the shop. The owner was a mentally challenged younger guy who was adopted into a wealthy family. The family had owned Winter Park Telephone in its entirety.

The business had existed for four years. In its best year, Silent World was so poorly run that the business lost $50,000. The mismanagement was easy to see. To explain the incompetency, the owner had recently married and let his wife take over managing the business. She also began to keep track of their family finances. Their personal checks started to bounce, so she began the research to find the cause. Her husband had written a check to the local volunteer fire department and had not subtracted the ten thousand dollar check from their ledger. When his wife asked him, "Why not?" he said, "Well, it's tax-deductible, so I didn't need to deduct it from the ledger, right?"

I'll leave that for you to figure out.

He also donated to every scam telephone call that he got, amounting to thirty thousand dollars per year. I'm certain the same phone bank called him asking for donations to things like the "Fireman's Relief Fund" and the "Disabled Whomever Fund."

It was endless, but he was so good-hearted and naïve that he always gave them money. After we bought the business, I fielded a steady stream of phony solicitations for a year.

We bought the business for a couple of reasons. When the family accountant realized the ineptitude of running the company, he demanded it be sold or shut down. Shutting it down would mean the end of my job, so the purchase interested me. The sale idea came to the accountant after I met him several times and conveyed my concerns about how the business was being run. He made an offer to me that I should take over management, have complete control, and at the end of a year, any money that was made could be used to purchase the business. In other words, buy their business from them with their own money. It was impossible to pass up.

I took over and overhauled everything. I sold one of the three boats, cut the insane advertising budget by 80%, cut everyone's exorbitant pay, among many other drastic changes. Several employees quit, but I hired more and kept on. When I entered into this agreement, I thought I was only doing it to preserve my job, but the bottom line changed so drastically that I realized this could result in a retirement. At the end of the year, I paid them for a business with assets of two hundred thousand dollars with only eight thousand dollars of mine and Janet's money.

Left to right: Janet, myself, Lilly, Captain Bob, Laura Lee.

Our dive customers would always ask us what there was to do while not diving. We sent them up the highway to a circus animal rescue in Homestead. The owners were so grateful for us sending business their way that we became VIPs. They would let us go behind the scenes for some close-up experiences. Whenever they had big-cat cubs, they would invite us to come up and pet them. It was a wonderful experience. Below is Janet petting a White Tiger cub and me with a Florida Panther cub.

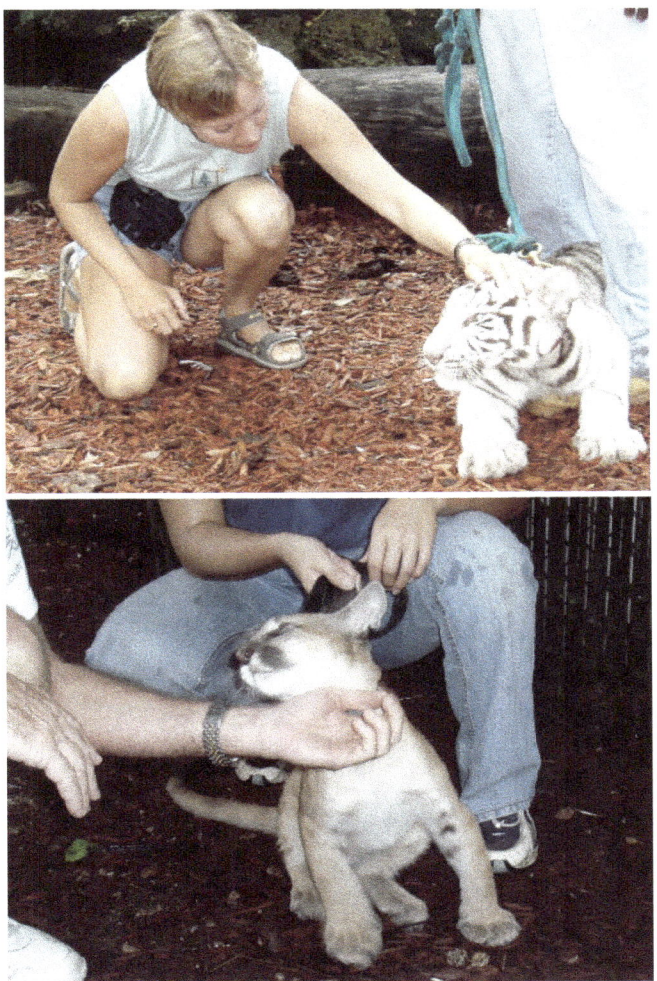

Phyllis

Before Janet came to Key Largo to be with me, I had, for a short while, a girlfriend named Phyllis. Phyllis was pretty, bright, and very smart, working as the restaurant manager at the Key Largo Holiday Inn. She moved in with me, and things were great for a while. The only thing I thought odd was that she thought it was acceptable to pee while we were in the shower together. Disgusting, but I let it slide.

The rental we lived in was a single-wide trailer. Due to space limitations, I had an upright freezer outside the back door connected by an extension cord to a power outlet inside the door. The cord went between the door and the door sill. I had about 75 pounds of fish filets in the freezer. One day, without saying anything and without looking to where the cord was attached, Phyllis pulled the extension cord plug out of the outlet and just pitched the extension cord out the back door. When I realized what she had done, the fish was spoiled. I was pissed, but again, I let it slide.

Phyllis had parents who supposedly owned a farm in the Midwest and wanted to visit us. According to Phyllis, they had to get one more corn crop planting done before it got too late in the summer. I said, "Okay."

Phyllis arranged to have them come down after the corn crop was planted. When her parents arrived in Key Largo, they came to the house with me at home and Phyllis at work. I sat them in the living room and began to get acquainted. After some small talk, I asked them, "So, did the corn crop get planted on time?"

They then looked at me like I had three heads.

I said, "The corn crop?"

Again, silence and incredulous looks.

"Don't you have a farm?" I asked.

They shook their heads. "No."

Mom worked at a convenience store, and Dad worked at a hardware store. They were dumbfounded at the farm questions. I continued as though things were normal, but things were swirling in my head.

Turns out Phyllis is what they call a compulsive liar, someone who lies for no reason whatsoever. I didn't believe people like that existed, but they do. When Phyllis got home, I confronted her about the "farm," but she only shrugged. Why would she lie like that, knowing it would soon be uncovered?

Also, during that conversation, it turned out that she had been fired two weeks before from her management position at the Holiday Inn. She had been leaving the house in the morning as if she were going to work and just going partying with her friends, not saying a thing to me. Someone I knew, in a position to know, had told me Phyllis got fired because none of her references were true.

I gave her a week to get out and ended things with her. During that week, two of my prize possessions disappeared: a Mickey Mantle rookie season baseball card worth $10,000 and a letter from Winston Churchill to my grandfather, Dr. Winton, thanking him for a gift of a box of Tampa hand-made cigars.

Unattached women in Key Largo can be a rough trade, so importing from the mainland is preferred.

Marriage Number Three

Not long after I moved to Key Largo, Janet and I met through a mutual friend, Mary Lee. I was going to be in Tampa for a weekend, and Janet and Mary Lee set up a dive trip to an offshore wreck in Naples, Florida. We got everything together but terminated the dive immediately due to zero visibility.

We had a drink at the waterfront bar and drove home. It was not a mind-altering afternoon, but the beautiful and smart Janet stuck in my head.

Janet

After nearly a year of no contact, I tracked her down and called her where she worked in Tampa. She answered the phone, and when I said my name, she said, "Who?"

I had obviously made a big impression.

We decided to meet, and I took her out for dinner that night. Things went very well. I was in Tampa for Kieffer's wedding and asked Janet if she'd go with me to the wedding the next day, which she did. We spent the rest of the weekend together: going to a party that her roommate was putting on, and then to Tarpon Springs for lunch the next day. Three months later, she agreed to move in with me in Key Largo.

The day she arrived and looked in our closet, she was taken aback by the fact that I had not cleared room for her clothes. I heard about that for a while.

Janet moved in August 1997. One month later, I took her out for dinner at a favorite restaurant. After we were home, she said she was headed for bed. I asked her to come into the living room before she went to bed. It was then that I asked her to marry me. She woke up at 4 am with food poisoning.

Sugar's Jealousy

When Janet moved in, I had several Siamese cats. The "matriarch," Sugar, disapproved of her moving in. When Janet and I would go to bed at night, Sugar would position herself between us. She would then move close to Janet, and in response, Janet would move closer to the edge of the bed. This would continue until Sugar had literally pushed Janet out of bed.

A few months later, Sugar was pregnant. When the kittens were born, Janet woke up that morning to find a placenta on her pillow, mere inches from her face.

Janet had been around cats her entire life. Her Dad loved all animals, especially cats and especially Siamese. Janet was not deterred, so Sugar failed to run Janet off. We believe Sugar began to think, "I'll outlast this bitch!"

Sugar lived to be 19 years old. On her last night on earth, it was Janet who stayed up all night with her and was there for her when she passed over to the Rainbow Bridge.

Two Boutonnieres

Janet and I married on the beach at Largo Lodge in Key Largo in May 1988. We had family and friends at a small wedding at noon on a beautiful day. I had my Bertram docked there so we could sail into the sunset with a story-book finish.

About an hour before the scheduled ceremony, my step-mom, Mickey, asked my friend Ben Ellis to go up to our room and get the two boutonnières. We all nearly fell over laughing when Ben strolled down to the beach holding two beers. When Mickey asked Ben to go get the two boutonnières, he thought she had said, "Go get two beers!"

He thought, "Wow, Mickey, that's my girl!"

The Propeller

Afterward, Janet and I sailed off in a glorious ending to the ceremony. We headed home, which was on a canal a couple of miles away, five homes down the canal. When we entered the canal, a blade on the propeller fell off, rendering the boat un-maneuverable. We had to stop at the first available dock, tie the boat up, and get off. Here we were, fully attired in wedding clothes, me in a suit and tie and Janet in her wedding dress.

None of that was particularly noteworthy, except that the person living at that address was my ex-girlfriend, Phyllis, who was there standing on the dock, watching the whole fiasco with a big, fat smirk on her face, me feeling six inches tall, and Janet wanting to be on another planet.

Honduras

Janet and I went on our honeymoon at a dive resort on Guanaja, Honduras, an island off the coast within sight of a more well-known island dive destination called Roatan. We were doing a lot of diving, and the Bayman Bay Club Dive Resort had a buy-one-get-one-free offer we took advantage of.

We flew into the airport in San Pedro Sula, Honduras, on an ordinary airliner. We disembarked over the tarmac into a small, ordinary terminal. In a few minutes, several crew-cut Anglo-Saxons with M-16s entered the airport and ordered about fifty of us into a room with no windows and no explanation. Our situational awareness went into hyperdrive. While in the room, we heard two C-130s land and take off. C-130s have a distinct sound that I knew from my Air Force days. About fifteen minutes later, the CIA types opened the doors, letting us back into the main terminal as though nothing had been out of the ordinary. This was in the time of Iran-Contra.

Iran–Contra was a political scandal in the United States that occurred during the second term of the Reagan administration. Between 1981 and 1986, Lieutenant Colonel Oliver North and others secretly facilitated the sale of arms to Iran, which was the subject of an arms embargo. The administration hoped to use the arms sale proceeds to fund the Contras, a right-wing rebel group, in Nicaragua. The resulting scandal was investigated and prosecuted by my uncle, Lawrence Walsh. President Reagan and VP Bush were implicated but not indicted. Eleven, including North and Caspar Weinberger, were convicted with their convictions overturned on the proverbial technicality. After Bush became President, he pardoned everyone.

This confusing, three-cornered, nefarious, arms deal, was ultimately aimed at the eventual release of seven hostages held in Lebanon by Hezbollah. The incident we witnessed at the San Pedro Sula airport was part of the arms deal.

When that dust settled, we boarded a vintage DC-3 for the short flight to a dirt strip on Island Guanaja. A short Jeep ride to a small boat took us on a twenty-minute ride along mangrove creeks to the resort.

The resort was built on the ocean-front hillside of the uninhabited side of the island. Individual accommodations for couples were separated by walkways surrounded by jungle foliage. There was no air conditioning, we didn't need it, there was a continuous onshore breeze that kept everyone comfortable.

The "cabins" were the bare minimum, with a small, open breezeway between the bedroom and bathroom. When we were taken to our cabin, there was a lovely mosquito net draped over the bed. Janet said, "Oh, how romantic!"

We discovered later it was to keep tarantulas out of the bed while we slept. I don't think Janet slept at all until the last day when she finally napped out of sheer exhaustion.

The dozen rooms spread over the hillside were connected to the common area where food and drinks were served to the guests. The trails led down to the dock where the dive boats were tied.

Our trip was perfect: weather, resort staff, dive crew, the food, and the diving. I experienced Montezuma's Revenge many years before, so I was careful not to drink the local water. I even used bottled beer to brush my teeth.

Everything could not have been better until the night before we left. Somehow, I had contracted an intestinal disorder. I was alarmed at the rate at which fluids exited my body. I could barely walk. I spent most of the night lying on the bathroom floor, watching hermit crabs crawl along their way in and out of the bathroom while an iguana watched over me from his perch on the light fixture.

The plan was to fly off the island to a larger airport on the mainland in San Pedro Sula. I was very weak, visiting the commode every fifteen minutes to deliver what was then a pure white liquid to the toilet, with nothing left in me but Montezuma's minions.

We were awakened early for our boat ride to the grass airstrip and DC-3 ride to San Pedro Sula. The idea of being more than two steps from a commode alarmed me. The couple that owned the resort were on the premises and were made aware of my predicament. They had diapers for their baby and suggested I wear one for the flight. I didn't want to miss the flight, who knows how badly further travel plans might get scrambled if I did.

I accepted the diapers and we got on the boat. The gunwale on the boat was only ten inches off the water level. I lay in the boat with a half-dozen sympathetic onlookers, my head over the side, regularly hurling very little into the water. Besides the embarrassment of wearing a diaper, nothing obscene happened on the flight to the mainland.

We landed and made it to the main terminal. I was so weak I didn't have the strength to sit in a chair, so I lay on the floor. A group of nuns soon noticed me, came to where I lay, kneeled, and asked if they could pray over me. I said sure, why not? It can't hurt. They prayed and left.

The airline from San Pedro Sula to Miami was Tan Sahsa, which the locals claimed Sahsa was an anachronym for "Stay at Home, Stay Alive."

Hardly reassuring, but there we were. On the flight, we sat in the last row with a stewardess and accessory cubby-hole just over our shoulder. With a slight turn of our heads, we could see the two female flight attendants taking turns chugging vodka out of a bottle. We didn't take much note of it, we were both thinking I could be on the verge of death. It was bad.

After we arrived in Miami, Janet cried as we went through customs. I was diagnosed with dysentery, which can be deadly, and I believed them.

Janet got food poisoning the night I asked her to marry me. I got dysentery on our honeymoon. Red flags were everywhere.

The Nineties

Some Caving

Around 1959, my parents took me and my sister on a trip to Mammoth Cave in Kentucky. I was twelve and fascinated by caves. Not long afterward, my short interest span made me forget about caves.

In 1997, Janet wanted me to go with her to see her mother in Virginia. I had been thinking of returning to Mammoth, so I said I'd go to Virginia, but I wanted to stop at Mammoth Cave on the way.

Janet called the Park Service to inquire about the types of cave trips offered. There were several 'tourist' trips, lights, paved pathways, etc. When the service mentioned a 'Wild Cave' tour during the conversation, knowing me, Janet said that sounded like what we were interested in, so she booked the trip. You had to be at least 16 years old, chest and hip measurement could not exceed 42 inches (if larger, you wouldn't be physically able to pass through the crawlspaces!), you could not be claustrophobic, nor should you mind getting dirty. You also needed some boots with ankle support and light-colored soles (so as not to mark the formations).

They provided helmets and lights. The park service bills this as the "most strenuous ranger-led activity in the National Park System."

It was about five miles underground, covered over about six hours. We ate like starved dogs at dinner after the trip. It was strenuous but tons of fun. We got the caving bug after Mammoth. For the next two years, we went on guided trips to obscure caves not visited by tourists. We caved at many spots in the TAG area (Tennessee, Alabama, and Georgia) and in and around Blacksburg, Virginia.

Some of these caves were easy walk-through caves with no crawling and zero danger. Most had an element of hazard. We did seventy-foot on-rope rappel drops into total blackness. Rappelling of any depth requires technical equipment, training, and some skill. Any mistake could result in a fatal free-fall onto broken rock. One reason we would take these adventures was that we are so focused on our immediate situation and the mortal danger we may be in, we don't give one second's thought to the crap that may be going on at home in our daily lives. You are in the moment.

Of course, once you are seventy feet down a rope into a hole, eventually you have to go back up. That requires more technical equipment. Climbing up a rope hand-over-hand is impossible for all but a minuscule set of our population.

One section of Mammoth Cave is a horizontal crack about fifty feet wide and one hundred feet long. This crack is the result of an immense rock separating from its upper half. The separation you must inch your way through is only ten inches tall. A requirement to take this tour is your chest and hip measurements must be 42" or less. To make matters worse, the crack is so small you can't go through with your head upright. You must turn your head to the side. This means you can't see where you are going. As you inch along with your toes pushing you, you have to trust where you are going and that it doesn't get so narrow you get stuck. The forty-two-inch rule is strict.

The above trips are called "dry" caves, meaning although you may have to wade through shallow water at times, you are never submerged. A "wet" cave is where you must get partially or fully submerged to continue into the cave. Some traverses are too long to do with only a breath of air; they require scuba equipment. This is an advanced level of caving. Janet and I have never done any wet caves.

However, Keiffer, Rob, Ben, and I did some full cave diving in the Ginnie Springs cave system on the Santa Fe River in North Florida. Cave diving on scuba is highly specialized, requiring intensive training. None of us had any cave training at all. We were experienced open-water divers, aware of the dangers and equipment redundancies required to dive in an "overhead" environment.

The land surrounding the access to Ginnie Springs is owned and controlled by a small company that allows access for camping, swimming, and scuba diving. The diving is strictly controlled and restricted to only those with cave diving certification or those under the direct supervision of a cave diving instructor. This level of diving is so dangerous that even the most renowned and experienced cave divers get killed in caves. Wes Skiles was the owner of Ginnie Springs and a world-famous cave diver. Years after my diving there, Wes was killed on a cave diving expedition due to equipment failure.

Arriving at Ginnie by land, none of us would be allowed to dive, so, we rented canoes upriver, loaded all our gear into them, and paddled down to Ginnie. Riverfront landowners only own the land down to the historic "high-water" mark on the bank. This technicality allowed us to tie the canoes off to the riverbank without any interference from the resort. We could get geared up and float a few yards downstream to where the crystal-clear spring water entered the brown, zero-visibility river water and enter the cave system.

The system is called the "Eye and Ear" due to having two entrances fifty feet apart that connected to the main cave thirty feet down. All four of us had done one dive into the system and had used the air in one tank each. After that first dive, we climbed back onto the canoes, rested, and waited an hour before doing a second dive.

When the hour was up, we hooked our breathing systems, called regulators, onto our second air tanks. Kieffer and I went first, together – the "buddy system." This "system" is the primary safety feature of scuba diving. The idea is for the two "buddies" to watch each other, be aware of their surroundings, and keep an eye on their own life-preserving equipment, like air pressure gauges and remaining volume of air. One procedure is to check the air in your buddy's tank prior to getting in the water.

Kieffer and I dropped into the river, then shortly down into the "Ear" opening. The main cave is about ten feet in diameter with a mild current until it reaches the split into the Eye and Ear. The combined diameters of the Eye and Ear are much smaller than the diameter of the main cave. This dramatically increases water speed, making it extremely difficult to get to the main cave. You have to kick your fins hard and also use the rough sides of the entrances to pull yourself in.

Kieffer and I arrived at the relative calm of the main cave and continued in. The flowing water is extremely clear in the main cave with no possibility of silting. When you get off into side tunnels, silting becomes a dangerous problem. One careless kick of the fins can immediately produce zero visibility. You can't see anything even with the strongest light and it takes hours to clear. Your air won't last that long. On serious ventures into side caves, a line is secured outside and everyone always holds the line as it is taken inside. I was in a side branch on another trip, took my hand off the line, the diver ahead of me kicked up a cloud of silt and I was immediately blind. I quickly slapped my hand to the cave floor and felt the line under my hand. My heart was hammering, but I soon felt relieved as we got out.

As Kieffer and I continued deeper, we saw a small hole on our right side. We looked in and saw a much bigger room just inside. We decided to explore, but only for a short distance. The hole was too small to enter without removing our tanks from our backs, keeping the regulator in our mouths, sliding the tanks into the room, then crawling into the room and putting the tanks back on. This took concentration and effort but we both made it safely inside.

Once inside, we gathered our composure and looked at one another. We were only a foot apart, looking into each other's eyes when Kieffer gave me the "out of air" signal. My heart pounded, and I thought, surely this is a joke. It wasn't. We both neglected to check his available air. He had hooked his regulator up to an empty tank.

The panic in me rose to brand-new heights. That moment taught me to be careful with whom you buddy. Panic in either of us at that moment could easily result in both of our deaths. One thing in your scuba training is to stop and think for a moment and assess the situation. That's hard to do when your life is at stake.

Another thing you are taught is how to combat an out-of-air situation with one of the dive team. There are two methods, one is the use of a spare regulator on everyone's tank that is always hooked directly to each tank. This allows both divers to breathe simultaneously off the same tank. The other is to "buddy breathe," meaning one diver takes a breath, then takes the regulator out of his mouth and passes it to the second diver to take a breath. This sharing continues until both divers manage to surface.

We took the second option due to the logistics of getting the tanks and ourselves through the hole into the main cave. Kieffer took a breath from my regulator, removed his tank, and shoved it through the hole. He turned back to me, took a breath, wriggled out the hole, and waited on the other side. I grabbed a breath, removed my tank, shoved it through the hole to Kieffer, and handed him the regulator. I pulled myself through the hole, out to Kieffer, and took a breath. We were still thirty feet deep and sixty horizontal feet to the surface.

We gathered our wits and proceeded upward. Divers cannot do uncontrolled, rapid ascents to the surface without a potentially fatal brain embolism. We continued in a controlled, deliberate manner until we arrived at the constriction and the rushing water. We bounced against the walls but made a safe ascent. That was our last cave dive.

Black Cows at Night

We went caving in rural Virginia, entering the cave mid-afternoon. When we exited, it was pitch black, no moon and no city light. We were on a farmer's property who raised black cows. When got in the car, I turned on the lights and illuminated several black cows near the car. Janet said, "Ooh, cool. Turn off the lights and I'll get a picture." She took the picture with a disposable 35mm camera.

Days later we had the film developed a prints made. Below is now the famous "Black Cows at Night," courtesy of Janet Clemons.

Four Corners

"Four Corners" is where four states intersect: Colorado, New Mexico, Arizona, and Utah all come together on Native American land. Several places nearby have dinosaur tracks in the rock that the Native Americans exploit for a living by doing tours of the tracks.

We hired one, and after the tour was over, we paid him. He then asked if we could give him a ride into town and we agreed to drop him wherever he wished. He steered us to the town liquor store, where we dropped him and watched him walk inside.

The Bates Motel

While planning one of our trips out West, Janet found a motel in the infancy of the internet just south of Sierra Vista, Arizona. She called the Sierra Vista motel to make a reservation and spoke to the owner. The owner told Janet that she had recently purchased the motel and had only one room renovated. She said the room was available on our desired date, so Janet booked it. Janet commented that the woman on the phone was very nice.

We arrived late one afternoon, very tired. We pulled into the driveway, which was overgrown with weeds. Avoiding some tumbleweeds, we pulled up to the office where the owner greeted us. She was in her 40s, sporting a completely shaved head and many tattoos on it, except for her face, which had many piercings. She looked somewhat disturbing but was otherwise very friendly and welcoming. She pointed out our room and gave us a key.

She also said we were the only guests that night and that she would have to leave soon and stay overnight somewhere else for a now-forgotten reason.

Most would have balked, but not Janet and I. We accepted the room key and went to the room. We entered and immediately thought this could not be the renovated room. It didn't look renovated at all. The bed looked like an antique hospital bed with the original array of wire and springs beneath the mattress that squeaked every time someone moved. There was no box spring on those old beds.

However, the bedding and the room were clean, so we stayed. Janet looked into the shower stall and saw a large spider crawl out of the drain, which was open with no strainer. Before going to bed, she went to lock the door and realized the door would not lock.

We usually take many pictures of our trips, but when we are in a threatening situation, there are few or sometimes no pictures. There is only one picture of this incident, that of a chair propped up against the doorknob.

When the sun set, we saw that there were no lights of any kind on the property. It was pitch dark and creepy. We rose early and bolted with dust and rock flying from beneath the spinning wheels of our car. It looked like the last scene of a horror movie with the victims getting away as fast as possible.

Deadbolt

Mount Hood, May, 2001

In May 2001, Janet and I went to Mt. Hood (11,240 ft.) with a professional guide, Jim Frankenfield. We stayed overnight at the Timberline Lodge, built in the '30s by the WPA. This place is a work of art—lots of gorgeous native stone and woodwork. The Timberline Lodge portrays the outside of The Overlook Hotel in the film "The Shining."

The next day was our wedding anniversary. Not thinking about the time difference from Virginia to Oregon, Janet's mom called us that morning before she went to work to wish us a happy anniversary and good luck on the climb. This occurred at 5:30 am EST, 3 hours earlier in Oregon. After the phone call, I had difficulty getting back to sleep. In the movie "Ghost," there is a scene where Carl meets his untimely end. Shadowy phantoms arrive and drag Carl away to Hell. I thought I was seeing the same shadowy phantoms in our room! The memory still makes the hair stand up on the back of my neck.

In the morning, we hiked up to about 8500 feet, pitched a tent on a moraine, and practiced self-arrest and crevasse rescue techniques that afternoon. The wind got going that first night, 20-25 knots, rocking the tent all night long, and we got very little rest.

At 3 am, Janet looked at me after getting no sleep and said she wasn't going. When I asked her, "Why?" she replied, "I'm miserable, I'm freezing, and I have to pee."

Nature's call can sometimes be an ordeal for females, especially when negotiating layers of clothing and trying to pee in a bottle. Janet looked like some wild, cornered animal, and it scared me that I was in an enclosed space with her. After this exchange, she dressed and didn't say another word about not going. I now figured the climb would be called off because of the wind. Not so. It wasn't that bad after moving up the mountain until we reached the Hogsback Ridge (the final ridge to the summit). We were suddenly buffeted by about 30-knot gusts of wind and blasts of ice crystals to the face that felt more like needles, threatening to knock us into the 'Devil's Kitchen' below. As we were starting the final push to the summit, Janet yelled at me and began shaking her head wildly. She was trying to tell me she didn't want to go any further. I just turned around and ignored her, thinking, "We're not getting this close just to turn around."

So up we continued and got to the summit of Mt. Hood.

There was a fatal accident just weeks before we arrived, a climbing team got to the top, which is a flat area maybe 25 yards across. It looks nice and safe enough for a young woman to unclip from her rope and walk toward the edge. What she had not considered was the possibility of a cornice.

Cornices grow through the winter on the leeward side of wind-exposed ridges and summits. Cornices range from small wind lips of soft snow to overhangs of hard snow larger than a school bus. They can break off the terrain suddenly and unexpectedly and sometimes be triggered from a distance. Overhung cornices can pull back further than expected onto a flat ridge top and catch people by surprise. While large cornices are quite destructive, even a small one can be deadly if it carries you over a cliff or rocky terrain below. One must travel cautiously on corniced ridgelines, giving cornices or unknown edges a wide berth.

The young lady seemed to be a safe distance from the edge and on solid ground, but she wasn't. She was standing on a cornice that chose that moment to give way, and she fell thousands of feet to her death.

There was another fatal accident that occurred in 2002 involving a rescue helicopter crash caught on video and played endlessly on TV. The helo crashed, rolled downhill, and rolled right over a climber who survived unhurt as the helo went over him. The open door framed him entirely, with the helicopter barely touching him as it rolled on.

Janet in the foreground, me in the background, Mt. Hood

Our Nemesis: Mt. Rainier

After a couple of years of caving, Janet and I had been talking about the possibility of getting into high-altitude mountaineering. We began working on a trip to Alaska, with the primary goal of attending a 5-day mountaineering class. The trip I created had many intricacies. Janet later referred to the Alaska trip as "a work of art."

In the days before our mountaineering class, Janet and I took a voyage on the Alaska Marine Highway, a blue-collar ferry system operating from Bellingham, Washington, throughout the Inside Passage and further up the Alaskan coast, all the way out to Dutch Harbor at the tip of the Aleutian Island Chain. Dutch Harbor was featured prominently in the TV series "Deadliest Catch." The vessels ferry people, goods and vehicles on several large ferries.

We boarded the MV Matanuska in Bellingham, and rather than book an expensive berth, we pitched our tent on the upper rear deck with several dozen other passengers. Showers and lockers were available. The tent could not be staked down, so we weighed it down at all times with the rest of our camping and mountaineering gear to prevent it from being blown overboard. Our ticket included three meals a day, which was delicious. The crew was great.

The northern terminus for our cruise was Skagway, which had seven stops in towns in between. After completing the trip, we took a ferry to Haines, where our mountain class was held. Haines is between the Chilkat Mountains and the Lynn Fjord, a gorgeous setting. The evening before our class began, we stayed at the Hotel Halsingland, former commanding and bachelor officers' quarters at Fort Seward, which was converted into a hotel in 1947.

In the morning, we ate breakfast at the hotel restaurant. I ordered coffee, but when it arrived at our table in a clear glass cup, I was surprised that the coffee was so weak that you could read text through the cup. You would think in Alaska, strong coffee would be expected.

We left the hotel and walked a short distance to the harbor. On the way, there was a tiny coffee hut. After the poor coffee experience at the hotel, we ordered a cup for each of us. The coffee was served in paper cups. The girl handed Janet a cup with a cardboard insulator around it. She then handed me the next cup but without the insulator. I asked her, "Could I have an insulator?" She responded, "I usually only give those to the girls." That, of course, reduced me immediately to a height of two inches. I slunk off.

In mid-May 1999, we spent the first week in Alaska sightseeing and the second week in the mountaineering class. The result was wanting to climb Mt. Rainier that fall.

September 1999, we found ourselves on a plane to Washington State. As we flew over Mt. Rainier, Janet and I pointed out the window and talked excitedly about our upcoming climb. We had no idea what was waiting for us.

One of the guides from the Alaska mountaineering class had agreed to go with us on the climb. The typical route up the mountain is called the "Disappointment Cleaver" route. Aptly named as, when you arrive at the base of "the cleaver" for a few hours of fitful sleep, you can't fathom going any further. When attempting to climb a glaciated mountain, the idea is to begin around midnight, climbing all night and, hopefully, reaching the summit around dawn. This is to avoid possible avalanches and rock falls on the descent. Once the sun is out and the ice and snow start heating up, the chance of avalanches and rock falls increases significantly.

We were awake at midnight and, by 1 am, were on the way to the summit. Our "guide" had told us that should one of us have to turn around, we'd all have to turn around. There would be no leaving anyone at any point to wait for the others to go on and then meet back up on the descent. About an hour after our departure, we were still in sight of camp. I felt I couldn't make it all the way and indicated that I'd like to return to camp.

Since we weren't very far away, it was decided that I could return to camp alone. The others continued. A few hours later, Janet had developed some massive blisters and felt there was no way she could continue. The "guide" put her in a sleeping bag and left her while the remaining four continued to the summit. Had I known the possibility of this being an option, I would have continued rather than returning to camp so early on.

After the team returned to camp, they all rested for a couple of hours, then we broke camp and headed down the mountain.

Everyone else was way ahead of Janet and me. Her blisters were excruciating, which made the descent slow going. About an hour from the parking lot, we made another rest stop. Janet was bent over, moaning in pain. A younger couple, who were day-hiking, passed by us and stopped to ask about our summit attempt.

After a brief conversation, the couple asked Janet if she'd like them to take her pack down for her. In Janet's mind, she's thinking: "I won't turn over a couple of thousand dollars' worth of gear to people I don't know."

She politely declined, and the couple started to leave. I then asked her if she was sure. Janet had no problem changing her mind and immediately handed her pack to the couple. When we arrived at the parking lot, the couple had found our group and had left Janet's pack with them.

We underestimated Rainier for three more trips. We skipped a year (2000) and went the second time in 2001, a third time in 2002, and a fourth time in 2003. By this time, the wait staff in the restaurant at Paradise Inn (the main hotel inside Mt. Rainier National Park) had begun to recognize us from prior visits. We planned a fifth trip for 2004 and decided to do some things differently.

In Key Largo, our training consisted of running three to six miles, three times a week, and walking up and down a short, 45-degree wooden ramp carrying 50 pounds of weight for up to an hour three times a week.

Before going to Rainier, we flew to Leadville, Colorado, at 10,200 feet. We needed to acclimate far better than we had in the past, and Leadville seemed like an excellent place to do that. We spent a week there climbing Mt. Elbert twice and Mt. Sherman once, both over 14,000 feet. These mountains are big day hikes on a well-defined trail with no glaciers or real danger. We stayed at a hotel in downtown Leadville called the Delaware, built in the late 1800s, a nifty old place. Carrying the luggage up just one flight of stairs was a shock, we could hardly catch our breath. We climbed every other day and ran on alternate days, and the acclimatization went well.

Janet and I then flew to Washington State and met a friend who had more mountain experience than we did. We had met Chris on our first attempt of Mt. Rainier when he was added to our group at the last minute. He had since climbed Denali in Alaska and Aconcagua in South America. Chris had just finished biking across the U.S. when he flew to Seattle to meet us for the climb. We (and he) were worried about how well he would do without acclimatization.

A side story:

Janet and I arrived in Seattle a day before Chris. We had reservations at a branded hotel and settled in for the night. We noticed that the door had no security bar or chain, so we secured the door with what was available and went to bed. I woke around 1 am to see a man standing in our room! I jumped out of bed (I slept in only tighty-whiteys) and lunged at the man, screaming at the top of my lungs.

Janet woke up and screamed. By this time, I was running down the hallway, trying to catch the man, but he had gotten away. The following day, we spoke to the manager about what had happened, but he seemed complacent about the event. Janet had made the reservation through a popular travel website. She told them what had happened, and our payment for the room was promptly refunded. We have yet to learn who the intruder was.

We picked up Chris from the airport the next day and headed for Mt. Rainier. We hiked the three miles into a campsite called Glacier Basin for the first night, which only took about two hours without much elevation gain. Our packs were hefty, probably 55 pounds, as we had to bring a 4-season tent, rope, crampons, a stove, fuel, food, and other equipment. The following day, we evaluated what we were carrying and left some food and gear on a bear pole, then left for Camp Shurman at 9,600 feet. The route up the Inter Glacier was uneventful, other than a couple of white-outs that didn't last very long. There was much less snow this year than last, and there was a large area that was hard, blue ice, which we had to skirt around. We made it to Camp Shurman in good shape, pitched our tent, melted snow, ate, slept, and rested the next day. After trying to get some sleep, which I couldn't, we got up at 10:30 pm and left camp at midnight.

The route is no more than about three miles, but much of it is very steep. I was nearly petrified for long stretches of 45-degree stuff where the boot track was only six inches wide. One miss-step by any of us could have been the death of all three. I swore I would never put myself in that much danger again. The Emmons Glacier route is the safest and least technical route on Rainier, so there aren't very many fatalities, but believe me, it still kept us very focused.

There are only two pictures made during the climb. About an hour into it, Chris got sick and puked on the trail for a few minutes, but he said he was okay and kept going. We were worried he might get even more nauseous. I know he wasn't feeling well, but he toughed it out.

We reached the top at noon, twelve hours after the start. It was very windy and cold on top, so I was ready to go back down within minutes of getting there. Some of the steep slopes on the way down were even hairier than on the way up. The snow and ice had grown slushier, and the footing was far trickier.

The acclimatization trip to Leadville was crucial, but Janet and I might not have made it on our own without Chris. He did some route finding that Janet and I might have needed help with. It took another six hours to get down. From there, it took another eight hours to return to the car, even with several nice, long glissades on the Inter Glacier. That is a total of 25 hours of hiking/climbing. I've never been so near complete exhaustion and near delirium in my life, and on top of that, my big toes took a painful beating every step of the way, which resulted in the loss of those nails.

It was 44 hours since I had slept. The last five hours were in the dark, on a remote trail with lots of fresh bear scat. In the last couple of hours, I would have welcomed a bear attack, but sadly, it never came.

Around 3 am, we finally arrived at the car. I was so knackered that I immediately got in the passenger seat and was asleep soon after. The rental car was in mine and Janet's names only, so Janet drove, and Chris was in the back seat. The first few hours were spent on a 2-lane road with deep forest. Janet was driving very slowly, and Chris asked her if she'd like him to drive. Being the prudent person she was, then; she declined his offer to drive.

A bit after that, Chris leaned forward and looked at the speedometer. Janet was driving about 25 mph, and Chris commented that she could drive a bit faster. Janet's following comment sounded like a crazy person. She said, "I can't drive faster, or I'll hit the zebras and elephants!"

Chris was now very confused and asked her what she was talking about. Janet didn't realize it, but she was a bit snow-blind from the climb. This was causing her to hallucinate, and she was seeing all kinds of large zoo animals on the road.

From left, Chris Moling, Janet, and myself, on the summit of Rainier.

Are We Taking the Dog?

Wheeler Peak, Arizona's Highest Geographical Point, has two main routes. One is shorter but steeper, and one is longer but shallower. The trailheads were two miles apart, with a parking lot at each. We thought, "What's the matter with the steep one?"

We parked at the foot of the shorter route and soon found out what the matter was. The last half of the climb was over loose scree, where you stepped up, but the footing was so loose that you slid back down a half-step.

We were at the summit resting when a group of three hikers behind us arrived with their dog. The dog could have been Toto's stunt double in "The Wizard of Oz."

We were dreading the route back down, and while talking about the route with the new arrivals, they mentioned that they had parked their car at the bottom of the shallow route and had gotten a ride back to the shallow trailhead. That meant they could go up the steep trail and down the shallow trail, then have their car there when they finished the hike.

The three hikers offered to take us back to our car if we went down the easier route with them. We took them up on that great offer and started down. There had been a heavy snowfall the day before, and nobody had been up the shallow route that day, so in places, we couldn't tell where the trail was. When we began to lose the trail, their dog took the lead and amazed us by continually finding the path all the way to the car.

We loaded our gear in the rear of the vehicle and climbed into the car. The driver started the car and put it in reverse gear when I looked down next to the car and saw the poor dog with a cocked head, a forlorn look on his face, and his tongue hanging out. I said to the driver, "Are we taking the dog?"

The laughter was deafening. We took the dog.

Rum Runners

On one of the many occasions when our friend Ben was visiting us in Key Largo, Ben and Janet decided they wanted to find the best Rum Runner in Key Largo. Rum Runners are typically a frozen concoction of light rum, dark rum, blackberry liquor, banana liquor, pineapple and orange juices, and grenadine, then topped off with a 151-proof rum floater.

I was the "designated driver" (this was during the years when I didn't drink alcohol), so off we went. After visiting four different bars, Ben and Janet decided that the fourth Rum Runner at Gilbert's Marina and Bar was the best. Four is a lot of rum runners. After we returned home later that night, I went to bed, but Ben and Janet were up to no good.

Janet was making wine at the time, and a 5-gallon glass carboy of Cabernet Sauvignon was on the kitchen counter, ready to be bottled. Ben and Janet thought it would be a great idea to drink this wine using the siphon hose for bottling as a straw. Of course, at that moment, neither of them was thinking about how a siphon hose actually works. So, it began.

The wine started flowing, and Ben and Janet couldn't keep up. They also weren't thinking about the gadget on the siphon hose that stops the flow. They were howling and spewing red wine all over our light gray kitchen. That woke me. I opened the bedroom door to see a wild scene of red wine everywhere and Ben and Janet laughing like crazy!

I shook my head in disgust, closed the door, and returned to bed. This caused Ben and Janet to break out into hysterics again. Needless to say, that kitchen was never the same.

Fall of the Berlin Wall

In 1989, I was a dive boat captain who sometimes took snorkelers out. I took a group out on a nice day with a German couple on board, who had been touring the US for a couple of weeks by the time they got to me and the snorkel trip. This was before the internet, so if you were visiting another country, you could easily be disconnected from world news. That was the case with this couple.

The fall of the Berlin Wall came very quickly in a matter of days, so being tuned in to world news, I mentioned to the Germans that the wall had fallen. The husband was vehement in stating, "There's no way that's ever going to happen."

I left it at that.

My Fingertip

My 28' Bertram had two 350 Chevrolet engines that occasionally needed work. I was in the bilge inspecting the fan belt condition and tightness. When checking fan belts, you need to press the belt section between the pulleys to determine whether they need tightening. Do this, of course, when the engines are not running.

In an inexplicable moment, I pressed the fan belt while the engine was running. The belt jerked my finger only briefly, but I knew something terrible had happened. I didn't feel anything but immediately grabbed my finger without looking at it. The blood began to pour out of my clenched hand. I opened my grip to see the damage and saw a half inch of my finger gone, just the flesh, and I could see the end of a finger bone looking up at me. The fan belt and pulley had pinched the flesh off.

I ran to our rental apartment and got our renter and friend to take me to the hospital. Janet was at work. On the way to the ER, I leaned out the window and hurled. In the emergency room, the doctor bandaged my finger and told me there wasn't much to do but wait until the flesh "granulated" back around the end of the bone. He gave me the unusable fingertip for a souvenir, which Janet shrink-wrapped and kept in the freezer for decades until it got lost in a freezer cleanout.

Three days later, I became concerned with the greenish liquid oozing from the bandage. I went to my general practitioner, who took one look at the wound and went green herself. She said, "Drive to the emergency room right now. I'll call them and tell them what to expect when you arrive."

The new ER doctor took a look and, a bit perplexed, began to insert numbing into my finger in several places with a needle and syringe. After a minute, he took a fingernail brush and briskly and firmly scrubbed the end of the finger. I had not been looking at this until he said, "Want to see?"

Without waiting for an answer, he pointed the pink, exposed fingertip toward me. My stomach went briefly to another planet. He said the original doctor had not even cleaned it. Bits of fan belt were still embedded in my finger, and the infection was nasty. He said this injury was common in the Keys, mainly with lobster boat apparatus being the culprit. He split the remaining skin into a "V," stretched it out over the exposed bone, and stitched it in place. He told me that even though the original fingernail was gone, there was enough nail bed to grow a fingernail. The finger was on the road to recovery.

A month later, I got an invoice from the original ER visit. I disputed the bill on the grounds of incompetency. I was told a review would be conducted, and I would be informed of the outcome. Another month went by before I got a response. The review concluded that the original examination and treatment were competent, and I still owed the money. The physician who conducted the review was none other than the original ER doctor conducting his own review. I never paid the bill and never heard another word.

A Snorkeling Trip

I owned a scuba diving shop in Key Largo and took a boatload of snorkelers out one afternoon. It was a perfect day: flat calm and blue water, primarily couples but also a couple of guys by themselves. After everyone got in the water, I sat in the captain's chair, hoping to chill and zone out. About ten minutes into the stop, I heard a scream right next to the boat.

I jumped up, looked over the gunwale, and saw a young woman in obvious distress. I got her attention and told her to return to the boat. She swam the short distance back to the transom and climbed on board. She walked over to a bench and sat down, her head in her hands, crying. I asked what was wrong, but I got no answer. After a few minutes, she calmed down, and I sat back down.

Once we returned to the dock, I approached a guy I knew was there by himself who I had seen near her early in the trip, and asked if he knew what had happened. He grinned and said that he was snorkeling along and felt a hand slide up inside his bathing suit and began to fondle him. He said nothing and swam along, enjoying things, apparently thinking this was all part of the perks of the excursion.

The young woman had lost track of her boyfriend and swam up to this other young man, thinking she was pleasuring her boyfriend.

My Favorite Customer

This girl was a "dancer" who worked in New York City and came to Key

Largo to get away and do some diving. She came to my shop and asked me, "Would it be okay if I dived naked?"

You may surmise my answer. I said, "I would be happy to take you out, but I think it best if we give you a private tour to avoid any gawking (other than from the captain)."

This we did several times, but I couldn't bring myself to charge her for the trips. I was all about customer service.

The Glass Bottom Boat

On another trip with a glass bottom for viewing, the boat I was on had an upper deck which mainly was shade for the guests, covering everything on the main deck out to the edges of the gunwales, but was also the captain's station and a place to get away from the guests. Occasionally, a guest would ask to climb the ladder and sit with me for a bit.

Today, a young woman asked to come up. It was a very calm day, but it takes very little at times for some folks to get seasick. After about 15 minutes, she said she wasn't feeling well. That statement gets a dive boat captain's immediate attention. I said she needed to go down the ladder immediately but she hesitated and began to vomit.

The upper shade deck had a slight crown, and the vomit started to slide toward the edge and run over the side. I looked over the side and down to where the vomit was dripping. It was dripping onto an older woman's blue-haired coiffure. I did what I could to stop the dripping, but the damage was done. I never went downstairs to see. I just ignored it.

Gomez and the Wolf Man

While Janet and I lived in Key Largo, we had some Siamese cats, one of whom was a chocolate point named Gomez. We were home on Halloween when some kids came by Trick-or-Treating. One small child came to the door in a very realistic Wolf-Man costume. Gomez was at the door when I opened it, took one look at the child, and got so bushed up and frightened that he was never the same after.

Ghost Pepper

Janet and I had a next-door neighbor in Key Largo who invited us for an afternoon barbecue. We had a great time, and while talking to the neighbor, Wayne, we mentioned we liked hot food and peppers. Wayne said he had raised peppers and asked if Janet would like to try one. Janet said no, not at the moment, so Wayne said to take one home for later.

The next day, while we were home, Janet decided to eat the pepper. After biting and chewing twice, she looked at me with this wild-eyed expression and ran to the kitchen sink. After she leaned over the sink for a few moments, she looked back at me, froth around her lips, with a look I can only describe as a look you might see on the face of a poisoned animal.

Smitty

Wayne's next-door neighbor was a 60-ish-year-old lobster fisherman named "Smitty." Before his Key Largo lobstering, he had a career involving NASA and Cape Canaveral. Every time a shuttle needed to be placed on top of a 747 for transport, NASA called him to come in and do the crane hoisting and attachment. Nice specialty gig.

'Bout What?

Janet worked at a souvenir shop in Key Largo that had gas pumps that were operated by an attendant. The owners were worried about credit card fraud, so they required the attendant to ask for identification from customers he did not recognize.

An unrecognized customer handed his credit card for payment, and the attendant said, "Do you have any ID?"

The answer was, "'Bout what?"

The 5k Race

Janet was a distance runner all during high school, running the 1-mile, 2-mile, and cross-country. She was such a good runner that her coach had her train with the boys' distance team so she'd have more of a challenge. For years, she held the record in the 2-mile at her school.

During the early 90s, Janet began to get back into running as she loved participating in 5K and 10K races. I hate running.

Florida. Just before she was leaving for the race, I appeared from the bedroom dressed in brand-new running clothes and shoes. She was stunned.

Immediately, she asked, "Where do you think you're going?"

I responded, telling her I would run the race with her. Then I heard, "You hate running, plus you haven't trained, and you'll hurt yourself!"

I was not deterred.

We arrived, and Janet told me she'd have to run at her own pace. Janet had only been waiting about two minutes at the finish line when I appeared. She looked at me, and her jaw dropped. She accused me of getting one of the race coordinators to bring me in a golf cart close to the finish, but not so.

Janet slept like the proverbial log back then. There could be a tornado on the next block and she would sleep through it. I'd been rising at 4 am, going out for a training run, coming home, showering, and getting back in bed with her having no idea what I'd been doing.

Janet's Sea Turtle Suitor

The open ocean is where sea turtles mate, not on dry land. The male sidles up behind a willing female, climbs on her back, and somehow manages to get the deed done.

Janet and I were offshore Key Largo scuba-diving and decided to surface. We were just a couple of feet apart when I looked at her to see a large male sea turtle over her right shoulder, his head just a few inches from hers. She was unaware, so I said, "Look to your right."

She looked, and seeing she was inches from a huge sea turtle, she freaked. These turtles have very poor eyesight from eating jellyfish, and this particular turtle had mistaken Janet for his girlfriend. The act was not completed.

Not so in a story printed in the Key Largo Reporter newspaper about an adult male snorkeler who was successfully sexually attacked by a local Dolphin. Locals widely dismissed the veracity of this story.

Wacissa River

The Wacissa River is a large, spring-fed stream in Jefferson County, Florida, Southeast of Tallahassee. Its headwaters are about a mile south of Wacissa, population 362, where the river emerges crystal clear from a group of large limestone springs. From its headsprings, the river flows approximately 12 miles south through a broad cypress swamp before breaking into numerous braided channels that join the Aucilla River a few miles further south.

The Wacissa is a popular swimming and canoeing river whose banks are mostly wild Cypress swamps. Civilization fades when you are on the Wacissa. There are three canoe rentals at the headwaters. Our friends, Ray and Sheila Fox, their young son R. J., Janet, and I rented two canoes for a trip down the river. The outfitter informed us there was a canoe pickup point about 12 miles south on the left. We were emphatically warned not to miss the pickup landing. If we did, the river splits into several smaller braided channels, one ending in a sump.

A sump is where the water swirls and disappears underground, reemerging further south into the Aucilla River. The outfitter warned if we missed the pickup and paddled into the channel with the sump, canoeing back out would be extremely difficult. The sump is in an inaccessible spot, and if we didn't have the strength to return upstream to the pickup area, we would have to be rescued and would possibly spend the night in a Florida swamp in the summer.

We launched and were quite aware to be on the lookout for the pickup spot. It was a beautiful day; the water was crystal clear. We had a great time paddling slowly down the river. We stopped to use a rope swing we could see tied to a tree at the edge of the river. The entire area was very flat, with the "banks" of the river being just the beginning of a shallow Cypress swamp that goes endlessly into the distance. There was no dry land for long stretches. In other words, you couldn't get out of the water if the canoe capsized. There is no turbulence on the river; it's flat-calm, serene, slow-moving water. Capsizing is not an issue.

However, no water in Florida doesn't contain alligators: the Wacissa is no exception. We saw many twelve-foot reptiles within arm's length from the canoe. The gators were concerning but not frightening until one of them swam directly under our canoe and banged loudly on the bottom.

The heavy thump freaked Janet and me because he could capsize our canoe.

At this point, there was no escape from the river. Janet banged her feet on the bottom of the canoe to frighten the gator away. That scared me, thinking we don't need a frightened twelve-foot alligator below our boat. I yelled at Janet not to do that. The gator swam on unafraid of us, and the scare was over.

Moving on to the next scare, we began to think we had missed the pickup point late in the day. This is a remote, wild area; you can't just get out of the boat and walk to a road to hitch a ride. This time was before cell phones. The specter of beginning a life-threatening night in an alligator and mosquito-infested swamp began to spook us all. After an hour of worry, we came to the pickup area.

On the way back to the outfitter, Janet asked the driver if they sold t-shirts. The driver answered, "At the shop, we sell a t-shirt with a map on the back of it."

The Wedding Ring

Janet and I exchanged wedding rings when we married. Mine fit perfectly and didn't come off easily, so I never took it off.

Offshore, headed to a dive site with mate Harry Sutherland on a 40-foot dive boat owned by Captain Slate's Atlantis Dive Center, Harry and I felt something wrong with the boat; it seemed heavy and sluggish. We moored up, got all the divers off the vessel, and opened the hatch. To our horror, we saw the bilge half-full of seawater and realized the vessel was in danger of sinking. All these boats have a small leak through the prop shaft to keep the shaft from overheating, so bilge pumps are a major safety factor.

Ours was not working, so I got in the bilge with a five-gallon bucket and frantically began to bail, handing the filled bucket to Harry to pour over the side. After thirty minutes of bailing, we reduced the level of bilgewater to a reasonable amount, got the divers back on board, and soon were back at the dock.

After rinsing the deck and the rest of the boat, I looked at my left hand and saw my wedding ring was gone. I thought, "Oh, no, my ring's in the bilge."

These boats are 40 feet long, and the bilge is big with lots of structure throughout, leaving lots of nooks and crannies for debris to collect. This boat was twenty years old and didn't have what you might picture as a smooth, curved bottom to it. It had a keel about fifteen feet long, four inches wide, and eighteen inches deep, which had never been cleaned. These diesel engines, especially this one, constantly leaked oil, leaving a thick, condensed, oily muck a foot deep in the keel over the years. After hours of deep-cleaning all the more accessible places to look for the ring, I began to dig the oil out of the keel. There were four or five gallons of this muck to sift through.

I finished cleaning that, and the entire bilge was clean to the point you could drop a sandwich on it, pick it back up, and eat it. No ring was to be found. From there, I assumed the ring had come off into the bucket and had been pitched over the side into the ocean. Soon after, Janet bought me another ring.

Canals in Key Largo are cut from solid coral rock, which underpins most of the Florida Keys. The cutting is done with what resembles a giant chainsaw, with the debris dumped up on the surrounding land to provide more elevation. When you want a dock at the edge of this cut, you construct a wooden platform to support concrete while it sets. After the concrete sets, you remove the wooden supports. Sometimes, concrete seeps out from under the outer support, and when the wood is removed, it leaves a small ledge, an inch wide, well below the low tide water line.

One year later, one of my duties as captain was to stand at the edge of the dock where the divers walk down a ramp onto the boat. The water is clear, and when things are idle, we all look down to see what sea life may be swimming by or sitting on the silty bottom five feet below. This particular morning, I looked down and saw a shiny object lying on the tiny ledge, two feet below the water line.

I reached down and retrieved what looked like a wedding ring. No bells went off while I walked the ring to the office to put it in lost and found. I absentmindedly slipped it on my ring finger. It fit perfectly. Then the bells sounded. I looked, and sure enough, Janet's inscription was inside the ring.

That ring had been washed off the deck as we cleaned it, landed on that ledge, and waited a year for me to find it.

Our Duct-Taped Airliner

Janet and I had checked into Miami International Airport for a flight to California. We were waiting at the terminal to board when they announced that the flight was canceled due to a mechanical problem. More than two hundred passengers were instructed to go to another counter to get booked on another flight. We did that, and while waiting for the new booking, we returned to the gate where our disabled aircraft waited and sat overlooking the gangway onto the aircraft.

The gangway was partially obscured, but half was clear of obstructions, and you could see anyone entering or exiting the plane. For twenty minutes, we watched and then saw a blue jump-suited aircraft mechanic walk onto the plane with a roll of duct tape in his hand. After five minutes, he walked back off the plane and into the terminal. The intercom came on two minutes later and announced the aircraft was repaired, and the flight was re-instated.

By then, all but twelve passengers had been re-routed to other aircraft, but the airline would run the flight anyway. At that point, we were an hour late, so the twelve of us wanted to get on the plane right away and get going. Not so fast, the attendants told us. When the flight was canceled, they had de-planed all the food and drink, so we could only take off once that was corrected.

All in unison we said, "We don't give a **** about food, let's get on the plane and go!"

You can't jettison protocol in an organization that large, so we waited the half-hour for the food and then took off.

The White Eagle Prank

Ben, Janet, and I took my 28' Bertram out fishing one day, and after wrapping it up, we headed home with Ben and Janet on the flybridge, driving. I was downstairs and thought up a prank for them. I hid in a small closet on board and waited for them to think I had fallen overboard. When they realized I was "overboard," they (Ben especially) panicked. Janet then realized it could be a prank, looked in the closet, and sure enough, there I was.

They were both pissed, especially since it had only been a few years since both Ben and I survived our lost-at-sea trauma. Not funny to them. I am embarrassed for doing it.

McGyver

When you arrive on a boat to a foreign country, as the captain, you must tell everyone to stay on the boat until you check in with customs. We arrived in Bimini for a few days and I did just that. I was told by the dock attendant to walk up the street to the customs office.

As I entered the office, I was the only one there except the three customs officers behind the counter. They were all watching the TV. I caught one's attention but was instantly told I would have to wait while the officers watched the end of an episode of "McGyver."

I waited.

Returning From Bimini

Ben and I took my Bertram to Bimini for a few days to dive and fish. Nothing noteworthy happened while we were there, but on the way back, something happened, foreboding an incident a little later.

Only a few minutes after departing Bimini Harbor, one blade of one propeller fell off due to hydrolysis and negligence. After a few moments to decide what to do, we felt the best way to proceed was to continue with one engine and one prop. Rigged that way, the boat would not get up on a plane and would only move looking like it was so heavily loaded that it couldn't plane.

We knew that running like this would double our return time and put us in Key Largo after dark. I was very familiar with the coastline and was confident traveling at night would be fine.

About halfway across the Gulf Stream, we saw an aircraft flying very low, coming up from far behind, directly up towards our stern. When it flew over us, we both thought it was most likely a drug interdiction aircraft that might be very interested in our boat's attitude underway. We were very aware this might mean something later on. However, things went fine until we reached Carysfort Reef Lighthouse, just south of The Ocean Reef Club on North Key Largo.

The Ocean Reef Club is a hyper-exclusive resort for the rich. I had been a charter captain there for a while and was familiar with all approaches to their channel. Just outside the reef line, a pair of blinding searchlights came on, and a gentleman on a loud-speaker ordered us to stop. We stopped, and when they tied up to us, two from their boat came aboard and briefly searched the vessel. Another Customs officer stood by with an M-16 at the ready. We weren't worried as we knew no contraband was on board, but they ordered us to proceed to the Ocean Reef Club main dock.

They followed us with their very high-end go-fast boat, probably having been previously seized by Customs from a drug smuggler. At that point, Ben and I both had convictions and had served time for Conspiracy to Import Marijuana, so when the search plane went over us, coupled with the seemingly overloaded boat and my name coming up as owner, it raised their collective heart rate and put the big bust in motion.

After mooring both boats to the dock, they ordered Ben and me off our vessel and had us sit to the side while they searched. They were surprised there was nothing to be found with a visual search, both above and below deck, so they removed all the side panels in the cockpit, again finding nothing. They then put some scuba gear on and inspected the hull from below, hoping to find a stash attached underneath. Ben and I sat there, at first amused, then as things went along, more and more irritated, knowing there was nothing there.

After about three hours of a fruitless search, several of them had a conference away from us and then came over and said we were free to go. There was no apology, nothing, just Ben and I wearing shit-eating grins as we departed.

As I mentioned earlier, I worked for a time before the above fiasco out of the Ocean Reef tackle shop as a fishing guide/captain, mainly for light tackle, live bait sail fishing during the winter, so I was in and out of the tackle shop several times a week. One year, 1990 or so, a Broward Yacht convention was held at Ocean Reef.

One day, during the convention, I was in the tackle shop. The only other person in the shop was Jacqueline Onassis, who was alone looking through the gift section. I left her alone and went on my way. That's how exclusive Ocean Reef was.

Ben in Bimini.

My 28' Bertram and I are at Brown's dock, Bimini.

Bimini by Air

Janet and I and our friends, Keith and Teresa, flew Chalk's Ocean Airways from its Miami seaplane base to Bimini in the Bahamas. They operated eight amphibious Grumman Mallards and Albatrosses in the 80s and 90s and held a spotless safety record until a fatal crash in 2005 ended the operation. At the time, they were the oldest continually operating airline worldwide. KLM now holds that record, beginning just after Chalk's in 1919. The Mallard carries a maximum of 17 passengers. If you get the chance, it's a fascinating way to fly.

We boarded the Mallard yards from the shoreline and briefly taxied until we were on the water. In another minute, we turned right and lined up for takeoff on the main Port of Miami channel. The seaplane rocks a bit like a boat with the waves until it begins to pick up speed. After a series of bumps on the waves, the takeoff smooths out, and you get a great view of the Port of Miami as you gain altitude. These flights are short, 50 miles, so you don't gain much altitude. I'm guessing, but 5,000 feet is about it.

That altitude is great, you can see ships and fishing boats as you cross the Gulf Stream. The Gulf Stream is a warm and swift Atlantic Ocean current that originates in the Gulf of Mexico and flows through the Straits of Florida and up the eastern coastline of the United States, then veers east near North Carolina and moves toward Northwest Europe. However, a significant problem with low-altitude flights can be the weather, you can't get above it, and you sometimes have to go through it.

Our flight began on a beautiful afternoon with clear skies and sunshine. Within minutes of taking off, we were forced to fly through a thunderstorm with the occasional lightning strike to unnerve us further. We were just feet from the pilots, who we could plainly see were actively fighting the controls. If we weren't buckled in, the lurching was so violent we would have bounced off the ceiling. We survived and rolled up onto the seaplane parking area where Bimini's main road dead-ends; King's Highway. You can look down this road from the aircraft parking in the final scene with Hannibal Lecter in the movie "Silence of the Lambs." Janet kissed the ground when we got off the plane.

Bimini is seven miles long and only two hundred yards wide, with two main roads, King's and Queen's Highways running the length. The four of us walked up King's Highway for a half-mile and came across a street vendor, but not your ordinary one. He was hawking a trick he did for a dollar. He asked if we wanted to see him open a coconut with just his teeth. We said, "OK, show us." It wasn't a real trick. He began bashing a whole coconut against his buck teeth and slowly tore it into pieces. It was stunning and painful to watch. We gave him five dollars.

We soon had another coconut encounter. We walked north from paying the five dollars several blocks and turned left, walked uphill one block to the other side of the island, and turned right onto Queen's Highway. We walked for a few minutes when we came across a dog. He was a friendly, mid-size dog who began to walk with us. We decided to call him "Sammy."

We walked past several coconut palms until the dog stopped at one and began to bark furiously toward the top of the tree. We looked up, expecting to see something, but we couldn't see anything moving, just coconuts. After a minute of barking and wondering what the dog saw or sensed, a coconut fell out of the tree to our feet. We looked toward the top of the tree and saw nothing but coconuts. How did he know?

For Ernest Hemingway, Bimini was a favorite place for an extended stay besides Cuba. He usually would stay at the Compleate Angler Hotel and Bar, just up from the docks. He wrote most of "To Have and to Have Not" at the Angler. Bimini was also the island in "Islands in the Stream," my personal favorite. He would do some drinking at the hotel bar, which he made famous until it burned to the ground in 2006, killing the owner. When we were there, we drank a bit of rum and a Kalik beer to toast Ernest, there was a ton of memorabilia on the walls. There is a more significant shrine to him in Cuba. His estate there is preserved, with many of his personal belongings available for visitors to see. You can't go in the house but can peer in the doors and windows with a steady stream of other admirers. There are about three acres of the estate to stroll through.

Hemingway used to blast his Thompson machine gun off the Brown's Hotel docks, where I usually docked my boat.

Underwater Fiasco

One of the specialties at Captain Slate's Dive Center, where I was working as a captain, was underwater weddings. We would take the wedding party to the dive site known as "Christ of the Abyss," a bronze underwater statue depicting Christ located at Key Largo Dry Rocks.

Everyone would begin to suit up in scuba gear, then get in the water for an underwater wedding. The couple getting married would sometimes bring their own marriage officiant to certify the marriage, or occasionally, they would use one of our instructors, a notary. The myth about sea captains being able to perform real weddings is just that: a myth. Sea captains could do temporary marriages, but that's outside our story.

At the time, in the 80s, there was a British TV show called "That's Life," one of the hosts being a gentleman named Gavin. Gavin had somehow learned of a young British couple that had booked an underwater wedding with us. He convinced the couple to let him and the TV show crew come along and film the entire thing for a segment on "That's Life."

The big day arrived, and the couple came with some of their friends and their presiding marriage officiant, along with Gavin's entourage, including the show's professional underwater videographers.

We loaded up all the humans and all the gear and headed out to the reef. It was a lovely day, the sea conditions being near calm. We anchored up at the dive site, and everyone began getting ready.

Getting everyone in the water on an ordinary dive trip usually takes little time. An objective of the dive crew is to get everyone off the boat as soon as possible. The longer a diver spends on deck before entering the water, the more likely they will get seasick. Even on flat calm days, people can get seasick. The problem stems from the difference between the information your brain gets from your eyes that have been looking around in the boat, which, to the eye, seems not to be moving, and the information coming from your ears, which sense the motion, however slight, from the movement of the boat. This conflict in the brain results in seasickness.

On board, when someone says they are starting to feel queasy, we tell them not to look around in the boat but to look at the horizon, which allows the brain to resolve the conflict between both eyes and ears, seeing and feeling the motion. The problem does not go away quickly; sometimes it works, but it usually just delays the inevitable ralphing over the side. We direct those afflicted to the "Fish Feeding Station" at the very back of the boat. The sight and smell of someone being seasick can be contagious, making other passengers sick who ordinarily would not have been so. It's in everyone's best interest to get everyone off the boat ASAP.

That brings us back to the moments after anchoring up with the wedding party. There's a bit of chaos getting twenty divers off a boat, even without all the problems of getting the videographers off the vessel. With all the delay caused by the wedding couple getting all their wedding clothing, rings, flowers, and such, coupled with the video preparation, people began to get sick. The bottleneck at the rear of the boat getting divers off made the situation worse.

Soon, most of the divers were ill, and some who were already in the water were also ill. Some still on the boat were hurling their lunch over the side, which landed on some of the divers in the water. I had a picture somewhere of Gavin having vomit falling on his head, but it's been lost.

Somehow, the ceremony was concluded, but the video aspect of the venture was a complete disaster. I doubt any video footage was usable. We gathered everyone up and headed back to the dock with a bad taste in everyone's mouth, literally. It was unanimous that the trip was a failure, the married couple being the angriest and most dissatisfied. We got everyone off the boat, and everyone went their separate ways.

There was some public interest in England preceding the trip, so when the couple returned to England, a TV station set up a publicly broadcast interview with them. The couple quickly denounced Gavin and "That's Life" for "ruining their wedding."

In retrospect, we should have used two boats, one with the film crew and Gavin's people, getting them to the dive site first and having everything ready for the couple to get in the water. Then, the wedding party could arrive on the second boat a few minutes later. That would have significantly reduced the confusion and chaos of everyone having to get off the same boat and the time everyone spent on the deck of a ship.

Gavin and "That's Life" disagreed with the accusations and the subsequent negative publicity, so they sued the couple for libel. The complainants and their attorneys paid for me (the Captain) and "Sparky," the first mate, to fly to England and put us up at a London hotel so that we could testify at the libel trial. The idea was that we, as the professionals on the boat, would say that it wasn't Gavin's or the TV show's fault for all the failures of the underwater wedding. They wanted us to testify that the root cause of everyone's dissatisfaction with the dive trip was seasickness, not Gavin or "That's Life."

Some delays with getting off the boat were due to Gavin and his crew, but the seasickness could have happened without all that. We testified for them, and the judge rendered on their behalf. I don't know what damages were assessed or anything else about the decision, but Gavin and the TV show were vindicated. The whole thing was just ugly.

A side note was that Sparky and I went to a SoHo bar one night. SoHo was sketchy then, but what could go wrong with just getting a beer or two?

We entered the bar, two naive Americans, and were seated next to two girls. We said hello, and they asked if we would buy them a drink. We said sure and also ordered one for ourselves. We were there only twenty or thirty minutes talking to them and listening to music when we decided to leave. We stood up and were immediately met by a gentleman who asked that we pay for the four drinks. We said, sure, how much do we owe you? Two hundred and twenty dollars, he told us. Shocked, we said, "What for?" to which they said one hundred dollars for each of the girls' drinks and ten dollars for each of ours.

At that moment, three more thugs closely surrounded us in a highly threatening manner. Sparky and I looked at each other and telepathically agreed discretion was the better part of valor and forked the extortion over. I'll bet those blokes laughed about it when we left. I'm sure it was a scam they pulled all the time. Sparky and I swore that we would never speak about it to anyone. This is the first time this story has been told, over thirty years later.

The Northern Light

It is a sport diver's dream to identify an unknown wreck. It is only a fantasy for all but a few, but it happened to me.

I worked as a dive boat captain in Key Largo for three years and had become bored by the local dive sites. I rarely dived anymore. So, when the after-work talk over a few beers with some fellow employees turned to finding a deeper, more exotic dive for us locals came up, I was interested. Both dive instructors, Joe Derrico and Bob Curtis, wanted to look for wrecks in deeper waters off the Elbow Reef Light.

The Elbow is a popular dive destination close to the deeper waters of the Key Largo National Marine Sanctuary. It seemed possible that there were undiscovered or unknown wrecks out there, but we were unlikely to find one. I found it fun and exciting talk, but only talk.

One day, we were in one of the many meetings at the local pub when Captain Dave Williams stopped by to talk with us. He was interested and knew of a rumor called the Elbow Wreck. He said he had heard that it had been dived once or twice many years before. It was very deep, 190 feet, and the divers had returned with stories of large tiger sharks and stiff currents, so it had remained unexplored and unknown for several reasons, including those mentioned. This tantalizing tale excited us, of course, so Dave said he would see if he could find the Loran numbers for it.

Wreck fever was building! Dave had found the numbers within a few days, and preparations were underway. It took Dave several days of searching to find the wreck because the numbers needed to be corrected, but he did find it. During that time, everyone inspected their gear, computed dive profiles, and rigged a heavy cylinder with the down line attached. Tension rose, none of us had been that deep before. We all had been to 150/160 before, but not 190. Anything below 160 is considered to be outside recreational diving limits.

On the morning of the first dive, it was Joe and Bob's plan to buddy up and go all the way to the bottom. Instructors Laddie Adkins, Nick Jenny, and I would drop to the top of the wreck at 150 and go down as much of the length of the wreckage as we could. Nick and Laddie would be taking a video.

The sea was calm, but the current was a little tricky. Joe and Bob descended first, and as my three-person team went down, we saw their bubbles rising from what seemed endlessly deep. At 150 feet, trying not to think of tiger sharks, I saw the wreck slowly appear in the low light. I first recognized a 10-foot-tall rudder and then a large hull, both heavily encrusted with coral. The overwhelming excitement mixed with narcosis was hard to control. My thinking was becoming fuzzy, and I had difficulty understanding my watch.

The wreck was bigger than I had expected and very impressive. When the ship sank, it had buckled in the middle, stayed hinged in the middle, and sank with the bow half resting upright on the bottom and the stern half collapsed upside down on top of the bow. We were all so narc-ed that it took a review of the video later to figure that out.

It was a steel-hulled vessel about 300 feet long by roughly 40 feet wide. On the bow, we could see a large winch. We saw a rudder on the stern but no sign of propulsion. Bob Curtis's research narrowed the possibilities to either being a sailboat or a barge in the shape of a sailboat. He found pictures of steel barges built just before 1900 that looked much like sailboats. Another dive was in order.

On the second dive, instructor Harry Sutherland took a second video, but it was only slightly better and provided no additional clues to the ship's origin. The third dive was to be the bonanza. I was the utility diver to set the down line for Bob and Laddie, so I had to sit it out while they tried to find something to identify the wreck. I watched from the boat as they decompressed and could tell they had something in their hands. I put my mask on and jumped in to verify. They had a round object shaped like a large deep dish in their hands. Although heavily encrusted, we could tell it was either brass or bronze. Little did we know how lucky we were.

When we were dockside, I took some muriatic acid and gently removed the encrustation. Bob, Laddie, Dave, and I watched in amazement as slowly, letter by letter, that single artifact revealed a wealth of information. Engraved by hand in three-inch letters on what proved to be an eighteen-inch brass windlass cover was the name of the ship, the Northern Light. Next, "1888" came into view, then the shipbuilder's name, Globe Ironworks Company, Cleveland, Ohio. Also, the artifact notes that the piece itself is a windlass cover built by the American Ship Windlass Company, New Providence, Rhode Island. It is absolutely unbelievable that we learned so much from the only artifact retrieved.

Then, after some research at the Miami Public Library, I found the details of the sinking. The Northern Light was a steel barge owned by R.P Hyams of Gulf Barge and Towing, New Orleans, Louisiana, carrying phosphate from Tampa to Wilmington, North Carolina. She sank south of Miami on November 10, 1930, with six crewmen aboard during a severe storm that also sank several other ships in the area. A Coast Guard vessel had reported 40-foot seas during that storm. The tug Ontario was towing the Northern Light when she sank, but she managed to save only one crewman. An air search for survivors chartered by R.P. Hyams proved unsuccessful in finding the other five.

In an odd footnote, on impulse, I called New Orleans information and half-heartedly asked if a listing existed for R.P. Hyams. To my astonishment, the operator said yes!

I immediately dialed the number, an elderly lady answered the phone, and I cautiously asked to speak to R.P. Hyams. After a few very quiet seconds, she told me that R.P. had been dead for many years and that she was his widow, nearly 90 years of age. She was cautious and reluctant to talk initially, but after I explained what we had found, she warmed up and reminisced with me at length about the Northern Light.

She remembered it well after sixty years. She told me that after the accident, she and her husband had become close with the lone survivor, a young sailor named J. Stewart. They eventually put him through college but lost contact with him during World War II. What a phone call to get 60 years after the fact!

So, divers, if you think it's all been done before, don't believe it.

I donated a large, professional photo of the artifact to the Key Largo National Marine Sanctuary, which is now on display in their office in Key Largo.

Capstan cover

Starbucks

I developed a terrific caffeine habit. I've loved Cuban coffee all my life, so two cups in the morning wasn't the issue. To combat the pressure of the dive business and function at a higher level, I gradually increased the amount of coffee I consumed. I coupled that with several Diet Cokes throughout the day, leading me to have sleep difficulty. I would drink so much caffeine I could only sit in a chair and vibrate, unable to function at all.

The source of the sleeping disorder finally dawned on me and I quit caffeine altogether. Soon, the withdrawal consumed me, and I had to start with the caffeine sources again and wean myself from them more slowly. That took a couple of months. A regular sleep pattern returned.

I drank no caffeine for many months. Going to and from Miami on our day off, Janet and I would stop at a particular Starbucks and I would get my favorite drink: a Venti Mocha Frappuccino Decaf. "Venti" is the largest drink Starbucks makes. We were somewhere unusual in Miami and stopped at a Starbucks we had never been to. I ordered my usual. About twenty minutes later, I was on another plane of existence. I was cheerful, talkative, and wittier than usual. I thought, "Why am I not always like this?"

It took some time to realize I had been served a caffeinated Mocha

Frappuccino.

Sugar and Sliding Doors

The house Janet and I built on the South side of Key Largo had large sliding doors that overlooked a canal that led to the ocean. I worked at Captain Slate's Dive Center on the same canal, on the other side, but closer to the Atlantic Ocean. When I went to work, I would drive around the dead-end of the canal and turn right, heading to work, passing my house, plainly visible on the other side of the canal. We routinely closed and locked the sliding doors when we left the house.

One day, after Janet went to work, I left after her and went to the store for something on the way to the dive shop. After returning from the store, I drove down the street to work and looked to my right toward our house. I knew I had closed and locked the sliding doors behind me, so I was alarmed that I could see the sliding doors were open. There were no cell phones then, so I drove to the dive shop and called the police. I waited a bit and soon heard sirens coming from my end of the canal. I waited a few minutes, then headed home.

When I arrived, there were several county sheriff deputies and a swat team vehicle. Some of the deputies were in my driveway and looking very relaxed. They told me no one was in the house, and nothing seemed amiss. We didn't know if I had just not remembered leaving the door open or whether someone had entered briefly and then left.

A few weeks later, Janet and I were sitting in the living room that overlooks the canal through the glass sliding doors, which were closed, when one of our cats, Sugar, walked up to where the two doors came together and hooked her claws in the seam where the two doors overlapped. She immediately began pulling and jerking the door until it opened enough for her to go out on the porch. These doors are heavy, and you wouldn't think a 9-pound cat could move those doors, but she could. Mystery solved.

Timi's Kittens

During the first 10+ years when Janet and I lived in Key Largo, we were breeding and showing Siamese cats. We named our cattery "Key's Siamese."

We had rented our downstairs apartment to a Monroe County Sheriff, Rob Palmieri, who soon became a good friend. He was very interested in our Siamese and had never seen a cat give birth. One of our females, Timi, was pregnant. He asked if he could come and watch when she started to give birth if he was around.

Janet was home when Timi entered labor, and she asked Rob if he wanted to come upstairs to witness the event. All went well until the first kitten's placenta came out, and Timi began to eat it, which is what cats do. Janet heard a groan and turned around to see Rob turning white and needing to leave.

Rob commented, "I didn't know they did THAT!"

Seeing Timi chew up the placenta had made Rob ill—big tough cop. We laughed and laughed and ribbed him mercilessly over it and still do, to this day.

Silent World III Sinking

In 1998, we owned a scuba shop in Key Largo with several commercial, Coast Guard-inspected dive boats, one named the Silent World III. Janet and I would take one day a week off together, which we would spend at the movies in Miami. The movie "Titanic" had just been released, so we wanted to see it. On April 15, by coincidence, the date of the sinking of the Titanic in 1912, we went to Miami to see the movie. Of course, that meant leaving the dive shop in the hands of employees to operate. It was a beautiful day, and there were several trips booked.

When we left the movie theater, I turned on my phone and heard several urgent messages to call the shop. When I called, I was informed that one of our boats, the Silent World III, had sank near the reef. While no one was injured, the sinking was a horrific blow. The boat was eventually salvaged, and life went on.

The event was noteworthy, but several coincidences make the story somewhat eerie. The Captain of the Titanic's name was E.J. Smith. The Captain of the Silent World III's initials were E.J. The date our boat sank was also the anniversary of the sinking of the Titanic. Janet and I were watching the movie "Titanic" when our boat sank, and finally, when we arrived home that day and retrieved our mail, a movie poster I had ordered of "Titanic" had arrived.

Evan Jackson

The concrete dock where we kept our dive boats also had a few private vessels and one "6-pack" dive boat owned and operated by Captain Evan Jackson. Evan would at times run dive trips for us, so we knew him well. One day he backed his boat in, tied it up and stood on the transom of his boat to step up a foot or two to get up on the dock.

His boat was wet from rinsing, and when he went to step up, he slipped and fell, hitting the edge of the concrete dock with his top row of teeth, knocking out both eye teeth.

Sparky, Liz's Sailboat

Two friends of ours owned a resort in Minnesota that closed during the winter. One winter, they bought a small sailboat and towed it down from Minnesota to Key West. The idea was not only to escape a Minnesota winter but also to enjoy the ambiance of Key West. Key West is much warmer than Minnesota, but it is still warm during the day, especially if you are cooped up in a tiny sailboat with no air conditioning. Liz especially found this to be profoundly uncomfortable, so she would go during the day to the local public library, sit in the back and nap. The experiment failed; they sold the sailboat and went home.

Cremated Ashes

A few times, our dive shop would get a request to take some mourners out and spread a loved one's ashes out at sea. On one of these occasions, I took a group of about eight out to the reef to do that. We arrived at the reef and moored up before the festivities. That takes a minute or two, so in the meantime, the mourner who had the ashes opened up the urn and was about to toss the contents overboard when I turned to look. I could see what was about to happen and yelled for her to stop. I was too late, she tossed the ashes into the air into the wind. The result was the ashes blew back onto the boat and covered everyone on board. Initially horrified, everyone soon began to laugh.

Buck

A dear friend of ours in Key Largo was called "Buck." One day, he was sitting, drinking beer with a friend of his on the dock behind his house. They got into an argument and stood facing each other. The friend swung his fist at Buck, hit him on the jaw and knocked him off the dock into the water. The friend turned and left, not looking back.

What the friend didn't realize is that he had knocked Buck unconscious, and Buck landed face down in the water and drowned.

The friend was arrested for manslaughter but the charges were dropped.

Genteel

Near our house was an animal shelter that cared predominately for cats. I would go in regularly to donate, usually speaking to an attractive woman who ran the place. I always had my best face forward, but it was always just a friendly conversation.

When Janet came home from there one day, she said the woman had complimented me, saying, "Your husband is so genteel!" Janet smirked as she told me this. "If only she knew! Ha!"

The 2000s

The Condom

Nearing 20 years into my marriage to Janet, our sex life had deteriorated into being non-existent. I felt paying for "professional services" might be an answer. I asked Janet if that was okay. Even though she agreed, saying, "Just don't tell me about it or bring any diseases home," I felt she thought I was kidding.

I was not.

I found a website that collects information and reviews on high-end escorts. Every bit of information you can imagine, every physical detail possible, everything they will and will not do, pricing, and most importantly, honest reviews of experiences with the girls. With all that, you could be confident in what you were getting into, with no danger or drama.

I've seen several and have nothing negative to say about them. A "Girlfriend Experience" is an interaction with a girl who will do what you want with enthusiasm, a smile, and the desire to please. I no longer hire these girls, but at the time, it was money well spent.

One of the first girls I saw was a Japanese girl I got along with so well that it became a regular thing. Sometimes, she would come to Key Largo, but mostly I would go to Miami to meet her. I met her at a hotel on one of the trips to Miami to see her. We drank some wine and did what we were there to do. None of these girls will have sex without a condom under any circumstances, maybe street hookers will, but not the high-end ones.

When we finished, she took the condom off me and pitched it on the floor. I dressed, grabbed the wine bottle with about a glass left in it, said goodbye, and headed home. I finished the wine while I drove. I would not have passed a breathalyzer and was driving too fast.

As I approached Key Largo, a couple of miles from the drawbridge at Jewfish Creek, I saw a county sheriff coming my way around a curve. I recognized immediately that he knew I was speeding. As I got around the bend, I saw about 12 cars stopped ahead of me, stopped by the guard rail that had just come down so the drawbridge could open. With the sheriff in my rear-view mirror with his lights on, at 70 miles an hour, I could see the bridge had started to open by just a few feet, so I swerved into the oncoming lane, went around the 12 cars, and onto the bridge at full speed.

The gap between the two halves of the bridge was about 6 feet when I successfully slipped the surly bonds of Earth and jumped across, the sheriff a little too far behind to follow, the gap being much more significant when he got there.

When I arrived home, my wife was sitting on a couch in our living room. I sat on the other couch, took my shoes off, and stretched out with my feet under the coffee table. We sat briefly when I noticed my wife looking at something under the coffee table. She pointed, so I looked down and saw what looked to be a used condom on the floor.

I knew immediately it was the one tossed on the floor at the hotel. I had stepped on it on my way out of the room, and it stuck to the sole of my shoe, waiting until the perfect time to fall off. The jig was up, as they say.

Selling the Dive Shop

The tension in my and Janet's marriage had begun to boil, so I started the urgent ordeal of selling the dive shop and our house in Key Largo. I knew things would explode if we didn't get rid of both and begin our planned move to Colorado.

The dive shop was profitable, but only if I spent 24/7 attending to it. We usually got one day off every week, but I spent every other minute with the shop. I was obsessed and sick with worry, tension, and anxiety. There was always a prevailing dread and worry for the safety and well-being of our customers. I had to rely on employees to keep them safe, but some of these employees were worrisome with their drug and alcohol habits.

The upkeep and functionality of my Coast Guard-inspected dive boats kept me up at night. They had to be safe but also dependable to take customers out every day of the year. I had to oversee those inspections and everything in our shop on US1. Scheduling crew for the boats, passengers for each trip, dive classes in the shop, booking for rooms at local motels and hotels, booking for trips, getting divers geared up for each trip, deciding which dive sites the trips would visit, coordinating divers with dive packages so they didn't go to the same site twice, inventory of scuba equipment of all kinds, t-shirts, monthly bills, outside boat mechanics, advertising, more monthly bills, operating the telephones, payroll, taxes and every other thing associated with a small business. It was a one-person shop.

The shop was profitable but took a toll on me. I was short-tempered and on edge much of the time. This extended to my home life. It only magnified my inability to express affection toward Janet, leading to the boiling point.

Janet and I knew we were in a mounting crisis with the clock ticking and needed a change or to get divorced. We had been to Colorado's Leadville/Twin Lakes and thought we would like to live in Twin Lakes. We bought a lot and found a contractor to build a home overlooking Twin Lakes, but we built it also as a two-room bed and breakfast which we named the Black Cat. As the building continued, so did the selling of the shop and our home.

Everything came together, but not without anxiety. The sale of the business went without much difficulty, with the only negative side effects being the loss of a sizable income from the business and Janet's employment as a dive instructor there.

The sale of the house and the construction of the new house posed a much more significant threat. This was 2008, the peak of the housing boom in the U.S. One of the biggest boom markets was South Florida and the Keys. We built the house on a canal for $175,000; we signed a sale contract for $1,000,000. The glitch with the agreement was that the closing was delayed for ten months. I can't remember why, but it was. Knowing what I did at the time about the real estate market and the impending implosion, I would have backed out of the contract if I had been our home buyer. Thankfully, they didn't. The buyers eventually lost their shirts on it after spending hundreds of thousands on the house and then having to sell it for far less than they paid. It was eventually repossessed. We had borrowed $400,000 for the construction of the Colorado home, and now, with no income and potentially no sale or cash from our Key Largo home, our finances would have collapsed, and we would have lost everything.

Everything went well in the end, so we packed up and moved to Twin Lakes. I thought I might never return to Florida, so I went on what I called my "Ex-wife Farewell Tour."

I visited both Michele and Stacey in Tampa to say goodbye.

The Black Cat and Wife #4

When Janet and I moved into the Black Cat, I had already created a website and a reservation program with multiple reservations pending. However, we had only been there briefly when things started to go awry.

Janet discovered the extent of my involvement with the Japanese "girlfriend," and then Janet revealed she had a boyfriend in Colorado, a guy we had known through our trips out there. She said she was moving out, and the B&B was now all mine.

My first thoughts were, "What now?"

"What should I do about the reservations?"

I realized that breakfast could not be hard, although I had never cooked anything before. Janet moved out, and I began my innkeeper career. I came up with some recipes and then discovered I like to cook.

Operating the B&B was fun, but otherwise, I was lonely. Assuming Janet was never returning, I soon began my account with Match.com without much success. The pool was small after you excluded women who smoked or owned horses or dogs. I never did date anyone off Match until I went worldwide in my search. Not truly worldwide, only China. Many men have a thing for Asian women, as did I.

I began a year-long dialogue with Jie Chen, culminating in a trip to see her in Beijing. She lived in South China but met me in Beijing. She met me at the airport with a car and driver who took us to a beautiful, very old traditional Chinese home, which had been converted to a bed and breakfast.

The B&B was on a hutong, a type of narrow street or alley commonly associated with northern Chinese cities, especially Beijing. The atmosphere in and around the B&B was exhilarating, worlds apart from my experience. The highly anticipated sex was great for both. It seemed quite natural.

We hit the high spots in Beijing, including eating street vendor food like scorpions, which were quite tasty. We also hired a car to take us out of the city to a little-visited and restored section of the Great Wall. The weeks-long trip was great for us both. Over the following years, I visited her twice a year, flying into her home city of Fuzhou.

The first thing we would do leaving the airport was get a foot massage. Foot massage in China is not a quickie. It's an hour-plus full massage. They give you drinks, fruit, and a small meal afterward. It's heaven for $8.

Jie and I traveled to Guangzhou, China, to sit for an interview for her fiancée visa. We were walking in the downtown area when we approached a street vendor. You see these folks all the time trying to eke out a living on the sidewalk, selling anything you could think of to be able to eat.

This woman was selling live white birds. I didn't recognize the type of bird; it was larger than a pigeon but smaller than a chicken. She had a female purchaser there who had bought a bird and wanted the bird's feathers plucked. The vendor was doing that as we neared. I saw the bird looking directly into my eyes, slowly turning its head and keeping eye contact. I'll never forget that bird's pleading, sad, defeated look.

Jie and some friends took me to a popular restaurant in the country. It was a large, modern affair. As we walked in, we passed several displays of water tanks filled with live fish. We also passed an ice tray with Ballyhoo displayed on top. Here in the States, Ballyhoo is purely a bait fish, absolutely not for human consumption. The following display was a large, water-filled bucket with a turtle standing on its back legs, with its front legs scrabbling on the side of the metal bucket in a vain attempt to escape. When we walked past the displays, we were asked what we wanted for the meal before being seated.

Eating at a Chinese restaurant for ordinary Chinese residents, city and rural, is an experience like no other. As is their custom, the Chinese will eat anything, so you must be on alert. Restaurants commonly have displays of their dishes, but no English and nothing to give you a clue of what the dish is or how it's cooked. It's a roll of the dice every time.

Jie's English was not good enough to help. Under the expectant eyes of Jie and her friends and not knowing what the rest of the dishes were, I pointed at the turtle. I was relieved of the pressure, and we sat down.

The Chinese often order many different foods and share on a huge Lazy Susan, especially in any festive setting. Everything was ready well before the turtle, so they served everything else first and we all ate. I ate too much, forgetting about the turtle, so when the turtle arrived, I couldn't eat anymore. Neither could anyone else, so that poor turtle, scrabbling his way to escape, was killed and went to waste. I feel the shame and think of that turtle to this day.

If you are a Caucasian in China, especially away from tourist China, bear in mind that every eye is on you in any setting, especially a meal. It's bad manners to express distaste for a meal in front of your host in any situation. Sticking out as I did, a representative of every American back home, I had to buck up and smile even though the taste, texture, or smell was threatening to make me vomit. More than once, I had to choke it down, smiling while being nauseated, verging on hurling. I came so close so many times. I even ate a disgusting garnish at one meal to the everlasting amusement of the other diners. Passing a McDonald's one day, I became ecstatic with the prospect of eating something familiar.

An unusual, useless fact I learned in China is that some Chinese, depending on their education, can read and understand much of Japanese text. Likewise, the Japanese can do the same. However, they cannot understand the other's speech.

Jie had been a successful business owner of a jewelry shop in Fuzhou. She was the first woman to graduate from college in her province after the Chinese began letting women attend higher education. She had been interviewed on television about that and at another time for her successful business. She had a sister and a twenty-something son who worked, but the family had little money. Jie and her son lived in a modern apartment, but her sister lived in far less, something you and I would find uninhabitable.

Fuzhou is a capitol city of eight million. Jie was very well-connected, and when I mentioned (on our long-distance video chats) that I needed three crowns and the cost was insane, she said I should have them done there in Fuzhou on my next trip. After arriving, we went to the dental clinic, which was unlike anything any American had ever seen.

It was a four-story building covering most of a city block, with hundreds of employees. The rooms were open bay, thirty by sixty feet, with twenty-five dentists working simultaneously on a floor that needed to be cleaned and had litter everywhere. I was worried about the level of skill, not to mention cleanliness, so I asked for only one tooth repaired. When he finished removing the broken areas of my tooth, he asked me to wait; they would create the crown immediately, and I would walk out with the finished tooth. I was so impressed with the result I asked if he could do two more today. He said sure, in Chinese with Jie interpreting, and continued. When he finished prepping the third tooth, I was asked which of the three grades of replacement I wanted; I said the top grade. After waiting about an hour for the crowns to be made, he installed them and put the four hundred dollars cash directly into his pocket for the work.

Months later, I noticed a hernia protruding from my lower abdomen. Not having health insurance, Jie said I should also have that fixed in China. She assured me she knew one of the top surgeons and gave me his name. I looked him up on the internet, and he was indeed one of the top surgeons in all of China. There was a lot of info on him, all good.

After arriving the next day on a Sunday, we went to the hospital. It was an impressive new building. We went to the surgeon's office, where he did a quick exam, saying my prior hernia repair was also in need of repair. I agreed to the surgery, and he said, "Okay, we'll do it right now."

Surprised but agreeable, he had an assistant take me to various labs for a urinalysis, blood work, x-rays, and an EKG. This was a fresh, new building

– sparkling clean, with a highly professional staff. It was the most excellent hospital I have ever visited.

Fuzhou is not a tourist city, so most citizens have never or rarely seen a Caucasian. I was constantly gawked at everywhere and stopped by strangers on the street for a selfie. It was the same in the hospital, but better. I was ushered to the front of every line at every lab, then taken to an executive or diplomatic suite reserved for upper-echelon Chinese. It was a complete, large apartment with every amenity.

Within two hours of arriving at the hospital, I was on a gurney, rolling toward the surgical suite. Except for my room and prep speed, everything about this experience seemed perfectly normal and familiar. An exception was the sheepish male nurse who shaved my red-haired pubic area. I'm sure he had never seen any hair color other than black.

I woke from anesthesia in my room with several nurses and Jie watching over me. In America, hernia repair is a walk-in procedure with no overnight stay, but it's a mandatory four-day stay in China. The surgeon did the two repairs and also removed a weird growth on my arm ad hoc.

Hours later, I began to have pain from the three sites and asked for a strong pain medication. I was told, "No, it will make you crazy." Ibuprofen was it. All ended well for seven hundred dollars.

The Monastery

On a tour of Yunnan Province, China, Jin and I visited China's most famous Tibetan monastery. Yunnan Province borders Tibet and has a large Tibetan population. The place is huge. At the top level, you come across two huge, identical temples side by side. About fifty visitors were milling about at the one on the left when we arrived . Jin and I separated for a few minutes, and I walked alone to the other temple.

These buildings were huge, open, fifty feet square, and forty-foot ceilings. I walked through the immense door and immediately heard a Tibetan monk chanting. He was sitting cross-legged in front of a large Buddha. I was the only visitor, along with a single monk, in that huge room. His chant was monotone but beautiful in its sound and simplicity, with no music.

Within a few moments, I was under his spell, transported to another time and dimension, and completely mesmerized for several minutes until the monk's cell phone rang. It snapped me back to reality in a millisecond.

At the end of another visit of my six trips to China, I came down with a virus that caused gastric distress the night before my return flight. Not wanting to get on a plane with diarrhea, we went to a hospital emergency room. I was seen by a gastroenterologist specialist, given several prescription medications, and released. The cost of the entire visit was seven dollars.

There was another worldwide viral pandemic problem at the time called SARS. The Chinese had installed infrared cameras for everyone entering or exiting every airport. If they detected a temperature, they quarantined you on the spot. I had to get on that plane, so I bought a hat and had a dishcloth soaked with cold water in my pocket. As I entered the inspection area, I wiped my face several times and walked through undetected.

Scorpions

After two years of this romantic, long-distance relationship, I decided to bring Jie to the U.S. and get married. After two years of setbacks and five hundred pages of paperwork, she was on her way.

Then things began to deteriorate. These marriages have a poor success rate, so I had a pre-nuptial agreement created, which I took with Jie to a Denver lawyer whose first language was Chinese. The contract was that if we divorced, I would pay all expenses to get her back to China and give her twenty thousand dollars. The Chinese Denver lawyer explained all this to her in Chinese because her English was poor, and we signed it.

On my trips before Jie came to the States, I would give her my cash so she could exchange it for Yuan and let her deal with all the expenditures. I handed her eighteen hundred dollars on one trip, but after a few days, she said she had no money. I asked what happened to the cash. She said she gave the eighteen hundred to her sister for a motorbike. I was fried about that, but I kept my mouth shut.

Her son wanted to give his girlfriend an engagement ring, so Jie asked me to buy it. I asked her, "How much do you want me to spend?"

The answer was five thousand.

I explained that although she knew there would be a trade-off between size and quality, the bigger the diamond, the poorer the quality.

We compromised. I bought a diamond from an old friend, Danny Hayman, aka Hayman Jewelers in Tampa. I had the diamond set and shipped it to her son in Fuzhou. A few weeks later, we got the ring back from her son, with him saying his girlfriend didn't like the quality. This burned my ass pretty badly.

I didn't comprehend what would be involved in marrying someone who spoke no English and couldn't do anything without my help and planning. It was just too hard for me to continue, so I began to plan how to exit with as little drama as possible. I knew she would return to China for her son's wedding in a year. That date was beyond the expiration date on her visa, which she was unaware of. You can leave the States without a visa, but you cannot return without one. I waited a year for that. I made an excuse for not going along with her, and she left for China alone. I was relieved and thought it was over and we would take care of the details internationally.

After seeing Jie off to China permanently, or so I thought, I had planned to go to St. George Island, Florida, at the end of October with friends Drew, Kay, Craig, and Anita. Janet always enjoyed this annual trip, so I asked her if she'd like to join us and offered to fly her down. She agreed. As usual, we had a great time, laughing and joking with our friends, enjoying the daily lunches of raw oysters and beer at Eddie Teache's, and way too much food and alcohol at Drew and Kay's island house.

Janet had to leave a couple of days before the rest of us. The day she left, I received a call from Jie that night that she was back from China and was at my house in Colorado. How could this be? When she went to China for her son's wedding, her United States visa had expired. I was stunned that she had somehow been able to weasel her way back into my life. I had to return, so I left St. George two days early, flying home the next morning.

In a tearful reunion with Jie, I told her I wanted a divorce. In an underhand, twisting, stabbing motion with her hand, she said she would kill me if I mentioned divorce again. I believed her. The Chinese notoriously use knives in disagreements.

I lay in bed that night as she entered the bedroom with one hand behind her back. I thought this was it, but no. The following day, I again said I wanted a divorce, and she went berserk. She picked up everything at hand; dishes, furniture, decorations, and flung them around the kitchen. Broken pottery and dishes were all over the floor.

We lived twenty miles from law enforcement, so when I called them, I didn't expect a thirty-second response, but a deputy was only a hundred yards away when he got the call. He showed up during Jie's peak anger, which was on full display from his viewpoint at the front door. She was angry and would not shut up when he tried to talk to her. She was still trying to break things when he cuffed her and put her in his squad car. He returned to our front door, and though I asked him not to take her away, he said it was beyond his control from what he had seen with his own eyes. State law demanded an arrest for domestic violence. That is what happened and I never saw her again.

The pre-nuptial held up in court. I sent her the twenty thousand and got the divorce without any contact with her. She wanted me but also wanted to legally move to the U.S. permanently, so she got half of what she wanted. Sustaining that marriage was beyond my capability.

Twin Lakes

Twin Lakes, Colorado, is a hamlet on the south side of Independence Pass, with Aspen on the other side of the mountains. When I arrived, only 30 or so full-time residents lived there. It is the last stop before travel up the pass. In the 1800s, it was a toll road with the toll collected in Twin Lakes at a log hotel built in 1879. It was built without a thought of it lasting 130 years, but the hotel is miraculously still there. The foundation is merely logs lying on the ground with no foundation. The result is that the lowest logs deteriorate at differing rates, gradually creating an uneven floor. However, it is still a functioning hotel, restaurant, and bar named The Twin Lakes Inn.

Since its inception, the inn has gone through many owners and operators, some for many years but increasingly shorter and shorter time frames. Before and during my time there, the inn had a series of owners that lasted two years. It was always difficult to succeed, the pass closed for icy road conditions six months a year. That meant no tourist or any other traffic for that time. All kinds of problems are associated with running a business for only six months a year, but the biggest is no income. How do you do that?

There were several valiant efforts made while I was there. The first owner I encountered held on and did an excellent job for two years. His biggest failing was hiring wait staff whose only qualification was that they were attractive, young females. Competence and experience were not necessary.

A friend of mine, Tim, took over from there with a lease-purchase agreement and renamed it Inn of the Black Wolf. He had been a top-end chef for many years before becoming the real estate salesman who sold me my property in Twin Lakes. Tim and his wife, Kayla, did an excellent job with the inn. They maintained a very high level of service. The restaurant was superior to anything prior.

I was operating my bed and breakfast and had begun making rum and Kahlua cakes for my guests. I brought one to the inn, and after Tim and Kayla tried them, I started selling them to them for sale by slice or as a whole cake to guests. My cooking had also branched into soups, a favorite being Italian Wedding Soup. Oddly enough, "wedding" refers to the marriage of flavors, not the marital kind.

Tim and Kayla would host a "Chef's Challenge Dinner" every year, inviting local chefs to create one for six courses. The courses were judged at the end of the meal by the guests. This event was very popular and sold out every time for about the four years of Tim and Kayla's ownership.

I am not a trained chef as the other entrants were, but being a friend of Tim's, I got an invitation. One year, I entered my Italian Wedding Soup and won the competition against all the real chefs.

Spring 2009 Twin Lakes Winemaker's Dinner Weekend

Inn Of The Black Wolf in Twin Lakes
Saturday April 18, 2009
Free Demos start at Noon
Dinner at 6:30 pm

The afternoon will be filled with cooking and a wine demonstrations by the featured chefs and the event will culminate with a six course gourmet winemaker's dinner.
Wine Importer Steve Berardi (featured in Food & Wine) will be joining us with specialty wines
from France, Spain and Italy.

Friday Chef's Challenge ~ Judged Competition
2 Chefs Making 3 Courses Each ~ $20 pp
Shawn Gower vs Victor Christian
Friday 4:30 through 8
Limited to 15 people viewing challenge

Free Demos Saturday

11:30 - 1:00 Shelley Long
Duo of Spanish Gazpacho Shooters
Santi Dimitri Cinciallegra Bianco 2007
Los Fraires efe Monastrel Rosado 2007

2:00 - 3:30 Greg Atkinson
Arancini di Riso with Tomato Pureee and Fried
Zucchini and Squash Blossoms with Balsamic Aioli
Jean-Francois Roy Valencay Blanc 2007
Fattoria di Petroio Chanti Classico 2004

4:00 - 5:30 Steve Berardi
Rare native and indigenous grapes
of the Mediterranean
Chasan-White from Minervois zone, France
Picpoul-White from near Montpellier, France
Pardina-White from southwestern Spain
Coccaciola-White from Abruzzo, Italy
Aglianico-red from Basilicata,Italy
Negroamaro-Red from Puglia, Ialy
Monastrell-Red from Valencia, Italy
Lagrein-Red from Alto Adige, Italy

Dinner $65 pp

Mallorcan Vegetable Flan
Shelley Long, Salida
Pierre-Luc Bouchaud Muscadet et Maine
Sur Lie 2007, Loire

Tuna Carpaccio
Joe Buchholz, Inn Of The Black Wolf
Uncastellum Tempranillo-Garnacha Rosado 2007

Italian Wedding Soup
Ric Altman, Black Cat B&B
Pierfrancesco Gato Barbera D'Asti 2006

Turbot Milaneses on Bed of Vegetables
Greg Atkinson, CMC Leadville
Michel Langois Coteaux du Giennois Sauvignon 2007

Pork Loin Souvlaki with Purple Potato
Mousse and Haricots Verts
Shawn Gower, Rosie's Leadville
La Legua Cigales Crianza 2003

Semolina Cake with Honey-Roasted Figs
and Mascarpone Cheese
Victor Christian, Inn Of The Black Wolf
Ronchi di Manzano Verduzzo Passito 2006

When Tim closed the Inn of the Black Wolf, it wasn't long before some completely incompetent owners took over and ran it into the ground. For the last 50 years, no owner/buyer has done any proper upkeep and have only patched things as cheaply as possible. The mechanical room was a nightmare and every inch needed work. When the owners after Tim gave up, the inn sat boarded up and continued to deteriorate. The locals were dismayed, it was the only place for twenty miles to get a meal.

A part-time resident named Mark contacted me and another pair of friends, a married couple that were friends of mine, and wanted to know if we were interested in partnering and buying the inn. He would be the 80% partner, and the other two would be 10% each. The other minority partners had been teachers all their lives and had limited electrical, mechanical, or carpentry expertise, which I had in spades. Mark said he would only proceed if I joined and was the on-site renovation supervisor. Mark would rarely be there.

The total cost, including purchase price and renovation, was about $700,000. We spoke to Building and Zoning to look at the project, and they said we would not have to bring it up to code; only the kitchen needed to be inspected.

In the amount of time to organize our partnership and to close on the property, the Building and Zoning officer's job had changed hands. When we arrived to arrange the permit, we were informed that we now needed to bring everything to code. That meant all new double-pane windows had to be installed, the stairway replaced, every door replaced with a fire-resistant metal door, and exit signs and fire escapes installed, among other smaller items. The upgrade would eventually cost us an additional $200,000, a punch in the gut, but we had no alternative but to comply.

At times, we had six contractors on the job. The building was so old, neglected, and ignored that nothing was straightforward. It was so bad, I rented a metal saw and cut everything out of the mechanical room to start fresh. My local partners were shocked, but it had to be done. There were 120 water line breaks. We stripped the place bare – everything. I had to field dozens of questions from contractors and make dozens of daily decisions for them. It was overwhelming, but I knew every single inch of the place when I was done.

I was there every day, all day, for six months. It was grueling and exhausting, but the worst part was dealing with the partners; we scuffled over everything. Sometimes, they would come after me and countermand something I had just told a contractor to do. It was maddening and greatly added to my stress. I honestly thought it was going to give me a heart attack. I have never worked harder at something but sold my shares and got out of it.

Aside from the renovation stress, a final straw triggered my exit. The other members of our partnership agreed to hire a chef for more money than he asked for and gave him the use of an entire residence attached to the hotel. The free rent included free utilities. All this was after a personal friend of the chef came to us confidentially to warn us that the chef had never held a job longer than six months in his life.

We saved that place. It could have collapsed into a pile of kindling if we had not intervened. A brass plaque should be engraved with our names on the wall, but nothing there reflects appreciation for our effort. It irks me to see photos like the one below.

I installed that sixty-foot deck and helped our carpenter install all the windows, the front door, and the beams above the deck. There are a thousand other projects you can't see. One notable endeavor was digging sixty feet of sewage drain with a shovel by myself. I put the signs up and had the main sign designed and made. With no public recognition, I still take personal satisfaction in my effort.

One of My 9 Lives

In August 2010, I drove from Twin Lakes, Colorado, to Montana to climb Granite Peak near a small town named Red Lodge. After meeting my guide, we did the two-day hike to base camp. You can't see the summit and the approach until you reach base camp.

I had attempted the climb twice before, but after getting to base camp and seeing how sheer and daunting the climb was, I twice turned around and hiked back out. This time, I was determined not to let the peak intimidate me. I promised to avoid looking at the peak and focus on the immediate area around where I stepped.

People do free-climb Granite, but some spots are too risky not to rope up and set anchors. I'm not a technical climber, so I hired a guide, Tom Turiano, who brought his girlfriend, Nancy, along. She is a very experienced technical climber with degrees in botany and forestry who also worked for the U.S. Forest Service.

On the hike to base camp, she continually pointed out the different flora along the way, including the many kinds of pine. There had been a fire through the area not long before, which gave the smaller, underlying growth a chance to thrive. Strawberries took full advantage of the new environment. They were everywhere. You could pick as many as you wanted, but these strawberries weren't the giants you see at the grocery store. They were far smaller but just as tasty and maybe even tastier.

Nancy's job at Forestry was collecting pine cones of several endangered pine trees. Forestry wanted to promote her to a higher-paying position, but it was a desk job. She loved the outdoors and what she was doing so much that she declined the promotion. She is also beautiful, tall, trim, and fit. Her black T-back underwear was fully visible whenever she squatted to pick berries or look at a flower. It was distracting, but a nice distraction.

Granite Peak, Montana.

Myself, Tom and Nancy

The climb was a bit strenuous at times but only frightening in a few places, where roping up and setting anchors was prudent. One was an ice bridge about thirty feet across, very narrow at about two feet wide with a sheer thousand-foot drop on one side and another sheer drop of about four thousand feet on the other. The rest of the climb was straightforward and a lot of fun. We enjoyed the beautiful vistas on top for a bit, descended, spent the night at high camp, and hiked out the next day.

After the mountain trip, I left Red Lodge on the morning of August 8. On my solo drive home, I took the rural route (rather than the Interstate), which was longer and more interesting. I was driving toward a small town named Meeteetse, Wyoming. Meeteetse is 35 miles southeast of Cody on Wyoming State Highway 120.

As I neared Meeteetse, I saw a hitchhiker, and out of the boredom and the need to stay awake, I picked him up. He was working as a carney and had just attended his mother's funeral. He was headed back to the carnival, which was now in Meeteetse. Ten minutes after picking this guy up, I saw another hitchhiker holding a sign that said "Casper," meaning Casper, Wyoming. I felt I had enough hitchhikers on board, so I didn't stop for him and drove on, dropping my carney in Meeteetse.

After I got home that night, the next day I saw an interesting story on TV.

From the Denver Post, July 9, 2010:

One of three convicted murderers who escaped from the Arizona State Prison in Kingman, Arizona, was captured today in Meeteetse, Wyoming, according to the U.S. Marshals Service. After escaping, the three killed an old couple in New Mexico a few days prior. Tracy Province, 42, was arrested at 6:20 am by a task force of U.S. Marshals and deputy sheriffs after being spotted walking through the town. At the time of his arrest, Province was carrying a hitchhiking sign with "Casper" written on it. Province has been linked by forensic evidence to the murders of the Oklahoma couple killed at a campground in Santa Rosa, N.M. The couple's camper was set on fire and discovered in Santa Rosa, while their truck was found abandoned approximately 120 miles away in Albuquerque. He was also found with a handgun.

Gives me the chills. I could be dead now. A friend said the first hitchhiker was my guardian angel. Could be.

We kept in touch.

During the few years with Jie, Janet and I kept in touch sporadically. In October 2012, Janet left her job in Inverness, Florida, and sold her home to move to Virginia to help her aging mom and oldest sister.

January 2013, I asked Janet if I could come for a visit. I wanted to spend some time with her, but I also wanted to see her mom and oldest sister, as I knew of their declining health. I asked Janet if she could please ask her mom and sister if it would be okay for me to visit. They both said that they'd love for me to come.

After a couple of days at her mom's, Janet and I took off for a night at Hot Springs, North Carolina, for some hiking and zip-lining. We visited The Biltmore House, then to Bristol, Virginia, where we did a cave tour before I returned to Colorado. The morning after I left, I received a call from Janet. She told me that after she woke, she was lying in bed, laid her hands on her chest, and felt a large lump under her right palm. This lump turned out to be stage 2B HER2+ breast cancer. Janet and I later joked, "Spend a week with Ric, get cancer!"

Janet's cancer diagnosis found her without health insurance, for the first time in her life, and no job. She moved without a job lined up as the need was great to help her mom and sister. I told her not to worry about finding a job until she found out what needed to be done about her breast cancer. Upon the advice of her mom's family doctor, she found a surgeon and oncologist at Welmont in Bristol, Tennessee.

A lumpectomy was recommended as the biopsy hadn't revealed the stage or type of breast cancer. The hospital offered a 60% discount on her surgery since she didn't have health insurance. I told her not to worry and that I'd pay the $20K for the surgery. The results showed clear margins all around the tumor, so she thought she was in the clear. The follow-up visit, with the surgeon, revealed that the margin against the chest wall was very close. In fact, too close for comfort.

A second surgery was recommended to take more tissue from the chest wall to be safe. Again, I told her not to worry about the expense and paid for the second surgery. Janet's oncologist was extremely caring and honest. She told Janet that if she had to get breast cancer, HER2+ was the best one as it was the most easily treatable.

Janet thought she had avoided chemotherapy as all of the margins were clear from her surgery. Preventative chemo was recommended as, without it, the chances of return were far greater in the first five years than without chemo. So now Janet was facing six chemo treatments at $57K a pop. Fortunately, the hospital offered a grant for patients in need. Janet was approved for this grant at 100%. She was very fortunate in that she never felt or was sick from chemo. She also had to endure 35 radiation treatments. From the day she found the tumor to the day of her last treatment, one year had passed.

After Janet's cancer diagnosis, I suggested that maybe we could find a bed and breakfast for sale close to her mom. This would provide her with a place to live and a job, and she'd be available to help her mom and sister. We spent hours on the phone looking for B&Bs for sale. Janet would go and do the reconnaissance and then let me know what she thought. We had looked at seven B&Bs, all with their plusses and minuses. None of them fit the bill. Then we found Aska Lodge Bed & Breakfast in the north Georgia mountains. It was a bit further away from her mom and sister than she wanted, but the house and the town were perfect. Everything was to the point that I suggested we should get back together. Janet was very agreeable to this idea, so we decided to give it a go. We also agreed that we wouldn't get legally married again: been there, done that.

I had some real estate friends move into the Twin Lakes B&B to run it while the property was put on the market, and I moved to Georgia with Janet. We closed on Aska Lodge in July 2013 and moved in that October.

Marriage Number Five

Janet and I got back together when we bought the Aska Lodge. After the purchase was finalized, there were a few weeks the sellers would be there training Janet before departing. Janet had moved her things in, but I was still in Colorado and had never seen the place. Before packing and moving, I flew in for a weekend. The place was perfect. I loved it. There were guests, with the original owners still running the place.

I walked past a table in the common area where the owner talked to a guest. I overheard the words "Sapelo Sound," which is where, on the coast of Georgia, our 18-ton pot bust took place.

I stopped and asked, "How do you know Sapelo Sound?"

He said he lived there all his life in McIntosh County, on the shore of Sapelo Sound.

He was in his sixties, so I prompted him with, "Do you remember a huge marijuana bust in the '80s?"

He said, "Of course, it was the biggest event in the county's history. Everybody remembers."

I told him of my involvement, and he asked, "Did you know there was a song written about the bust?"

"No," was my answer.

He said to look it up, it's by a local named Vic Waters, who has been a songwriter and has had a band all his life. The title was "The Great Sapelo Bust."

It's on YouTube and it's hilarious.

Another small world note: Vic's band played in Tampa regularly in the sixties, and I was one of their fans. Vic and I caught up on Facebook and had a good laugh. He still lives there.

Rental Car

Janet and I took a trip that started in Pittsburgh, Pennsylvania. We rented a car and drove first to Centralia, Pennsylvania, a town with a terrible, troubled past. I first heard about it while reading "A Walk in the Woods" by Bill Bryson. Centralia is a borough and near-ghost town in Columbia County, Pennsylvania, United States, part of Northeastern Pennsylvania. Its population declined from 1,000 in 1980 to five residents in 2020 due to a coal mine fire burning beneath the borough since 1962.

The cause of the fire is disputed, but it burns today beneath the town and adjacent hillsides and will continue for another two hundred and fifty years.

Centralia with toxic smoke and gas rising from the ground.

All that sounded like a great side trip, so there we went. It was eerie, the streets were there, but only a couple of houses. We got out of the car and felt the hot pavement. We then went up a hill where we could see smoke coming from the ground. The short trip through rough terrain and up the hill was tough on a low-slung rental car, but we made it carefully. Seeing the smoke rising out of the ground was surreal. We looked around a bit and went on.

The next stop was a tourist attraction that took you inside a coal mine. We were taken down into the mine in original coal cars fitted with seats, possibly to take miners down. They gave us the history, stopped briefly, and turned the lights off to give us a pitch-dark experience. It was a nice experience.

When we left the attraction, it was only a few minutes before our car's oil light came on. I thought it needed oil, so I stopped at a convenience store, went in, and bought two quarts of oil. I stood at the front of the car with the hood up, pouring the two quarts into the engine, when I casually looked down at my feet and saw a stream of engine oil running between them. Stunned, I looked underneath and saw a hole in the oil pan under the car. It was punctured when we were on the way up the hill in Centralia to look at smoke rising from the ground.

Coming up with a "Hail Mary" plan, I parked the car out of the way and walked down to an auto parts store on the next block. I purchased a spray can of de-greaser and a tube of J-B Weld, a putty-like product that adheres to metal and hardens in short order.

At that point, the oil leak was down to a drip, but you can't apply J-B Weld to oily surfaces. When the drip slowed, about an hour later, I repeatedly sprayed the oil pan with the de-greaser until the surface seemed clean enough to apply the patch. After a few minutes, I filled the crankcase with oil and started it up. There was a small leak, but we went on our way.

After the two side trips, our stop was Mount Davis, Pennsylvania, in a desolate area accessible by gravel road. Janet was driving up the gravel road when suddenly, we saw orange cones blocking the road. We were only a mile from the trail to Mount Davis, so Janet exited the car and moved the cones before I suggested it. What could go wrong?

After a minute or two of driving past the cones, I looked back down the road, which was tarred black, but could see two white lines following us up the road. We could hear particles of something raining down on the car. The cones were placed there to block anyone from driving on the freshly tarred road. I got out of the car and, realizing the situation, looked over the car and saw we had slung tiny bits of tar covering the entire vehicle, even forward onto the headlights. The tar was very sticky and couldn't just be wiped away.

We did the short hike to Mount Davis, came down, and drove on. I was mulling over another "Hail Mary" when I realized I still had a can of de-greaser. When we stopped at our motel, one of the remaining Wigwam

Hotels in Cave City, Kentucky, I planned to test the de-greaser on the tar. It worked just great! I wiped and cleaned the whole car and then went to get the tar off the hubcaps. I sprayed one hubcap, a second, a third, and a fourth. When I came around the car to the original hubcap, the plastic lug nuts were all lying on the ground, detached from the hubcap by the de-greaser. The lug nuts were merely glued on from the factory but with a machine that got them perfectly straight.

Here we go again. We bought some glue, and I glued the plastic lug nuts to the hubcaps. My alignment skill with the lug nuts was far from the factory specs, so they were ridiculously misaligned at close inspection, not one being at the same angle as another. However, it might pass a cursory examination by a low-pay, hourly employee at the rental car agency. I had also managed to screw up a couple of the original lug nuts, so early the following day, we went to the local Chevy dealership and bought some more lug nuts, attached them, and problem solved. We went on for the rest of our trip to Maryland and West Virginia.

That one rental car had been savaged three times: a poorly patched oil pan, paint that was cleaned up nicely, and a cringe-worthy job on the lug nuts. We would be fortunate to exit the car rental without paying thousands for repairs. We had, of course, declined the damage insurance when we rented it.

The moment of truth came and went without any problem, and we briskly walked out of the rental car place with tails between our legs. For years afterward, when standing at a rental car counter trying to rent a car, we fully expected some loud horns and flashing red lights to go off, but that never happened.

The Ferry

Janet and I took a ferry from Charlotte, Vermont, to Essex, New York, crossing Lake Champlain. While on the twenty-five-minute crossing, I walked around the boat and found a large brass plaque on the wall. Reading through the huge plaque, it said the vessel had been refurbished and extended twenty feet at the Tampa Shipyard with Elliot Fletcher as the naval architect. I was the paperboy for that same Elliot Fletcher in Beach Park in the '50s.

We exited the ferry and went to a hotel near Lake Placid. While checking in, I noticed the proprietor had a nametag saying, "Ric."

I had spelled my nickname "Rick" all my life until I was hired at Atlantis Dive Center, where they looked at my full name, Fredric, and heard "Rick," then put "Ric" on the name tag. That change stuck. I mentioned this to the proprietor. He looked surprised and told me that is exactly what happened to him. His given name was Fredric, he had gone his life as "Rick," and late in life, a mistake somewhere permanently gave him "Ric."

Midgets

Janet and I were vacationing in a mountain cabin with our friends Craig and Anita Burch and Drew and Kaye Smith. We were at a restaurant having dinner and enjoying some talk. I don't hear all that well, so when Drew said something about pigeons in his attic, I heard "midgets."

I looked up immediately and blurted, "There are midgets in your attic?"

Everybody lost it, with Anita spewing Coca-Cola from her nose. She then commented that she also thought Drew had said "midgets."

We laugh about it still.

Adriano and Isabella

In the summer of 2015, Janet and I went to North Bend, Washington, with Janet's cousin Dean and his husband Jim for the Twin Peaks Festival. Twin Peaks is a show that aired on HBO for two seasons starting in 1990.

The festival was small, with a limited number of 300 tickets. The Twin Peaks Festival is not only about the Twin Peaks Festival, it's also a celebration of David Lynch's career. Another favorite of his fans is the movie "Blue Velvet." Isabella Rosellini is the actress who played Dorothy Valens's part in the film "Blue Velvet" and sang a haunting version of the song "Blue Velvet."

One of the festival attendees we met was a young Italian man, Adriano. He was somewhat shy and demure, but we enjoyed his company and talked about Twin Peaks and our love for the director, David Lynch. One of the events during the festival was a barbecue and karaoke night. Adriano happened to be a cross-dresser/drag queen and operatic singer.

When we arrived at the barbecue event, Adriano had somehow assembled a costume from local stores that he needed to portray the character of Dorothy Valens from Lynch's film "Blue Velvet." Adriano was strikingly beautiful and a dead ringer for Isabella when in character. Adriano has since attracted international attention for his portrayal. He has met and attended shows with Isabella since.

When he walked into the barbeque event, I didn't recognize him. Janet did and asked him to sit with us at our table next to me. We had saved a seat for him. I asked him if he dated older men, and he said the answer was "Yes."

He said he was a gay man who liked to dress in drag and portray female characters and never gave thought to becoming trans-sexual. He enjoyed being a man.

He confided to us that he'd love to sing for the karaoke but didn't feel confident enough. Janet and I encouraged him by telling him that none of these people knew him and that he would never see any of them again. Then, the karaoke was canceled because it was raining, and the inside space was just too small for the karaoke part of the night.

Janet kept telling Adriano, "Just get up and belt one out."

He finally succumbed to our wishes, and his performance did not disappoint! Two hundred people were there, and everyone went quiet when he started. It was a mesmerizing, beautiful performance.

Adriano

Tate's Hell

As we travel down Highway 65, a long stretch of highway with no internet reception, to St. George Island for our biannual trip with longtime friends, we always pass Tate's Hell.

Tate's Hell is a Florida state forest just North of Apalachicola, Florida, in the panhandle. When you are on a sixty-mile-long road with nothing but trees, a name like that catches your attention. We have made this trip many times, and on this particular trip, we decided to explore more than just the beach and the local bar. Tate's Hell immediately went on this list.

It was a cold and windy Halloween as we turned down the road. We were the only visitors that day, except for the one empty pick-up truck. It was late in the day and getting dark quickly when we made this decision, probably after a beer or two. The observation area was spectacular, with beautiful views of wildlife and marsh. We immediately noticed the trails among the weeds – alligator trails. Most of them ended at the elevated observation deck. That's when it first became spooky.

It was sundown and we decided we should probably head back. The Land Cruiser was still the only car parked in the dirt lot. That was when we realized we were almost out of gas, had no cell service, and had no road signs. We passed the pickup truck once again and thought we were on the right track. As we passed the empty truck again, we knew that we were lost. All the roads looked the same. We began to recall horror movies we had seen and were laughing hysterically. At the same time, there was an edge of fear. Fear of being stuck in the forest overnight with the lone truck driver on Halloween.

I had been in a survival situation before, and this had me worried. After all, Tate's Hell was named for a guy lost in the woods for days along the Forgotten Coast. When he finally exited the forest, he told people his name was Tate and he had just escaped Hell.

'Possums

Janet and I have slept in separate bedrooms for a long time. The breaking of glass woke Janet late one night. She came into the bathroom and yelled for me to wake up and come to the bathroom. I looked in the bathroom and saw a baby possum sitting on the bath counter, calmly looking at us. We had an outdoor cat, so I didn't want to catch the baby and pitch him outside, knowing a competent predator lurked. So, I found a cardboard box, coaxed the possum into it, and sealed it up with the idea of letting him go in the morning when we could keep the outdoor cat inside.

I woke up that morning and immediately told Janet, "I had the strangest dream last night." When I was fully awake, I realized it was no dream. We let him go.

We wondered how he got in the house. Our cat door only opens when it detects a registered microchip in one of our cats. Janet had noticed over the previous three days that there was what resembled black rice in the water bowl. We hadn't thought much about that until we learned possums put their poop in water to hide their scent. The baby possum had been living inside our couch for at least three days, but how did he get in? He had no marks on him.

The cat door was in a window adjacent to our TV. One evening a month later, we were watching TV when Larry the Cat popped up outside the door with a baby possum in his mouth. We both screamed, and Larry dropped the possum and bolted. We went outside to rescue the baby, brought him in, put him in the cardboard box, sealed it, and let him go the next day. He was completely unhurt. Larry had been gentle with him while catching and bringing him in. We realized that was how the original possum got in the house and that Larry was being motherly by bringing a lost kitten into the house.

Janet said we needed to make a sign saying "Larry's Home for Wayward Kittens" to put outside by the cat door.

Aneurysm

From Janet's perspective:

Ric and I had been sleeping separately for a while back then. Between snoring and "leg antics," one of us usually wound up on the couch. It was 1 am when I woke up on the couch in a cold sweat. Sleep had not come easily, and I had been restless. My sweet kitty Nathan had been snuggling with me, and his purring comforted me.

I woke up around 1 am in a terrible cold sweat, and my stomach was cramping. I sat up momentarily, then got up to go to the bathroom. I noticed that I felt a little dizzy and was bumping into things. I got to the bathroom and sat down on the toilet. The cold sweat was becoming worse, and my abdomen was cramping painfully. Nothing was happening, so I got up, returned to the den, and sat on the couch.

I called out to Ric, but he didn't answer. I'm now thinking that I seriously need to go to the ER. I get up and stumble into the kitchen, get my med bottles out of the cabinet, go into the bathroom, and, as I'm standing at the sink, I call out to Ric to tell him that he needs to get up and take me to the ER.

I go over to the closet in the bathroom to get dressed; the next thing I know, I wake up slumped into the corner of the bathroom and find I'm sitting in a puddle of urine.

Ric is standing over me, telling me that I've just had a seizure and that EMS is on their way. I distinctly remember thinking, "Did you pee on me?!" and then thinking, "Did the cats pee on me?!"

The litter box was directly next to me in the bathroom, so I thought maybe the cats had been the ones to pee on me. Ric asked me if I thought I could get dressed or put on some shorts. I could hardly move. My body felt like jelly. I crawled to the middle of the bathroom floor and lay back on the bath mat. I grabbed one of the handles on the vanity with my left hand, trying to pull myself up, but I couldn't. I turned onto my right side, my left arm flopped over on me, and I realized that my vision was fixed. My heart rate slowed to a snail's pace, and I knew my blood pressure was bottoming out. It's funny what you can remember going through your mind at such desperate times, but I remember thinking to myself; "I'm going to die staring at the base of the toilet."

I remember gripping Ric's hand and asking him to stay with me. I clearly remember thinking, "I am going to die right now."

<End Janet's narrative>

When I turned the corner into our bathroom, I saw Janet slumped in the corner next to the linen closet. I immediately recognized a seizure. I called 911 and waited for a minute or two until the seizure subsided. Her thousand-yard stare became more focused, and she was able to talk. Her first words resonate today, "Did you pee on me?"

I had missed an opportunity.

After extensive testing at the hospital, her doctor came in to say there was nothing conclusive from the tests as to what had caused the seizure. We were hoping for an explanation but got none. The doctor told us that the tests had shown a deviated septum, but not the kind that needed to be fixed. He then said that her right carotid artery was 50-55% blocked and that she just needed to have that checked with a cardiologist once a year. The doctor then started to leave the room, stopped, turned toward us saying, "Oh, and you have a brain aneurysm!"

We looked at each other like, "Uh, what was that last thing?"

We consulted an aneurysm specialist who soon did a repair that should be permanent. The procedure begins by going up through the femoral artery (in your groin!) to your brain to place a coil to block off the aneurysm. Janet has regular check-ups with her vascular surgeon, and all seems well.

Fake Blood

Janet is a big fan of Halloween, so I thought of a good trick to pull on her. She likes to stop at these pop-up Halloween decoration shops, so while we were in one, I bought a tube of fake blood without her knowledge.

When we returned home, we were in the last stages of renovating our kitchen. There were hundreds of board-feet of lumber and wood trim. Every board had to be squared and then trimmed to length with a table saw. Table saws are notorious for cutting carpenter's fingers and thumbs off. I was inside and outside doing just this and thought this would be a good time for the trick.

I squirted the fake blood over my hands and screamed to Janet for help. She ran outside to the table and saw where I was standing with the "blood" pouring from my hands. I stood there momentarily, doubled over, holding my hand with a pained grimace. I waited until the horror of the situation sank in, then laughed and laughed. Janet was not amused.

Karma exists.

A month later, I was doing the last cut on a piece of trim for the kitchen. Rather than walk the extra two paces to the chop-saw, the proper tool for the cut, I stopped at the table saw. It was a small piece of trim, too small for the table saw. It happened so fast that I don't remember how it happened, but my entire thumbprint was gone. I was bleeding profusely. I screamed to Janet, who strolled outside to where I was with a fat smirk on her face.

It took a while to convince her that I had actually injured myself. We then began to look through the sawdust for the thumbprint. We found it and brought it with us to the emergency room. The verdict at the ER was it was too thin to re-attach and just to let the skin granulate back in. That resulted in a badly scrambled thumbprint.

Our Friends, the Dillards

I made a beautiful Black Walnut full-size desk for our good friends, Tim and Kayla, who live in Breckenridge, Colorado. When Tim and I initially talked, I offered to create a piece of furniture for him for free so he could give it to his wife, a small coffee table or nightstand, something not bulky that could be shipped through ordinary, inexpensive means.

I said I would pay for the shipping regardless of the cost. He asked if I could make a desk. I was startled but didn't want to seem like a cheapskate, so I agreed to the desk, a more significant, costly, complicated piece, and the full shipping cost to his house. However, it would have to be shipped freight, which was expensive, so I planned to send it terminal to terminal, with him picking it up in Denver.

Now, I should have mentioned that to him. So, after completing much of the desk, I told him he could pick it up at the Denver freight terminal, which was the first time he heard that. He said he didn't want to do that, that he didn't have a vehicle capable of that and didn't have the time either. He then asked what extra it would cost to ship it to Breckenridge.

I got back with the freight company and got a quote of $325 to drop it at his house. I called Tim with this, and his response was, "That's just too much money."

Then he suggested that I should sell the desk here in Blue Ridge. The desk was custom-made for his wife, to his specs, so selling it here would not be simple. The confusion over who pays for what shipping was my fault, and I told him I was sorry. So, after the back and forth about shipping, I finally agreed to pay for all the shipping. If it hadn't been for my friendship with his wife, Kayla, I would have just canceled the whole thing and sold it here, as he suggested.

However, I got irked when I realized the desk was not worth $225 to him. That's okay, times can be challenging, and a gift for your wife for a couple of hundred bucks might not have been in the cards. I did it for Kayla, not him.

I love them both, but I also have a valuable friendship with Kayla. She was very dear to me, so I was willing to do something nice for her. I had about 60 hours and $1800 in the project, materials, and shipping, for which I wanted nothing back.

A few days later, he texted me that the desk arrived safely and that Kayla was out of town and knew nothing about the gift. She would be home in two days and would then see the desk. A week went by without hearing anything from either of them.

Janet texted Kayla, suggesting Kayla should thank me by phone. Kayla replied to Janet, "There is a lot going on here right now, and I have days I can't keep up, your text didn't help. Please stop beating me up."

Nearly two weeks after the texts between Janet and Kayla, I received a handwritten note in the mail from Kayla. The first thing she said in the note was, "I emailed Janet asking her to thank you for the desk. I'm not sure why she didn't share that with you."

Then the note ended with "Thank you for the beautiful desk."

The note would have been appreciated had she not started by saying she had thanked me via an email to Janet. A two-minute phone call would have been appropriate.

Our Friends, the Graysons

In 2020, after owning the Aska Lodge Bed & Breakfast for seven years, we sold it to guests Sam and Missy Grayson, who, after being guests several times over the years, had become our friends. In 2018, after they asked how much we wanted for it, I came up with a price of $575,000. Janet and I didn't want to sell then, and they didn't have the cash or borrowing power to buy it.

However, in 2020, when the planets aligned, Janet and I decided we wanted to sell, Missy's dad died, leaving her some assets, and Sam retired from the police force.

From the start, I had told them I could finance about half of the sales price if they couldn't find financing. Financing a B&B with a commercial lending institution is difficult under ordinary circumstances, but with 50% down and no other real debt, it should be able to happen.

However, with my promise to finance in the background, I saw no real effort to get commercial financing, so, in effect, they forced me into funding it for them. We signed the paperwork in late 2020, moved out, and they moved in.

One wrinkle: since I quoted them a price, the area had gone through a real estate boom, leaving the B&B worth about $100,000 more than I had quoted. After wrestling with my misplaced sense of honor, I kept the sales price at the original amount, probably forgoing $100,000.

At closing, they were $100,000 short, but Missy had a piece of property left by her dad that was up for sale and would sell within a year. We structured the loan with a balloon payment of $100,000 due in one year.

When we structured the note at closing, I assumed that the monthly payment would drop accordingly when the balloon payment was made, but they wanted to continue with the higher payment so the note would get paid off sooner. So that's how the note was written: $2,400 a month until the principal was paid.

I told them at the closing table that I was worried that this monetary commitment between us could eventually lead to the end of our friendship, but we pushed on, and the sale was finalized.

Only a few months into the mortgage, they were a few days late on a payment. It wasn't just oversite; it was because they didn't have the money. I was a bit alarmed. Having run a small business, I knew carrying a reserve fund of at least several thousand dollars was good business practice, so I told them just that. Good business practice demands a reserve fund for unforeseen circumstances, so you could incur some unplanned expense or shortage in sales and continue to pay your bills, especially your mortgage.

I also told them that running a small business wasn't easy and that unnecessary expenditures must be avoided. I assumed that this was such good advice that they would take heed. Still, no. They continued to purchase things for the inn that Janet and I thought unnecessary, and even more importantly, they also blocked out prime dates and weeks so they could take vacations and have family and friends stay at the lodge. A blocked week in prime time would approach $5,000 in lost revenue, but they continued, apparently oblivious to the long-term threat that meant.

Over two and one-half years, the late payments continued, all with the explanation that they didn't have the money. They were never more than about a week late, but that foretold what was soon to happen.

In June of 2023, they were late again. On about the tenth of the month, with the payment due on the first, Missy came to our house, tearfully saying they couldn't make the payment. There was no contact until she returned to our house on the 26th to explain they still had no money for the payment. This was only five days until the next payment was due. That broke my patience. I texted them saying that if they couldn't catch the payment up today, I would hire a lawyer, reminding them they would eventually reimburse me for any money I spent. An hour later, an angry, agitated Sam showed up at our house with cash.

It became plain from their point of view we were the assholes. They never spoke to us again. The subsequent mortgage payments were never late again by even one day. Imagine that.

The DMV Caper

When I moved from Colorado to Georgia, I had a new Colorado tag on my car. Rather than pay Georgia again for the same year, I waited almost a year to get a Georgia tag, but I did get a Georgia driver's license as soon as I moved there.

At the DMV office to get a tag, they looked at my driver's license and asked, "You moved here a year ago and didn't get a Georgia tag for your car?"

I said no.

She informed me that I owed an additional $400 penalty for not registering when I first arrived. The date of issue on my driver's license was the trigger. I sat for a moment and said to the clerk as I left, "I'll be back when I figure out how to get around this."

You must prove you live in a particular state to get a driver's license in that state. I had paperwork showing I owned a home in Tampa. The following day, I left early and drove the five hours to the DMV in Madison, Florida. I told them I was moving back to my house in Tampa and needed a Florida driver's license. I showed them my home ownership papers, surrendered my Georgia license, and got a Florida license.

The same day, I drove back to Blue Ridge, Georgia, and arrived at the DMV at 3:00 pm. I told them I had gone to Florida for work and had gotten a Florida license, but the job had immediately fallen through on the same day, and now I needed my Georgia license back. They gave me a new license for no fee, and I left.

The following day, I went to the Georgia DMV and said I needed a tag for my car. The same clerk who had seen me the previous day looked at my nice, fresh Georgia license and gave me a tag for $20, with no penalty.

Ukraine

The Dutch Salomonson branch of my family came to Holland from Ukraine. With the 2021 Russian invasion of Ukraine, I felt a grossly misplaced sense of duty to my homeland. I contacted the Ukrainian Embassy in Washington and volunteered to fight in the Ukraine Foreign Legion, telling them I was 76 years old. It took them a week to reply and say, "You are too old."

I replied that I could help as a medic with my battlefield medical training and didn't have to carry a Kalashnikov. They answered, "You are too old."

I replied again, saying I would be happy to help in a hospital, but again, they said I was too old.

I'm happy they didn't accept – it would have been disastrous.

Family In Need

Very close to our Georgia B&B, there is a rental house that we drove past every day. A Mexican family lived there for several years. I never spoke to them, although I waved to the father occasionally when I drove by. One day, as I passed by, I could see the horrific aftermath of a house fire that had gutted the entire interior of the home.

I called a neighbor to ask if he knew anything about the fire. He said no one was hurt and that it was an illegal Mexican family of three that had been burned out. He knew nothing else. I had never felt the urge to help anyone in any significant way before, but I wanted to help them.

I drove to the Blue Ridge Fire Station and met with the Chief. I asked the Chief if he knew anything about the family or how to contact them. With a large Confederate flag on the wall behind him, he said they were indeed an illegal Mexican family of three that had been taken in temporarily by another local family. I wanted to know how to contact them, so he took my number and said he would forward it to the foster family.

I got a call later that day from a woman who identified herself and asked how I wanted to help. I asked, "What do they need?"

"Everything," was her reply.

They had no time to get anything out of the house. She assured me this was a hard-working, salt-of-the-earth family. I asked her to arrange a time for the family to meet me at Walmart.

Janet and I went to Walmart and met with the woman fostering the family and the mother and son. I told them to go into the store and get anything they needed, regardless of cost. The mother was initially hesitant, but then we asked what she needed, and she accepted. She gathered some kitchen items, toiletries, and some clothing.

I took the young son (probably around 14) back to electronics, and we picked out a television together. I purchased the cart for them, and Janet gave them $100.00. The mom was tearful with appreciation. We learned later the family had recently lost a younger daughter to a medical issue. I've known three illegal immigrant families who have all been the salt of the earth.

My Favorite B&B Guests

Our bed and breakfast had guest rooms on the second floor. One of the guest rooms had a small balcony above the main entrance that overlooked our front yard. Much of the time, I avoided guests by leaving the property for one excuse or another.

One morning, I walked out the front door, under the balcony, and onto the lawn. I walked toward the parking and heard a sound from above. I turned and saw an attractive young woman standing on the balcony with a big smile. While looking directly into my eyes, she opened her robe to show me her nude full frontal. Walking to my car, I never broke stride or looked back. Men love crazy women.

Our B&B was also a popular destination for a "Girls Weekend." Women friends sometimes like to get away for the weekend to have fun and leave their husbands at home. Our rooms had only one bed each, kings or queens, so any two staying in the same room would have to sleep in the same bed.

We had two thirty-something females leave their spouses at home and come to stay with us for a few days. After they checked out, I stripped the bed and found underwear deep between the sheets. This bit of underwear was not an ordinary underwear garment. It was a black, tiny, lacey, sexy thong.

My immediate question was, if you were sleeping in the same bed with a same-sex friend, what is the scenario where your underwear was to come off and be forgotten? Frankly, I can't think of any that don't involve sex.

When I picked the thong up and looked at it, I did what any red-blooded male might do, I put it to my nose. I kept it as a souvenir until Janet found it and disposed of it, to my sorrow.

5-Star Michelin in Paris

Janet and I had a European trip planned for the Spring of 2023. Our trip was to begin in Krakow, Poland, then Berlin, Paris, and London. We both love to cook and have taken many cooking classes. I wanted us to have the experience of a Michelin 5-star restaurant in Paris. After some research, I came up with the restaurant Pur'-Jean-François Rouquette. Janet and I looked at the website and agreed on the reservation. The restaurant is open from Tuesday to Saturday from 7:45 pm until 9:30 pm. Dinner is six to nine courses with wine pairings. There is only one seating per night.

We arrived in very casual street clothes after a day of sightseeing. The Maître d seemed unaffected by our appearance and seated us. Our waiter arrived and greeted us, asking if we'd like still or sparkling water, a cocktail, or a glass of champagne. Janet ordered a glass of champagne. After our beverages arrived, the waiter brought menus and instructed us on ordering based on whether we wanted six courses or nine. I excused myself to visit the men's room. While I was gone, Janet took note of the waiter retrieving my napkin, refolding it, and placing it back on the table. When I returned, we both were still perplexed about how to order and asked the waiter to explain a second time.

Janet's champagne arrived, and she commented to me that it was "ok."

I asked Janet what she'd like, and she told me that her menu had no prices. I commented that my menu did have prices. Janet was a bit taken aback by this due to the day and age in which we live.

The waiter then brought us six exquisitely hand-made complimentary hors d'oeuvres and asked if we'd like to order. Still not understanding how to order, we asked for a third explanation. After the waiter left, Janet said to me that she thought we were a bit in over our heads. We both surmised that this dinner cost would be anywhere from $800-$1,000! Janet suggested that we ask for our check and politely excuse ourselves. She also commented that we'd never see any of these people again and we should just cut and run. We did just that.

When the check arrived, one item was on it: Janet's glass of champagne, which was $50 for a single glass! Janet has loved cheap champagne since college. She later told me she was thinking how many bottles of Andre's she could have bought with $50.

We still needed dinner after leaving Pur'-Jean-François Rouquette with our tails between our legs. We walked several blocks and saw an exclusive hamburger restaurant. We went in and had a great time and a great burger—burgers for two cost over $50. After what we'd just experienced, we felt it was a bargain.

The next day we had a private guide for a tour of The Louvre. We told her about our experience at the Michelin Star Restaurant. She then told us about a couple from Texas she had guided who had traveled to Paris for their 40th wedding anniversary. The husband made dinner reservations at the same restaurant we went to. He had told our guide that the food was so scant when the appetizers arrived that he felt like they had been brought a dirty plate. He also commented that the portions were so small that he could only think, "I want a huge piece of meat!"

Our guide told us the Texas couple's dinner cost nearly $3,000!

The very best food we had on the entire trip was in Krakow. Not to mention that Krakow was the cleanest city we've ever been in, and the people there were incredibly friendly.

Brushes with Greatness

"Butch" Gallagher

Leo Anthony Gallagher Jr., known mononymously as Gallagher, was an American comedian who became one of the most recognizable comedic performers of the 1980s for his prop and observational routine that included the signature act of smashing a watermelon on stage with a wooden sledgehammer.

For over 30 years, he played between 100 and 200 shows a year, destroying tens of thousands of melons with the sledgehammer he called the "Sledge-O-Matic." This last sketch was meant to poke fun at infomercials who peddled similarly inane products and whose popularity apexed in the late 70s/ early 80s before waning during the 90s. (Wikipedia)

Leo Gallagher

Known in high school and to me as "Butch," he was a good friend for years, as was his brother, Jerry.

Judy Collins/Stephen Stills

I met Judy twice after her concerts in Leadville a few years ago. I had been reluctant to see her perform because, being a fan for 50 years, I worried her voice was not what it once was. I was right and wrong. Her voice was even better than her early singing, "richer" is the only way I can describe it.

Anyway, at the "meet and greet," which is a quickie handshake and photo op, I told her I had a funny story about Stephen Stills if she was interested. Celebrities tend to zone out during these obligatory things after a performance. My suggestion didn't register, so I left it alone.

Here is the story: I attended the same high school as Stephen, Plant High in Tampa starting in 1965. He was two years ahead of me and an upperclassman on my first day of high school. Walking out of the orientation on the morning of the first day with all three classes, my friend Gary Woodworth said: "Do you realize what happened?"

I said, "No, what?" He told me Stephen Stills walked up behind me and spit a big loogie on the back of my head. I felt, and sure enough, it was there—my only exchange with the Great Stephen Stills.

Judy and I, backstage in Leadville.

Muhammad Ali

I attended a Muhammad Ali boxing exhibition in Orlando in the early '70s. I was a huge fan of his stand on the Vietnam War. The bout was standard fare, but as he left the arena, he walked down the aisle I was on and passed just inches from me. From anyone's perspective, he had an impressive physique, but from inches away, he was eye-popping.

Photo by Fredric Altman
1971 Exhibition in Orlando
Angelo in corner

Reverend Jesse Jackson

I met the Reverend and his wife in the Atlanta Airport. They stood by themselves as I approached them and introduced myself. I thanked him for his service to America and spoke to him briefly. He was quiet, but his wife was very sweet and talkative.

Jeff Foxworthy

I sat next to him while we waited for a flight from Denver. I left him alone.

Phone Company Stories

African Bull Elephant

I worked for the phone company in the Gibsonton/Riverview, FL, area in the 60s/70s as an installer/repairman. In the winter, carnivals and circuses would shut down, and everyone would go home until spring. Gibsonton was the favorite town for the "carnies" to winter. I met many and found them good people and fun to talk to.

So, you could find any animal used in a circus in someone's backyard. One day, I went to install a telephone extension in an outbuilding at a home in Gibsonton.

Then, "Gibton" was primarily rural, with many trailers on big, multi-acre lots. I met the property owner, who walked me around the house into the huge backyard. The first thing I saw was an African bull elephant. The owner told me not to get anywhere near him; he was mean and dangerous. They used these as tractors to erect tents and for other heavy work.

This elephant was chained with a long, heavy chain fastened to the ground with a wooden stake. While installing the phone, I was carrying a ladder and other assorted tools around back and had forgotten the warning not to get close to the elephant. Suddenly, from behind, I heard an elephant bellowing like in a Tarzan movie, and I could feel the ground shaking with him charging me. The ladder and tools flew when I took off running, fearing for my life.

What went through my mind was what would happen when the chain ran out. Would it hold or pop out of the ground and let the beast catch me? I could tell he would have killed me if he were to catch me. The stake held.

The Dairy

After 50 years, the memory is fuzzy, but there was a dairy south of Hwy 60 above Riverview on 301 on the west side of 301. I was there to put an extension in the milking building, a big concrete structure with two rooms. One held the cows while being milked, and the other a smaller room with a large refrigerated holding tank where all the lines from the cows emptied.

The owner was there to show me where the phone went, but while there, he asked me if I wanted a glass of milk. The only way to get a fresher glass of milk would be straight from the cow's udder. This was 50 years ago, but I remember it like yesterday, the delicious taste of that milk. I haven't had that taste since.

Giant's Camp

After picking up my telephone work orders in the morning, I used to go straight to the Giant's Camp to eat breakfast (on the clock). I never knew the giant, Al Tomaini, but I regularly saw his wife, Jeannie. She was a good person.

Al and Jeanie Tomaini

After about five minutes with her, you forgot she had an infirmity.

One day, I had an order to put an extension phone in her personal kitchen. She was there the whole time doing some cooking. Without legs, she bounced around that kitchen like you wouldn't believe. She had a vibrant personality and was fun to talk to. Al Had been long dead by the time I met Jeannie.

The Cucumber

In Gibsonton, one day, I went to a woman's house to install a telephone jack next to her bed. She had something to do with a carnival, which I think was hairless cats. She was standing behind me as I kneeled next to her bed and nightstand when something caught my eye just under her bed. It was a large, fresh cucumber. Now, no matter how badly I wanted to say: "Hey, lady, do you know you have a cucumber under your bed?"

As difficult as it was, I kept my mouth shut.

The Disconnection

In the '60s and '70s, to disconnect a phone for non-payment, you sometimes had to go directly to the subscriber's house, go up the pole out in front of their house, and physically disconnect the line to the house.

In Riverview, I was doing precisely that when the subscriber came out of his home with a shotgun, pointed it at me, and told me in no uncertain terms that I was not to disconnect his phone and that I needed to get off the pole immediately and leave.

Of course, I did just that. My boss called the sheriff's office, but I don't remember anything beyond that.

B-17

A camper migration from Northeast America and Canada arrives every winter in South Florida, "snowbirds." Many want a temporary telephone for their winter stay. I went to install one at a campsite in Bradenton for an American in his 60s.

While talking to him, he said he had met his camper neighbor a few days ago, and even though this neighbor was born and grew up in Germany, they found they had some things in common. My American had been a crewmember of an 8th Army Air Force B-17, stationed in England during World War Two. I don't remember which position he held on the bomber. The Air Force was part of the Army at the time. The 8th Air Force had the job of high altitude, daylight bombing in Europe and eventually in Germany. The 8th had the highest mortality rate of any American unit in the war, 77 percent killed or wounded. The Marines weren't even a close second.

The Americans flew 30 bombing missions over Germany against a ferocious anti-aircraft defense consisting of fighter aircraft, but the most feared defense was "flak." We've all seen footage of these raids, much filmed by William Wyler. The puffs of black smoke are the flak. These puffs are exploded shells coming from an 88-millimeter cannon used by the Germans in many versions.

Aside from the anti-aircraft version, they used one in the heavy version of the Tiger tank, the most feared tank in the war. The anti-aircraft versions of the shells were designed to explode into 200 fragments at a particular altitude and were very effective. Fifty percent of the casualties were from the 88mm flak. This was the only German cannon that could reach 30,000 feet, an expected altitude for a B-17 bombing.

The American's German neighbor, also in his 60s, was a gunner on an 88mm anti-aircraft installation on Germany's border, crossed over by the American in his B-17 several times. It was more than likely that this German had fired at this same American more than once. They looked like lifelong friends.

The Family

The Holocaust

When Jews immigrated to America in the 1800s, they were escaping the "pogroms" going on in Eastern Europe and Russia. Pogrom is a Russian word meaning "to wreak havoc, to demolish violently." Historically, the term refers to violent attacks by local non-Jewish populations on Jews in the Russian Empire and other countries. When they immigrated, many would disavow their Jewishness in an attempt to blend in here in America. I was in my twenties when I realized I had a Jewish background, never once being mentioned by anyone in the family. My Salomonson family came from Ukraine, running from the pogroms when they found a home and success in the Netherlands.

While doing my genealogy, I could never get (and still can't) any further back than Frederick's father, Lodywyk, but dawning on me finally I realized there had to be a link from my Jewish family in Holland to the Nazi invasion of Holland and subsequent deportation and extermination of Jews there. My father was a fighter pilot in WW2 in Europe, so the war was something I was well aware of but had no serious link to.

I found websites dedicated to those murdered by Hitler in the Holocaust. The Germans kept excellent records because millions of names, dates, and places are listed on these sites. I began to immediately find dozens and dozens of blood relatives murdered by the Nazi regime. Three-month-old babies, their parents, their grandparents, and even great-grandparents all from the same family were murdered. I found relatives killed at almost every Death Camp you can name. Sobibor, Treblinka, Auschwitz-Birkenau, Bergen-Belsen, Buchenwald, Dachau and others. As a result, my perception of WW2 has dramatically changed, and it's now very personal. These findings made me ill, and I was unable to do any more genealogy for a year.

Dr. Mac R. Winton

The Tampa Cuban community revered my mother's father, Dr. Winton, husband of Marie Francis "Mollie" Salomonson, surgeon and general practitioner. I worked as an installer/repairman for General Telephone in the late sixties and seventies. I was regularly in Cuban homes and would mention Dr. Winton's name for a little conversation. I had two people immediately pull their shirts up and show me their appendectomy scars. I had another Cuban descendant woman tell me she had been hit by a bus, which mangled her leg. The other doctors wanted to remove the leg, but Dr. Winton said he could save it, and he did. He maintained an office at the Centro Espanol long after he had quit surgery when a long-term patient of his needed an appendectomy and would not let anyone do it other than Dr. Winton.

He was about 86 when he performed the surgery. Before he did the operation, he called me and asked if I wanted to observe. I agreed, and he picked me up, took me to the hospital, and let me watch. He was a small man and had to stand on a stool to reach the patient as the tables wouldn't lower. I was thirteen years old and vividly remember the scalpel slicing through about six inches of fat. That was it for me. I don't remember masks or gloves in the operating room. I certainly didn't have a mask on. Dr. Winton was very old school.

After finishing the surgery, he drove me home but had a stroke while driving and barely made it home. He spent most of his last nine years in bed, unable to speak or do anything else. I had many of his patients tell me he never charged them. I still have his stethoscope and a beautiful, small wooden box that held some instruments from his military days, which I know nothing about. He loved and grew orchids. I can still smell his hothouse. He had a pecan tree in his backyard, which the local squirrels loved. But he used to shoot them with a .22 rifle with rat shot while sitting on his back porch.

Salomonson Side of Family

F. A. Salomonson

My mother was born Florence Winton, daughter of Dr. Mac R. Winton and Marie Francis "Mollie" Salomonson, daughter of the flamboyant 3-time mayor of Tampa, Frederick August Salomonson.

F. A. Salomonson was born in 1860 in Almelo, Netherlands. In 1882, he arrived in Florida as a representative of a Dutch syndicate that had purchased land in Florida. He decided to remain in Florida and moved to Jacksonville, where he worked for a railroad company for two years. In late 1884, Salomonson relocated to Tampa, establishing himself in the real estate business.

He was twice elected to the City Council. Immediately following his last term on the City Council, F. A. was elected as Tampa's 28th Mayor, served from 1893 until 1894, and was elected to two more terms.

While mayor, he purchased the Tampa Bay Hotel (Now the University of Tampa). After submitting a deposit and signing a contract, the next day, he sent the Tampa police to evict everyone from the hotel. This began a massive, immediate outcry, most notably from the Tampa City Council. Using the police department for your personal needs is unacceptable. The council threatened impeachment if something weren't done. A lawsuit ensued, and somehow, Frederick wriggled out of the purchase agreement with a tidy profit. The council relented and reduced the impeachment to a censure.

At some point, he purchased an adult male lion from a European carnival, shipped it to Tampa, and kept it in his backyard on prestigious Bayshore Blvd. There are no further details about how this endeavor went.

Salomonson had developed a personal relationship with the Tampa Fire Department and one day took a quantity of beer and whisky down to the Department. After everyone was good and drunk, Frederick went home and immediately called in a false fire alarm. It's unknown if this was something pre-planned or spur of the moment, but in any event, he thought this was great fun. I don't know of any repercussions from this.

After being elected in 1904 for a third term, he became ill with tuberculosis and spent time in Colorado in an effort to improve his health. Unfortunately, he was unable to overcome the illness, returning to Tampa to die.

My Father

Lardner Ewell Altman, Jr. was born in 1918 into a working-class family of six brothers and sisters, with whom he moved to Tampa from Wauchula in about 1915, when dad, Lardner Sr., got a job with Seaboard Coastline Railroad. In 1923, Lardner Sr. was killed, leaving a wife and six children, soon to go through the "Great Depression."

Excerpt from the lawsuit:

This was an action by the plaintiff in error to recover damages for the death of L.E. Altman, which occurred while he was an employee of the defendant and acting as a brakeman on a freight train. The death of the deceased was attributed to the negligence of his employer in permitting the brakes on a freight car from which the deceased was thrown and killed to be in a defective and dangerous condition. The evidence adduced was to the following effect:

When an attempt was made at night to couple the end car on the train on which the deceased was a brakeman to a car on a side track — called the L. & N. car, which was loaded with lumber — the coupling was missed, with the result that the L. & N. car and an unloaded car a few feet beyond it on the side track were caused to run down the side track towards a tank car, which was standing on that side track, and which was to be taken from that place. Thereupon it was the duty of the deceased to get on the L. & N. car to set the hand brake thereon for the purpose of stopping it. When the deceased reached the brake wheel, he was 150 or 200 feet from the tank car. If the brake was in good condition, the car should have been stopped within the distance of two or three car lengths, the average length of a freight car is about 36 feet. The L. & N. car and the car beyond it continued to move until the latter collided with the tank car. When the impact occurred, the deceased fell on the track between the two cars and was killed.

The Sea Cloud

Dina

Screenshot of 14-year-old Nedenia Marjory Hutton (Dina Merrill on the stage and in the movies) of the movie camera footage shot by my dad on the Sea Cloud in 1936 somewhere on Europe's coast. My dad was 20, so she was a little young for a romantic interest, but they became friends and kept up a pen-pal relationship for 50 years. Her mother, Marjory Merriweather Post, the wealthiest woman in American history, built Mar-A-Lago as a personal residence.

Some notable movies Dina was in:

The Young Savages

The Sundowners

Butterfield 8

Catch Me If You Can

Operation Petticoat
Don't Give Up the Ship

L.E. Altman

My Dad on the fantail of the Sea Cloud yacht in 1936, owned by Marjory Merriweather Post.

Uncle "Eddie" Walsh

Lawrence Edward Walsh married my mother's sister in 1936. He was nominated by President Dwight D. Eisenhower on April 6, 1954, to the United States District Court for the Southern District of New York. After he resigned from the federal bench, he served as Deputy Attorney General in the Eisenhower administration from 1957 to 1960. He went into private practice at the end of the Eisenhower administration.

In December 1986, he was named the independent counsel of the Iran-Contra investigation. His investigation led to the convictions of both former Assistant to the President for National Security Affairs Vice Admiral John Poindexter and Lieutenant Colonel Oliver North. However, both convictions were subsequently reversed on technicalities. He also brought an indictment on two perjury counts and one obstruction of justice against former Secretary of Defense Caspar Weinberger in June 1992.

On the eve of the 1992 presidential election, on October 30, Walsh obtained a grand jury re-indictment of Weinberger on one count of false statements. President George H. W. Bush was implicated in that indictment. Some believe that Bush had been closing the gap with Bill Clinton and that this event stopped his momentum. This indictment was dismissed later for being outside the statute of limitations. Weinberger's pardon by President George H. W. Bush in December 1992 preempted any trial. Walsh denied that the investigation was politically motivated, while Bush and others criticized it.

Uncle Eddie died at the age of 102.

Some Cousins

ALTMANS "HIT LIST"

I've done a lot of genealogical research for over thirty years. At the moment, there are 145,000 people in my family tree. I found two blood-relative Altmans mentioned in a "Hit List," a document in the Georgia Revolutionary War records issued by the "Executive Council" in 1784. At the time of the Revolution, not all Americans approved of it. They were called "Tories." This described persons who supported the British government during the American Revolution.

During the American Revolution, the Tories were bitterly denounced. They believed separation from Britain was an illegal act that would ignite an unnecessary war. After the war, these Americans were relentlessly and mercilessly hunted, even hung and stripped of all possessions, including any land. It's hard to tell if the Altmans, James and Thomas, were hunted due to supporting the Tories or whether they were only murderous criminals.

The warrant says:

"WHEREAS, there are a number of notorious characters, who infest the roads and other parts of the State, and are continually murdering and plundering the virtuous inhabitants of the same, and in order to the more effectually expelling and totally annihilating those enemies to mankind (those hellish and diabolical fiends) from the face of the earth.

Therefore,

ORDERED that any person, either employed in the public service or otherwise, shall not only be released from his term of enlistment, but also receive the sum of ten guineas as a reward on his producing to the Governor and Council in Savannah the body, or good and sufficient proof that such of the under-mentioned persons are absolutely and bona fide killed.

Of the 22 listed, brothers James and Thomas are there. They fled Georgia to Baxter, Florida, near Jacksonville. Some of their progeny became the Notorious Altmans, one of whom is mentioned in an obit below.

Florida Times-Union, 26 November, 1909. Obituary (of sorts):

> Jacksonville has been rid of a disturbing character in the killing of Jesse Altman, shot down after he had cut two men to death. Altman has figured in a majority of the serious affrays which have decorated Jacksonville's recent criminal record.

(Jacksonville has been rid of a disturbing character in the killing of Jesse Altman, shot down after he had cut two men to death. Altman has figured in a majority of the serious affrays which have decorated Jacksonville's recent criminal record.)

Cousin Frits

Also, under the heading "Beware what you find searching your ancestry," I found some history of a cousin, Frits Salomonson. My mother's mother was born Marie Francis Salomonson, daughter of Frederick August Salomonson, three-time mayor of Tampa. Frederick (where I get my name) was born in Almelo, Netherlands, and had family living there. One family cousin is Frits Salomonson, born about 1940, went into the military, later became an attorney, and eventually became Queen Beatrix's attorney. Beatrix had a husband named Claus (Prince Claus of the Netherlands, born Jonkheer van Amsberg), who became a good friend of Frits.

Claus was a member of such Nazi youth organizations as Deutsches Jungvolk and the Hitler Youth. In 1944, Claus was conscripted into the German Wehrmacht, becoming a soldier in the German 90th Panzergrenadier Division in Italy in March 1945. He was taken prisoner of war by the American forces at Meran before taking part in any fighting.

I had met Frits only once when I was about ten. Frits came to America to visit his family in Tampa. I only remember a little about him until he became famous as the Queen's attorney. My sister and I went to see him in the seventies and met him for dinner in Amsterdam, but we lost touch until recently. My interest in that family branch got me interested in finding Frits again, so I searched and searched and called every similar name in Holland but found nothing. I had given up until, while bartending at a 1978 Colorado hotel I helped renovate, I heard a Dutch accent from a young couple sitting at the bar.

They were sightseeing here in America when they stopped for a drink at my bar. I told them the story of my famous cousin Frits, attorney for the Queen, whom I was trying to find in Holland, and how I needed help finding him. They said when they got back home, they would look for him.

I thought, yeah, right, but a couple of weeks later, I got a call from Holland. It was the couple! They said I was correct, that my cousin was famous. My chest began to swell, so proud, remembering a picture of Frits standing beside the Queen in his military uniform. They then said he was famous but for all the wrong reasons. He had been at the center of several financial scandals in Holland, but that wasn't the worst part. According to several online accounts, Frits had become lovers with Prince Claus, but that footnote aside, he and Prince Claus had been importing young Moroccan boys as sex slaves, keeping them in a sex dungeon in Frits's house.

The resulting public uproar from this scandal was horrific. There were rumors of complaints by neighbors about freshly poured concrete and gunshots heard at Frits's home. The Monarchy covered up as much of it as possible, and Frits self-exiled to Belgium, where the couple found him. I had his contact info but soon lost it and never contacted him. I wanted to ask him, "So, what's new?"

Frits on the left, with Prince Claus.

Frits in uniform with Queen Beatrix.

Thomas Mayhew 1593-1682, 12th Great Grandfather

In 1641, while engaged in business ventures in the vicinity of Boston. Mayhew bought the islands that now constitute Dukes County and Nantucket County, Martha's Vineyard, Nantucket, and the Elizabeth Islands for 40 pounds and two beaver skin hats.

Mayhew established himself as governor of Martha's Vineyard in 1642. Together he and the younger Thomas established Martha's Vineyard's first settlement and called it Great Harbor, now Edgartown.

Mayhew and his fellow settlers found a large and economically stable native population of about 3,000 living in permanent villages. Relations between the first settlers and their Wampanoag neighbors were peaceful and courteous. Under the leadership of his son, a minister, they instituted a policy of respect and fair dealing with the Wampanoag natives that was unequaled anywhere. One of the first of Mayhew's orders was that no land was to be taken from the native islanders, the Wampanoags, without their consent or without fair payment. From this time forward, the colonial settlers and Wampanoag lived without the bloodshed that marked the history of European colonies elsewhere in the New World. From the beginning, Mayhew had worked to preserve the original political institutions of the native population. Much of the above courtesy of Wikipedia.

None of that value remains 12 generations down the line. I would like to arrive in Martha's Vineyard and order everyone off my island, but no.

Salem

I have many connections the Salem witchcraft trials, mostly by marriage. All the below are related by marriage except those with 4 stars, those are blood relatives.

Elizabeth Booth-accuser
Thomas Boreman 1601-accuser
Ann Carr-accuser
James Davis-accuser
John DeRich (Rich)-accuser
Mary Cross Herrick-accuser
****John Howe-accuser
Joseph Hutchinson-accuser
Margaret Jacobs, gdaughter of George Sr. testified against him
Margaret Wilkins Knight-accuser
Abigail Martin, Jr.-accuser

John Proctor-accuser and executed
Ann Putnam, Jr.-accused and survived, also accuser
Ann Putnam, Sr.-accuser
Edward Putnam-accuser
Hannah Cutler Putnam-accuser
****John Putnam, Jr.-accuser
John Putnam, Sr. (married blood relative)-accuser
****Jonathan Putnam-accuser
Nathaniel Putnam-accuser
Thomas Putnam-accuser
John Wilkins B1667-accuser
Samuel Wilkins-accuser
Bray Wilkins-accuser
Thomas and Mary Jacobs-accusers
Ann Putnam, Jr.-accused and survived, also accuser
Mary Bassett de Rich-accused and survived
George Jacobs, Jr.-accused but evaded
Susannah North-executed
Sarah Solart-executed
George Jacobs, Sr.-executed
Elizabeth Jackson Howe-executed
John Proctor-accuser and executed

Letter to My Ex-Wives

There is a lot of water under the bridge between us, but something has been eating at me for years now, and I need to tell you a story.

You may have wondered at least briefly decades ago why, after wanting badly to be close to you, married to you, and live with you, that once that happened, I began to push you away until finally, we were apart. I've wondered that many, many times myself with no answer.

I couldn't trust, be close, or let my guard down. It wasn't because I didn't love you, because I did. I always chalked it up to being immature. Still, after the third marriage began to fall apart, I had an epiphany that profoundly changed how I see things and interact with people, but with loved ones in particular.

I had been pushing Janet away for many years until she had finally had enough and wanted a divorce. I asked her to go with me to see a therapist. She was cool with the idea but eventually agreed to go.

We only went to a few sessions, but during one of the first ones, the therapist remarked that there seemed to be a pattern to all three marriages. I desperately wanted to be close, but once close, pushed away. The conversation drifted away from that for a while. I don't know why it came up because it was just an offhand comment about something I found going through some old family stuff. I said I had found my year-end grade school report cards, and there were comments from each teacher on those cards. I mentioned that in grades 1, 2, and 3, the teachers all remarked that as a child, I was happy, talkative, outgoing, and even disruptive at times in class. But the 4th, 5th, and 6th-grade teachers wrote that in their classes, I was almost completely silent, withdrawn, and rarely talked at all. I had also started stuttering. I was relating a childhood anecdote, but the therapist perked up and asked if anything unusual happened in the summer between the 3rd and 4th grades.

I had to think briefly, but "Yes" was the answer.

I was molested by a neighbor's relative several times during that summer. In those days, things like this were just hushed up, and emotional care for the victim was unheard of. My dad threatened the guy, and he moved out of the area. That was the end of it, and it was never mentioned again. I never believed anyone could block out memories until I remembered this one. I had blocked it out for many, many years. Also, it never occurred to me that there could be profound, lasting effects.

The therapist was somewhat stunned but then told me that the most common and profound side effect of child molestation is that the child stops trusting. He stops trusting everyone, keeps everyone at a distance, and when he does have the chance to get close to someone, it's impossible to maintain.

It took a few minutes for what I had just heard to sink in, but things slowly began to make sense. The amount of damage that man did to me over my entire life (and to your life) just can't be calculated. I mentioned that these realizations were an epiphany, but that word isn't strong enough. That session changed my life. Understanding all this doesn't make the effects immediately disappear, but at least now I know what has been happening in my head.

I can usually keep the walls from going up, and it's easier to trust. It's made a huge difference in my life. I routinely talk to strangers now, which I never, ever did. This has been an enormous relief. I can't overstate how big. There's been a fifty-year trail of emotional wreckage in my life.

I know this all sounds like deflecting, trying to absolve myself of guilt, but not so. I had free will then and made some decisions I shouldn't have.

I hope this brings some understanding.
  Yours Sincerely, Idiot Ric

My favorite quotes

D.H. Lawrence:

"The proper way to eat a fig, in society, is to split it in four, holding it by the stump, and open it, so that it is a glittering, rosy, moist, honied, heavy-petalled four-petalled flower. Then you throw away the skin which is just like a four-sepalled calyx, after you have taken off the blossom with your lips. But the vulgar way is just to put your mouth to the crack and take out the flesh in one bite. Every fruit has its secret."

John Huston in "Chinatown"

"Politicians, ugly buildings, and whores all get respectable if they get old enough." screenplay by Robert Towne.

Mark Twain (Janet's cousin)

"There is nothing to be learned from the second kick of a mule."

Play it Again, Sam

"Allan: That's quite a lovely Jackson Pollock, isn't it?
Museum Girl: Yes, it is.
Allan: What does it say to you?
Museum Girl: It restates the negativeness of the universe. The hideous, lonely, emptiness of existence. Nothingness. The predicament of Man, forced to live in a barren, Godless eternity like a tiny flame flickering in an immense void with nothing but waste, horror, and degradation, forming a useless, bleak straitjacket in a black, absurd cosmos.
Allan: What are you doing Saturday night?
Museum Girl: Committing suicide.
Allan: What about Friday night?"

—Woody Allen, Play It Again, Sam

Unknown:

"Better to cut off the sleeve of your favorite sweater than to disturb a sleeping cat"

This saying refers to a well-known story about the Islamic Prophet Muhammad. The story goes that one day, when Muhammad was preparing for prayer, he found his cat, Muezza, sleeping on the sleeve of his prayer robe. Instead of waking the cat, he chose to cut off a piece of the sleeve so that Muezza could continue sleeping undisturbed.

While this story is popular, some scholars and religious figures dispute its authenticity, noting that it doesn't appear in early Islamic texts like the Hadith. However, its widespread circulation reflects the reverence and care for cats within Islamic culture and among cat enthusiasts in general.

Regardless of its historical veracity, the phrase underscores the understanding and respect cat lovers have for their pets' need for uninterrupted rest and comfort.

Unknown:

"A certain sadness touches me, in thoughts too deep to share.
It's not that I never loved you, but that I cease to care."

From Stacey

My time with Ric was a roller-coaster of events and emotions. Amazingly, I still call him my friend for life! What a ride!

From Anita

When I think of Ric Altman, the phrase Renaissance Man comes to mind. Ric was probably born at the wrong time on the wrong continent. He is a person interested in the Arts and Humanities. He is a man of few words who plays violin, loves "out there" music with deep lyrics, writes, reads thought-provoking books, does woodworking, is an excellent cook, tinkers with engines, is capable of remodeling a house, and is a total "Cat person." He is kind and caring for his fellow man and has endured much suffering. When Ric is your friend, he's "your friend.

From Janet

Ric,

I often wonder if you know just how much you mean to me. The love that I have for you is immeasurable.

Several weeks before I met you for the first time in 1986, I had broken up with a man I thought I loved to the point that I wanted to spend the rest of my life with him. That panned out otherwise since I broke up with him to preserve my dignity and sanity.

When you showed up, I had given up on men and love. I was jaded. I didn't realize that our mutual friend, Mary Lee, was trying to play "matchmaker" when she introduced us. So, when you phoned me at work nine months later, it didn't register with me that you wanted to see me and hadn't forgotten about me. When you said your name, I uttered, "Who?" It wasn't that I'd forgotten about you, I think I was in shock that you had called after so many months had passed.

I remember our first date at an Italian restaurant on Davis Island. When you took me home that evening and walked me to the door, you asked if you could kiss me, to which I replied, "I'd be disappointed if you didn't." Then we went to Kieffer's wedding the next day. The older man sitting to my right gave us a look of shock when you reached over my crossed legs and laid your hand on my thigh.

I invited you to my roommate Jan's party that night. She was going to ditch making rumaki, but then you volunteered to make it. I remember you and I in the kitchen making the rumaki. Then, later, we were in the den looking through albums. We put on Meatloaf's "Bat Out of Hell," and when "Paradise by the Dashboard Lights" came on, I sang every word, and you commented, "I guess you weren't kidding when you said you loved this song!"

We picked Ben up the next day to eat in Tarpon Springs. You wanted to stop by your Dad's on the way. Several months later, when I moved in with you, your stepmother, Mickey, revealed she had thought I was Ben's girlfriend and wondered why I would be moving in with you?!

You always have been, and always will be, the "living end" for me. During the six years that we were apart, I dated very little. It wasn't that I compared other men to you, it was just that deep down, I knew that I'd never meet anyone as unique as you.

I'm so happy that you came back into my life. You are the most incredibly unique person, not to mention the sexiest man that I have ever *met or ever will meet. I love your/our crazy sense of humor. We've shared such enthusiasm for discovering everything we've done together: diving, caving, hiking, backpacking, climbing, and traveling. You have compassion, empathy, patience, and generosity for others and for me. I love our life together.*

While you were writing this book, we shared previously unknown things about our lives, accepting those things and making our peace with them. Still, after 36 years, we have learned more about one another and have grown even closer because of it.

I love you more and more every day.

Always,

Janet

Acknowledgments

Janet, for her patience, support, edits, and story contributions.
Anita Long Burch, for "Tate's Hell."
Michele, for forgiveness and reminding me of some of my unsavory acts that I would have preferred to have forgotten.
Stacey, for her friendship and help with details.
Po Morgan, for details and other things.
Jei, for not knifing me.
Stanton Phillips, research and contributions.
Lee Montgomery, for his friendship and memory.
Irek, for editing.
Debra Getts, support and advice.
Akhtar Baig Mirza, for complete editing and support.

Posthumous thanks to Ben, Ray, Rob, Allen, Mike, Pedro, Gary, Tricia, and Sylvia.

www.ingramcontent.com/pod-product-compliance
Lightning Source LLC
Chambersburg PA
CBHW042030050526
44107CB00128B/1492/J